Effective curriculum management

Effective curriculum management

Co-ordinating learning in the primary school

Edited by John O'Neill and Neil Kitson

London and New York

First published 1996
by Routledge
11 New Fetter Lane, London EC4P 4EE

Simultaneously published in the USA and Canada
by Routledge
29 West 35th Street, New York, NY 10001

Routledge is an International Thomson Publishing company

Selection and editorial matter © 1996 John O'Neill and Neil Kitson;
individual chapters © the contributors

Typeset in Palatino by Datix International Limited, Bungay, Suffolk
Printed and bound in Great Britain by Biddles Ltd, Guildford and Kings Lynn

British Library Cataloguing in Publication Data
A catalogue record for this book is available from the British Library

Library of Congress Cataloguing in Publication Data
Effective curriculum management : co-ordinating learning in the
    primary school / edited by John O'Neill and Neil Kitson.
        p.   cm.
    Includes bibliographical references and index
    1. Curriculum planning—Great Britain.   2. Education, Elementary–
–Great Britain—Curricula.   I. O'Neill, John.   II. Kitson, Neil.
LB2806.15.E366   1996
375'.001'0941—dc20   95–25969
                                                                         CIP

ISBN 0–415–12409–3

Contents

Part III The extended curriculum

Introduction

John O'Neill and Neil Kitson

We are of the view that it should be part of the ordinary duties of virtually every primary school teacher to act as co-ordinator in some aspect of primary school work.
(Science and Arts Committee of the House of Commons, 1986, *Achievement in Primary Schools*)

In recent years the role of the subject or curriculum co-ordinator in the primary school has emerged as an essential element in the management of a quality learning experience for all. However, the various models of the role of the co-ordinator which have been developed during the last decade, certainly in the minds of practitioners in schools, are often viewed almost as flights of fancy. Seen through nostalgic eyes they may appear to belong to a former age of comparatively generous funding of a national education service, when it was optimistically assumed that time and resources would be in sufficient supply to enable co-ordinators to support the work of less confident colleagues as and when necessary. Or, alternatively, these models are dismissed as purely academic constructs which represent unrealistic and unattainable demands on the skills and persistence of co-ordinators, and which fail to reflect the very real difficulties of observing and attempting to support colleagues at the point of delivery – in their classrooms.

This volume is intended to help co-ordinators plot a practical route through those potential difficulties. It celebrates excellence and lasting achievements in primary school curriculum practice and, by doing so, allows subject co-ordinators to reflect and analyse the fundamental issues associated with the provision of quality learning experiences: effective policy making, the promotion of confident and consistent practice throughout the school, and the efficient use of limited resources.

Nevertheless, there remains a readily apparent paradox in the role of the primary subject co-ordinator which is all too often ignored in the prescriptive models. The potential benefits of enhanced pupil learning and the professional development of teachers in the school via an 'in-house' expert, 'on-tap', and possessing the confidence and motivation to lead 'by example', are very alluring. The rather more sober reality is that these models ignore or, at best, only partially address the needs of busy practitioners. Lack of time, opportunity, confidence, support and resources conspire to militate against the easy application of neat theoretical models to fragmented primary school realities, and the more instrumental concerns of overloaded teachers.

A more likely scenario is that in primary schools which have actively developed a caring and nurturing *learning environment* for both children *and* adults, the necessary preconditions for effective subject co-ordination will already exist:

- openness;
- trust;
- a willingness to support colleagues in times of personal stress or professional insecurity; and
- a clearly articulated set of guiding values or principles.

These factors describe a school culture in which the work of the subject co-ordinator is regarded as important and is carried out in a relatively unproblematic way. Conversely, where those preconditions are absent, where teachers work in isolation from each other, and where fear of failure outweighs the desire to experiment and perhaps even risk the occasional disaster, then, in these schools, subject co-ordinators are more likely to encounter resistance, hostility, a reluctance to move away from the safe mediocrity of 'the way we've always done it'.

We would argue that any attempt to prescribe a checklist of co-ordinator responsibilities is doomed to failure, if only because it would fail to account for the range of unique professional and social environments in which primary teachers work. Transplanting successful practice from one school to another, without regard to context, is difficult, if not impossible. Suggestions for action, change and development can only ever be suggestions together with an offer of support if meaningful and enduring improvements are to result. Willingness to change, adapt, move forward are not qualities or attitudes which the co-ordinator can demand of colleagues by right of office.

As many subject co-ordinators will attest, change and development can only take place when expertise and enthusiasm on the part of the co-ordinator is matched by open-mindedness and a sense of willing co-operation amongst colleagues. Hence, the contributions in this volume have been commissioned and edited from an unashamedly pragmatist perspective. They are designed to offer a range of signposts and strategies to harassed co-ordinators whose recent memories of the 'management of learning', via the introduction of a National Curriculum, are of continually being told what to do only to have the ground rules changed once the initial directives have been successfully implemented.

This is not a 'how-to-do-it' book. Readers will be only too aware of, on the one hand, the plethora of published material and 'experts' ready to offer instant solutions on the implementation of the curricular 'flavour-of-the-month' – at a price – and, on the other, the frustrations of having to modify or completely scrap practices and procedures which had only painfully been learned or adopted. The purpose of this volume is to offer conscientious co-ordinators a set of conceptual frameworks within which they can better understand their own practice and an indication of the essential elements of high-quality learning which permeate all effective primary school learning experiences.

The ultimate intentions of the contributors are to promote, through analysis of the various issues, excellent learning environments and experiences for children in primary schools. The more narrowly defined aim of this book is to enhance the management capability of curriculum co-ordinators. We argue that in order to do that, co-ordinators need

- an overview of primary school curriculum management issues;
- a clear agenda for delivering quality learning in each area of the formal curriculum;
- an awareness of the implications of whole school planning demands; and
- access to lines of support and information in the wider educational community.

The book is divided into three parts. We now explore the rationale for each.

PART I THE WORK OF THE CURRICULUM CO-ORDINATOR

This part gives a 'management of learning' focus to the role of the co-ordinator.

Maurice Galton's keynote chapter offers an exploration of the nature of teaching and learning for staff and the generic whole school issues which need to be considered in attempting to manage effective curriculum innovation.

John O'Neill examines the development of theoretical models for the role of the co-ordinator, identifies how these conflict with the realities of everyday practice for many practitioners, and suggests how the role might be redefined.

Tom Whiteside introduces some empirical data to illuminate current co-ordinator experiences in terms of awareness and confidence about their role. This is linked to evidence drawn from other research projects into the realities of the co-ordinator role.

In *Sally Featherstone's* contribution, a practising Ofsted inspector reviews the framework for inspection and early reports of experiences of the process. She relates these to the focus for discussions between inspector and curriculum co-ordinator. She makes an important distinction between development and maintenance modes for areas of the curriculum.

The chapter by *John West-Burnham* uses the principles of total quality in the audit of classroom management practice. He suggests that total quality enables primary schools to enhance the quality of learning on offer in classrooms.

Finally, in this part, there is an acknowledgement that changes in employment patterns and teacher training systems in the primary sector have a significant impact on the role of the co-ordinator in terms of developing subject expertise amongst colleagues.

Roger Merry outlines some approaches to the development of practitioner confidence by looking at three distinct groups of new teachers: initial teacher trainees, newly qualified teachers, and returners to the profession.

PART II PROMOTING A QUALITY CURRICULUM

In this part each author sets out the *key* areas of

- knowledge, skills and understanding;
- teaching styles; and
- learning approaches

across the key stages which need to be developed and applied consistently in order to contribute to a high-quality learning environment for all children. The editors argue that these fundamental principles of excellence constitute an essential framework for teaching and learning which transcend any short-term changes in statutory curriculum requirements. The strength of the book, we feel, is that it doesn't start from the point of offering templates for planning and action in order to deliver the National Curriculum.

> This book is meant to help teachers in their work. However, it is not a 'How to do it' book rather it is more of a 'What might be worth doing?' book. [Its] chief aim is to help teachers critically reflect on current practices and to be able to act more confidently and competently as a result. [. . .] Through practice we may develop confidence. Through reflection we may develop wisdom.
>
> (Rowntree 1992, p. 2)

Neil Kitson in his chapter on English examines the role of language across the curriculum and points out the importance of a whole school policy. He considers the development of writing, reading and speaking and listening in the primary years and looks at significant ways in which the co-ordinator can help colleagues improve their own practice.

Mike Price and Rose Griffiths investigate the attitudes to mathematics and the breadth of mathematical information necessary for individuals to cope in the modern changing world. They address the range of teaching styles and approaches to be encouraged by a co-ordinator and show, by drawing on case studies, some of the characteristics of successful maths co-ordination.

In her chapter *Tina Jarvis* tackles one of the key issues of science teaching today, which is that many primary teachers lack the self-confidence necessary to teach the subject. She suggests that the science co-ordinator not only needs to ensure an appropriate curriculum and suitable materials but must also develop the skills and understanding of his or her colleagues.

Aileen Dunkley's chapter examines design and technology as a medium through which children may develop and apply their knowledge and skills. The co-ordinator's responsibility to encourage colleagues to develop 'capability' amongst children is examined. The chapter also examines progression in skills development, in the experience of using a range of materials, in gradual and increasingly complex technological applications, and in the ability to work independently.

In *David Walker*'s contribution he considers the nature of history as presented within the National Curriculum and demonstrates the ways in which excitement and vigour can be fostered through the introduction and development of appropriate teaching techniques. He addresses the notion of historical learning by encouraging the co-ordinator to question the concept of historical understanding. He also offers advice on the resourcing and assessment of the subject.

John Stout examines the nature and purpose of geography as an essential part of the primary curriculum. He challenges the limited interpretation of geography as seen merely in terms of mapwork and lists of exotic names. He provides guidance for co-ordinators to foster a spirit of enquiry amongst both colleagues and children alike in order to enable children to understand and question the world in which they live.

The chapter by *Angela Wortley* on PE begins by placing current practice in an historical context. She suggests a variety of ways in which the co-ordinator can work with colleagues in order to develop their teaching so that it is structured, challenging, planned, purposeful and stimulating. This is considered first in general terms and then by looking at the specific areas of gymnastics, dance, games, athletics, swimming, and outdoor adventure activities.

David Williams focuses upon the nature of the art curriculum and the need to develop the necessary confidence amongst colleagues. He stresses the importance of a whole school plan which builds upon the skills of experienced teachers and which creates high expectations of the children.

David Wheway addresses some of the issues for co-ordinators related to curriculum music and, in particular, the areas of performing, composing, listening and appraising. In the second part of the chapter he examines some of the management issues for the music co-ordinator and considers in detail the challenges surrounding the development of specialist music with non-specialist teachers.

Mark Lofthouse discusses the nature of RE co-ordination in schools. Starting with an examination of the complexities of the legal and legislative frameworks he then unpacks the approach 'Understanding Religion' and examines good practice in terms of its relationship to 'Fitness for Purpose'. After addressing the unique nature of this subject he offers advice on resources.

PART III THE EXTENDED CURRICULUM

This final part reinforces the twin notions that

- each subject co-ordinator is but one member of a whole school team of 'curriculum managers'; and
- the complexities associated with the management of learning increasingly demand an infrastructure of support on which the subject co-ordinator can draw at need.

With this in mind the editors have identified a range of contributions which address planning, integration and support from a broader whole school perspective. In the first chapter of Part III *Neil Kitson* offers some practical suggestions for getting started as a co-ordinator.

Sylvia McNamara focuses, in her chapter, on the ways in which the role of the special educational needs co-ordinator can act as a model for other co-ordinators through its focus on the needs of both teachers and individual children.

Jean Underwood's contribution reinforces the theme of IT as an increasingly essential support for a complex learning, administration, and management environment within which the primary school curriculum continues to evolve and change. She illustrates the differences of approach to IT which are likely to be found in primary schools.

The chapter by *Margaret Riley* maps the range of LEA and other support services which, in the age of autonomous schools, constitute a powerful network of advice and expertise. This network, actively maintained by the subject co-ordinator, is seen to provide a point of access to the myriad of external resources to support classroom learning and continuing professional development within each subject area and the school curriculum as a whole.

The advocates of a 'how-to-do-it' approach, mindful of the practical needs of the busy co-ordinator, might point to the absence of planning schedules, model policy documents, and outlines for schemes of work, lessons, topics and staff development sessions amongst the contributions. We would argue quite forcibly that it is precisely *because* teachers and co-ordinators have been offered *too many* prescriptions rather than structured opportunities to reflect on the real 'core' of effective primary school practice, and to articulate their own perceptions about how to plan, organise and manage those essential learning experiences, that anxieties and uncertainty persist. We argue that co-ordinators need to be clear about their understanding of what their role is intended to achieve, and of the tasks that need to be undertaken. It is this understanding which sets an agenda for review and planning, action, monitoring and evaluation. The procedures and working practices which are actually undertaken within each primary school will depend far more on the values and norms of those who work there than they will on any manual of prescriptive guidelines.

The editors assert that the volume as a whole acknowledges and addresses the statutory obligations schools are required to fulfil. There is, hopefully, due recognition of the fact that a statutory curriculum framework and associated inspection arrangements offer useful templates for reflecting on, and challenging, preconceptions about the quality of existing provision within schools. What emerges, however, is the principle that, underpinning this framework, there needs to be a shared, articulate, professional interpretation of the way in which the statutory frameworks may be used to develop the whole curriculum offered within each school. That, in essence, is the work of the primary school curriculum co-ordinator.

Part I

The work of the curriculum co-ordinator

Chapter 1

Teaching, learning and the co-ordinator

Maurice Galton

INTRODUCTION

This chapter will review the recent research evidence concerning the role of the primary school curriculum co-ordinator, here defined as an appointment from within the staff of a school. However, any consideration of this research cannot be divorced from the studies of the roles of advisory teachers, here defined as externally appointed consultants. During the early 1980s when the main emphasis was on the use of advisory teachers, many of the issues which are now germane to the work of the in-school co-ordinator began to emerge. In this chapter we shall begin by looking at the similarities and the differences of the two roles.

THE ADVISORY TEACHER

During the mid-1980s a 'cascade' model of professional development began to emerge, whereby the adviser passed the necessary knowledge down to the advisory teacher who then passed it down to the school post holder who then disseminated it to other staff. Following the 1988 Education Reform Act, and the shift to local financial management in schools, the role of the internal post holder as a subject co-ordinator has assumed increased importance.

Whichever method of support for the development of classroom teachers was preferred, little direct observational evidence has been collected about the success of these attempts at improving the curriculum. Insofar as success or failure can be inferred from data about changes in practice, collected in different contexts, it must be concluded that the role of the advisory teacher and the in-school co-ordinator has not been altogether successful. Evidence in support of this proposition comes from the general findings of research that there have been few signs of change in classroom practice over time (Galton *et al.* 1980, Mortimore *et al.* 1988, Tizard *et al.* 1988, Alexander 1991). More recently, with the advent of the National Curriculum, there is evidence from the PACE studies (Pollard *et al.*, 1993) that, for the most part, teachers have continued to 'bolt on' their existing practice to these new curriculum initiatives.

Various suggestions have been put forward to explain these failures to bring about identifiable changes in patterns of teaching and learning in the primary school (O'Mahony and Sollars 1990, IPSE 1988, Stillman and Grant 1989). A major shortcoming is that both advisers and advisory teachers are expected to learn on the job. It is assumed, by those appointing them, that their reputation as 'proficient practitioners' (the main reason why they were appointed in the first place) will be sufficient to persuade colleagues back in the schools to accept their advice and to imitate their practice.

Other reasons for the advisory teachers' limited success have been attributed to the temporary nature of the posts, particularly the lengths of appointments. Harland (1990) has argued that the lack of a satisfactory career structure leads advisory teachers to opt for short-term rather than long-term goals. Reorganising a school's resources or developing a new theme pack were tangible results of a secondment which could be mentioned at subsequent interviews. Concentrating efforts on aspects of practice which were slow to change, and where it was difficult to demonstrate success in the short term, was a considerably less 'marketable' achievement.

However, neither Harland (1990) nor O'Mahony and Sollars (1990) single out a further reason why advisory teachers or co-ordinators tend to enjoy limited success. In almost all cases, those responsible for appointing to these posts ignore the underlining power structures which exist within the primary school system and which determine not only how the advice will be received but also how it will be delivered. For example, Galton *et al.* (1991) describe the response of an advisory science teacher who avoided any discussion with the headteacher of a small rural school after an unsatisfactory lesson. When asked why she had not attempted to intervene nor discussed the lesson with the headteacher afterwards, the advisory teacher replied, 'Well she's the head! I've only been a teacher for five years.' Asked in a follow-up question about how she hoped to bring about a change in the headteacher's practice, the advisory teacher replied, 'By letting her see what I am doing. I hope through team teaching that something of what I do will rub off on her practice next time.'

This theory of 'osmosis', where it is hoped that a natural diffusion of the expert's practice to the less competent teacher will take place, appears to be the main way in which advisory teachers, and school co-ordinators, attempt to change existing classroom practice. In Galton *et al.*'s (1991) study of curriculum innovation in rural primary schools many of the advisory teachers spoke of the difficulties of power relationships both with the headteacher and with more junior colleagues. Very often, advisory teachers stated that they needed to begin by establishing their credibility. This they did by taking lessons to demonstrate their competence. Only when they had established their credibility in this way did they feel able to proffer advice.

Harland (1990) identified a number of ways of providing this advice. He notes that, at its simplest, the role of the advisory teacher was to provide resources or to offer information about how such resources should be procured or constructed. This Harland called the *provisionary method*. The second method of advising consisted of oral or (more rarely) written communications which passed on information, advice or ideas. This *hortative* mode was used regularly during debriefing sessions or during talks to staff, for example as part of a 'Baker Day'. The third mode, which has already been described, was that of the role *modelling* mode where advisory teachers either demonstrated some aspect of practice or worked alongside the classroom practitioner. Clearly, as Harland indicates, there are links between all three modes. For example, in the SCENE project, Galton *et al.* (1991) recorded an incident where an advisory teacher demonstrated the use of the concept keyboard by taking a lesson. Throughout the lesson, however, the interaction with the pupils was continually interrupted by a stream of advice directed at the classroom teacher concerning the best ways to set up the apparatus or to overcome technical problems.

The fourth method noted by Harland was termed the *zetetic* mode. Here, the advisory teacher attempts to explore with the classroom practitioner the latter's view of practice and to establish, first, why things are done in a particular way and, second, whether these ways might be changed to the mutual benefit of both the teacher and the learner. In its fullest form this model is similar to the idea of the teacher as a 'reflective practitioner' (Schon 1983) whereby teachers attempt to theorise about their own practice. The distinction between reflecting and theorising is, however, not always obvious (McIntyre 1992). Generally, this approach has its antecedents in the concept of the 'teacher as a researcher' where the classroom is viewed as an experimental laboratory. Teachers arrive at explanations, for example, when children fail to learn, create hypotheses of the best way to remedy the situation, test these out, observe further and then modify the hypotheses if necessary. Studies of this 'action research' approach (Galton and Williamson 1992) do not suggest that up to now it has been totally successful even in the hands of skilled consultants. The success of this approach in a situation where, as reported earlier, few advisory teachers had any serious induction training, is clearly questionable.

THE SCHOOL POST HOLDER

The role of the school post holder has also been the subject of research. In all cases there are similarities with the problems experienced by externally based advisory teachers and internal co-ordinators. Campbell (1985) notes, for example, the tension between the formal status of the post holder, as described by the headteacher, and the perception of this status by colleagues. Most teachers, while accepting advice, did not wish to be observed implementing this advice in the classroom. Post holders often experienced conflict between their advisory role and their position as class teachers. Post holders also experienced stress in an educational context since they were held accountable for the quality of the school's provision in their subject. Not only were they required to identify their colleagues' shortcomings but they were also expected to provide the necessary resources to enable corrective action to be initiated. When colleagues performed well the post holder received little credit; when things went badly he or she took the blame (Campbell 1985, pp. 68–76).

Similar problems emerged in one of the largest intervention programmes involving internal appointments, the Leeds Primary Needs Project (PNP). By far the largest proportion of the £13 million allocated was used to appoint an additional teacher co-ordinator to each of the participating schools. In the first year some of these teachers had not managed to gain access to their colleagues' classrooms (Galton 1994). Some appointments were strongly resented because the co-ordinators had not previously worked in an inner city classroom. Headteachers were puzzled by the ambiguities of the co-ordinator's role in comparison with that of the deputy head. In some schools, headteachers tended to see the appointment of the co-ordinator as indicative of their own failure to manage the curriculum successfully. Subsequently, Alexander (1991) reported that there was very little change in these perceptions throughout the five years of the project. As in other cases, co-ordinators undertook the task of supply teacher, partly to improve their credibility and partly to gain access to the pupils. When eventually co-ordinators did establish their credibility then, as in Harland's study, the modelling strategy was most frequently used to demonstrate improved practice.

One of the most puzzling features of the subject co-ordinator's work is this reluctance to engage in direct instruction with colleagues although this teaching approach is often used in his or her own limited training. Part of the reason for this reluctance is, as Campbell (1985) has argued, to do with the nature of the power relationships within the school and the need for the co-ordinator to be seen to be at one with colleagues, both in the interests of harmonious daily relationships and also for future promotion prospects. But a more deep-seated reason may have to do with the co-ordinator's lack of any deep understanding concerning theories of curriculum change, or of theories about the ways in which expertise can be developed in teachers and, more importantly, of the way this development can be fostered by different INSET approaches.

In any school teachers will be at various stages in their development. Yet it is rare for any school based INSET approach to attempt to differentiate between these different levels. Usually, one approach is offered with the consequence that, although some teachers may appear satisfied, there will be others who find what was offered either too facile or irrelevant to their needs. As Eisenhart *et al.* (1991) argue, a weakness of teacher training is that it is not based on any theory of how teachers *learn to teach*. Eisenhart and colleagues single out initial teacher training but the same criticism can be applied to INSET in that there are also no theories of how experienced teachers *learn to teach better*. It is to these two issues, the nature of curriculum change and the nature of expertise in teaching and its development, that we now turn.

THE NATURE OF CURRICULUM CHANGE

Studies of the change process, as it affects individual teachers during the adoption of a new curriculum, suggest that it consists of a series of interrelated stages. In the SCENE project, although the particular issue concerned the development of collaborative structures within clusters of rural schools, the implications of what was observed during this process have a bearing on all curriculum change. Briefly, the SCENE project established that teachers proceeded through three main stages in their thinking during a curriculum innovation. During the first stage, termed the *initiation* stage, teachers operated according to what Doyle and Ponder (1977) described as 'the practicality ethic'. This refers to the balance between the teacher's estimated costs of an innovation as against its perceived benefits. Only if the benefits are perceived to outweigh the personal costs will teachers agree to proceed in a positive fashion. The more benefits outweigh costs the greater the enthusiasm on the part of the teachers. For example, in the SCENE project where teachers were asked to plan jointly curriculum initiatives, the extra workload involved in attending 'after-school' planning meetings was set against the perceived benefits of ending personal isolation and of pupils working with the other children from the surrounding villages. At this stage, the main objective of the co-ordinator or adviser is to ease the additional workload. For example, in the SCENE project, teachers needed time to talk to one another in order to plan joint activities and if this time was to take place during the normal school day, then support was required for supply cover. At this point, therefore, little expertise other then general good classroom competence is required from the advisory teacher or co-ordinator. Theirs is a generalist role.

Once, however, there has been general acceptance of the value of the innovation the teachers begin to move to the next stage, which in the SCENE project was called the *consolidation* stage. Here the main objective is to achieve success in ways which satisfy the objectives of the innovation as closely as possible. At this stage, teachers require specific expertise in those parts of the curriculum which are undergoing change. In Harland's (1990) terms the help is mostly provisionary and hortative (see p. 13). Teachers need to know how to procure the necessary resources. They need advice on how to use these materials. Advisory teachers at this stage will, therefore, usually be specialists in the particular subject area where innovation is taking place. The emphasis will be on learning to use new materials and procedures and evaluating their effectiveness. For the most part, 'direct instruction' (i.e. demonstration followed by practice) should be the predominant mode of training.

In many cases, innovation may not proceed beyond this stage. Even after five years in the SCENE project, only a few clusters of teachers moved to the third phase involving *reorientation*. Here teachers ceased to think about meeting the objectives of the innovations as closely as possible and instead began to consider how to adapt the innovation in ways which advanced pupils' learning more effectively. There was now less emphasis on the subject matter content and more interest in the nature of the learning processes involved and how best to enhance it. This requires teachers to engage in reflection in the manner proposed by Schon. More importantly, the resource for supporting the change should now mainly come from within school rather than from outside. Well trained in-school co-ordinators now have a key role. A sense of ownership of the process by those involved is now very important because any changes in practice which are considered necessary to enhance the learning process will, inevitably, involve a debate between the teachers about their beliefs and philosophies. This debate can be heated and for some teachers threatening.

In this situation, change is sometimes only superficial, as a result of what Galton (1989) has called the 'common market' approach on the part of the headteacher. Just as negotiators in the European Union often agree a form of words in policy documents which do not involve any serious change in an individual state's present practice, so too schools draw up policy guidelines without defining in sufficient detail the meanings attached to key words. Thus all teachers may agree that the school should increase the proportion of collaborative group work in the classroom. But unless what this involves is clearly spelt out, teachers can return to their own classrooms and continue to operate grouping arrangements which are at variance with the intended policy. Only insiders are able to penetrate this surface level of behaviour and, providing they have the necessary skills, confront colleagues whose practice is at variance with the agreed norms. Managing curriculum change effectively requires those offering advice and support to adopt these generalist, specialist and negotiating roles according to the stage of a teacher's development.

DEVELOPING EXPERTISE IN TEACHERS

The changes in teachers' thinking during the process of curriculum inno-vation appear to be a specific example of a more general process of teachers learning to teach. The transition of novice teacher to experi-enced expert have been the subject of considerable research effort in recent years (Berliner 1992). Novice teachers find it difficult to focus on several elements of classroom activity at the same time. Consequently they have difficulty translating general advice into practice during train-ing. Novice teachers also rely heavily on predetermined planning and are therefore largely very inflexible in their approach. Galton (1989) has described this overreliance on the use of *entry* strategies and contrasted it with the expert's use of *exiting* strategies. For example, if a novice finds that a lesson is too long he or she will go back to the material and look for ways of shortening it, only to find, in all probability, the lesson still does not finish on time. Experts, on the other hand, recognise that there are always unforeseen events which waylay even the best laid plans. They, therefore, don't bother with precise planning but rely on identify-ing a point where it is convenient to engineer a closure. As a result, the lesson looks well planned although the various moves required to bring this about are largely improvised. For this reason, experts have been described by Borko and Livingston (1989) as 'improvisational performers'.

As novices become competent and gain the necessary experience to be able to 'read' events in the classroom, their ability to solve problems increases. Unlike the expert, however, this problem solving takes place through the use of what have been termed 'maxims'. Galton (1989) has argued that these maxims or procedural rules often involve 'two stage theories of teaching'. Stage 1 sees the competent teacher behave in a particular way until pupils reach a certain state of readiness whereupon stage 2 behaviour is instituted. An example of this process involves guided discovery where teachers first set tasks which require a high degree of support or guidance in the belief that once pupils have gained confidence by completing the task they will be more prepared to complete a second similar activity without the same degree of support. Experts, on the other hand, have only one maxim, namely that circumstances alter cases, and therefore they react to different classroom situations by trying to understand the causes. Thus pupils may behave badly, having come into class in a highly excited state because of an incident in the playground during the lunch hour. Expert teachers, while not condoning any disruptions, will make it clear to the class that they understand the reasons for this behaviour.

According to Kagan (1992) this model of developing expertise is preferable to others because it is based on the changing cognitive state of teachers as they move through the various stages. In the full model there are five stages with advanced beginner straddling the novice and competent stage and the proficient stage straddling the competent and expert levels. However, the distinctions between the five stages are not as clearly defined as might be desired. For this reason only the novice, competent and expert stages are considered here. Clearly the cognitive states of these stages bear some similarity to those identified in the SCENE project when, during curriculum change, teachers move from initiation to consolidation and reorientation. As with the initiation stage, so too novice teachers are self-focused and concerned to deal with their own personal problems and to judge situations in terms of the practicality ethic. Competent teachers are more task oriented in the manner of those passing through the consolidation stage. Expert teachers, however, are more pupil focused as are those engaged in the reorientation stage of curriculum change. Berliner (1992) suggests that these links between curriculum change and expertise might be more easily identified by carrying out an experiment where expert teachers were observed attempting to teach in novel situations. For example, an expert teacher in the top junior class might be asked to teach the reception children.

Some research using this model of expertise has been undertaken by Benner (1984). She, however, studied clinical nursing where expert nurses, like their teacher counterparts, are improvisational in their performance. In seeking clarification for various courses of action, Benner found that expert nurses could not articulate clearly the reasons for making particular decisions. Instead they would reply, 'It just felt right.' She found that the novices required strong coaching which made use of direct instruction. Competent teachers, however, benefited from the use of case study material in which they could compare and contrast aspects of their own practice with that of colleagues. Benner stresses the need to provide a suitable framework for the discussions of these case studies. Without a systematic review no firm conclusions are likely to emerge. Instead the teachers involved will simply agree to disagree and continue to argue that classroom practice should be a matter of personal preference. By the third stage, the reorientation stage, teachers should be, in Berliner's (1992) terms, 'student focused'. Everything is now judged as to how it affects pupils rather than how it affects the teacher. Consequently, Benner recommends that reflection and action research can now be used with this group of teachers.

A number of other pointers also emerge from Benner's analysis. First of all, it suggests that it is better if the teacher involved in mentoring is not too far ahead in his or her own development from that of the trainee when a 'modelling' strategy is used. Co-ordinators should, therefore, be chosen carefully so that their own practice is not too far ahead of colleagues undergoing training. Where this is not possible co-ordinators should be aware of these principles and demonstrate the appropriate rather than their own preferred strategy. These differences in development between the trainer and trainee help explain why attempts to get the latter to model practice upon the former can sometimes fail. Novice teachers, for example, may not be able to think through the logic behind the expert teacher's approach to a problem. They will therefore put down the expert's success to characteristics, such as personality, and conclude that the approach is beyond them. Competent teachers on the other hand can benefit through involvement with expert teachers in the same way that competent musicians improve considerably through attendance at 'master classes'.

SUMMARY

Theories of curriculum change and models of expertise in teaching suggest that the failures to implement new curriculum reform through the use of advisory teachers and co-ordinators is not due solely to a lack of suitable training in their subject specialism or in the acquisition of counselling skills prior to their taking on the role. It is also necessary that co-ordinators are shown how to match training approaches to the cognitive state of the learner, in much the same way as teachers attempt to do with pupils. In the past, little attention has been paid to identifying the stage of development of a particular teacher and to ensuring that the ways in which the co-ordinator offers new ideas about practice are 'in tune' with that teacher's thinking. Without the use of these models of teacher development to guide the planning and execution of INSET programmes, it is likely that the contribution of school co-ordinators to the improvement of teaching and learning in the primary school will continue to be a marginal one.

Chapter 2

The role of the co-ordinator

John O'Neill

INTRODUCTION

The first review (Dearing 1993) of the National Curriculum provides a timely perspective on the constraints which can be placed on the teaching and learning process by unconfident management at school level:

> In the event, we have created an over-elaborate system which distorts the nature of the different subjects, which serves to fragment teaching and learning in that teachers are planning work from the statements of attainment, and which has at times reduced the assessment process to a meaningless ticking of myriad boxes.
>
> (Dearing 1993, p. 61)

A quality curriculum depends on teachers having the time and encouragement to engage in discussion about the values on which it should be based, the appropriate balance between content and process, and how to ensure consistency in terms of access, continuity and coverage. Throughout the existence of the National Curriculum, the role of the subject co-ordinator as someone able to provide support, guidance and reassurance for the work of colleagues has remained a seductive model of effective primary school curriculum management (DfE 1992a), yet without any clear idea of where the role of the classroom teacher ends and that of the co-ordinator begins.

The purpose of this chapter is to examine the extent to which such a model can work in practice. In doing so, we focus on three key areas:

- the *contexts* within which co-ordinators work;
- the *role* of the co-ordinator; and
- *tensions* and *opportunities* in role management.

THE CONTEXTS WITHIN WHICH CO-ORDINATORS WORK

The issue is that simple models of the role struggle to reflect the range of different school contexts within which co-ordinators work. It is possible to argue that any definition of the role of the co-ordinator will prove inappropriate and, indeed, ineffectual, unless it is modified and adapted to meet the particular needs of the school in question. For example, if you have worked in more than one school you will know that norms and behaviours, ways of working with colleagues and the terms in which teaching and learning are discussed vary considerably. At a very basic level, in some schools it is acceptable to admit that you are struggling with a particular topic, class, child, parent or colleague. In other schools, teachers work in isolation and such issues are never aired publicly. In yet others, success is celebrated with colleagues on a regular basis.

Every primary school is in many ways, therefore, unique. A supply teacher, for example, working in two apparently similar schools serving adjoining catchment areas, after a brief time in each school, would be able to list an almost infinite number of differences concerning 'the way they do things over there'. Equally, a group of student teachers, having completed their first teaching practice, routinely exchange anecdotes and compile their own pecking order of the 'best' schools to work in. Many of their judgements are based on the levels of encouragement, support and advice they received from staff in their host schools, to enable them to 'fit in'.

A related process takes place, in many instances, amongst teachers who come together from different schools either for INSET, school cluster group work, or moderation processes. You will know, from your own experience, that the initial sessions are invariably halting, tentative affairs whilst individual teachers work out what is expected of them, the extent to which it is acceptable to disagree with colleagues, how much of your school's work you can legitimately share with others, and so on, until or unless mutual trust and openness can be established:

> there was a wall of suspicion, the tremendous lack of confidence that prevented people making a contribution and we have changed. There is no doubt about it.
> (Teacher's comment, quoted in Galton et al. 1991, p. 88)

This collective hesitancy is about the move away from a working environment where people are familiar with the values, norms and behaviour patterns which are expected of them in their day-to-day working routines. And it is the familiarity of working routines and expectations which provides security for teachers within the classroom and co-ordinators throughout the school. In the 1990s, the difficulty for primary school teachers is that the National Curriculum has undermined perceptions about the way in which the curriculum should be planned, delivered and assessed (Alexander et al. 1992) within individual schools and, in a very real sense, caused all teachers to question their personal educational values and professional judgement.

The notion that curriculum co-ordinators can help overcome many of the anxieties of classroom teachers and provide some level of professional certainty and leadership through their subject expertise is an attractive but incomplete perspective for, as Nias *et al.* (1989) reveal, the culture of the school as a whole is a more likely source of the support, reassurance and challenging models of good practice needed by individual teachers.

Nias *et al.*, in their study of five 'successful' primary schools, identify a culture of collaboration which is perceived to provide a personally secure yet professionally demanding context within which the management of learning could take place. The key elements of the culture are set out below:

- individuals take strength from the notion that they are valued both as people and for the unique contribution they make to the work of others;
- belonging to a group and working as a team help create a sense of interdependence;
- a feeling of personal and professional security leads to open expression of emotions and opinions;
- shared values and goals create a high degree of trust in others; and
- a willingness to be flexible and adaptable enables staff to cope with uncertainty and crisis.

> It encourages a sense of team pride and so of hard work, and it facilitates relaxed, spontaneous co-operation over teaching and other professional responsibilities.

(Nias *et al.* 1989, p. 53)

Unfortunately, this cameo of the primary school working environment may not be the norm for many readers and, clearly, a fully collaborative culture is only one of a range of contexts within which teachers work and co-ordinators are expected to function. The model of management cultures (Figure 2.1) developed by Day *et al.* (1993) provides a more complete picture of the challenges which co-ordinators are likely to face in carrying out their role.

Individualism

In a fully collaborative culture individuals, both as classroom teachers and co-ordinators, are likely to feel part of a closely knit team of professionals, with a clear idea of where they are going in terms of curriculum development. At the opposite end of the continuum, individualism characterises the working context for both teacher and co-ordinator:

> In this school there is a sense of professional isolation, habitual patterns of working alone, no feedback to teachers on their effectiveness

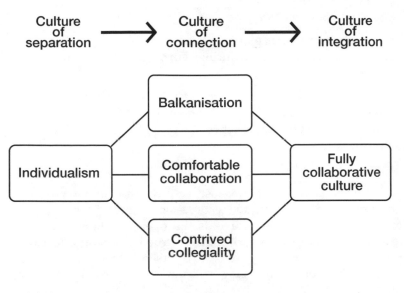

MANAGEMENT CULTURES

Figure 2.1 School Cultures
Source: Day, C. *et al.* (1993), *Leadership and Curriculum in the Primary School*, London: Paul Chapman

> from outside the classroom, safe, non-risk taking forms of teaching.
>
> (Day *et al.* 1993, p. 9)

Here, the opportunities for the co-ordinator to observe and influence colleagues' practice are likely to be minimal. Cultures of separation are highly resistant to the reductions in teacher autonomy demanded by central government interventions such as

- school development planning;
- teacher appraisal;
- Ofsted inspections; and
- the National Curriculum.

These cultures constitute a debilitating constraint on the ability of the co-ordinator to promote meaningful change and development.

Balkanisation

For curriculum co-ordinators, balkanised cultures might usefully be characterised in terms of disputes over

- access to financial and material resources, and
- the relative status of core and foundation subjects;

and a questioning of the need for

- detailed cross-curricular planning, and
- rigorous approaches to ensuring curriculum continuity between classes and across key stages.

In balkanised cultures, co-ordinators are likely to work only with groups of like-minded colleagues and to create pockets of common practice rather than whole school approaches.

Comfortable collaboration

Where comfortable collaboration exists co-ordinators undertake a limited role by offering advice and suggestions on request. Their support for colleagues is non-threatening, avoids the open questioning of existing practice and is a supportive rather than a true leadership role. Comfortable collaboration, in many senses, offers a veneer of professional co-operation without challenging colleagues to move beyond merely adequate levels of classroom management. In these sorts of cultures the role of the co-ordinator is valued within the school in terms of the ability to organise and maintain resources, to produce policy documents and schemes of work to satisfy external demands and to reinforce the status quo.

Contrived collegiality

Contrived collegiality, at one level, also presents a veneer of efficiency and effectiveness, primarily to outside observers, who may well see a lot of 'activity' on the part of co-ordinators but are unlikely to uncover many changes in practice as a result:

> It may be recognised by sets of formal, bureaucratic procedures which increase attention given to joint planning and consultation.
>
> (Ibid., p. 10)

Given the size and complexity of the National Curriculum, particularly in small primary schools, it is tempting for teachers to concentrate on issues of curriculum implementation rather than engage in reflection and debate about how to adapt a curriculum area to fit within a framework of existing school values or the extent to which statutory curriculum requirements challenge accepted teaching and learning styles.

Thus, in cultures of contrived collegiality, development planning, appraisal, the use of directed time and policy development are amongst those aspects of curriculum management where external requirements are complied with but which contribute little to meaningful changes in the quality of teaching and learning.

Hargreaves (1994, p. 208) suggests that forms of contrived collegiality are manifested:

> [. . .] in terms of teachers not meeting when they should, of meeting when there is no business to discuss [. . .]. The inflexibility of mandated collegiality makes it difficult for programs to be adjusted to the purposes and practicalities of particular school and classroom settings. It overrides teachers' professionalism and the discretionary judgement which comprises it. And it diverts teachers' efforts and energies into simulated compliance with administrative demands that are inflexible and inappropriate for the settings in which they work.

Although describing experience in North America, the parallels for England and Wales, post National Curriculum, are clear. The dangers of contrived collegiality for curriculum co-ordinators are that

- they may find themselves leading INSET workshops or being released to support colleagues in order to use up appropriate quotas of directed time, rather than when they are needed;
- 'policy development' becomes 'document production' to satisfy Ofsted demands; and
- the focus for the appraisal of classroom performance will be determined by the preferences of the classroom teacher rather than the development priorities of the school or the particular teaching and learning challenges posed by different areas of the curriculum.

Day *et al.* (1993) suggest that contrived collegiality can also be seen in a more positive way because it provides a necessary structure for teachers who are attempting to move towards full collaboration, but lack successful experience. In this sense, meeting patterns, clearly defined formal roles for co-ordinators and procedures for collaborative development planning can help provide a secure structure within which staff groups begin to develop the skills of collaboration.

At the heart of the problem for co-ordinators in particular is being able to observe and influence the practice of colleagues. In teaching this presents particular difficulties:

> When teachers meet only occasionally on questions of logistics, broad curriculum outlines or school-level matters, they are unlikely to engage in close mutual examination of how they think about teaching, plan for teaching or handle teaching demands in the classroom. Closer to the classroom is also closer to the bone – closer to the day-by-day performances on which personal esteem and professional standing rest. The prospects for conflict are high.

> (Little 1990, p. 180)

A co-ordinator role which tries to get 'closer to the bone' is profoundly threatening for many teachers; hence the variety of management cultures (see p. 23) in schools which settle for arrangements which are less than effective in terms of supporting and, at the same time, questioning individual practice. Nevertheless, I wish to suggest that the basic test of the value of the work of the curriculum co-ordinator is the extent to which it helps:

- overcome the normal working isolation of classroom teachers;
- enhance collaborative curriculum development within the school; and, crucially,
- improve the quality of teaching and learning.

With that in mind, we turn now to examine the role of the curriculum co-ordinator.

THE ROLE OF THE CO-ORDINATOR

The most enduring generic model of the role of the co-ordinator is provided by Campbell (1985). He suggests that curriculum co-ordinators need a combination of curriculum and interpersonal skills:

1   *Curriculum skills,* that is those skills and qualities involved in knowledge about the curriculum area for which the postholder has responsibility.
    (a)   Knowledge of subjects. The postholder must keep up to date in her or his subject, and must know its conceptual structure and methods, etc.
    (b)   Professional skills. The postholder must draw up a programme of work, manage its implementation, maintain it and **assess its effectiveness**.
    (c)   Professional judgement. The postholder must know about, and discriminate between, various materials and approaches in her or his subject, must relate them to children's developmental stages, manage the school's resources, and **achieve a match between the curriculum and the pupil's abilities**.
2   *Interpersonal skills,* that is those skills and qualities arising from the postholder's relationships with colleagues and other adults.
    (a)   Social skills. The postholder must work with colleagues, leading discussion groups, **teaching alongside colleagues**, helping develop their confidence in his or her subject, advising probationers, etc.
    (b)   External representation. The postholder must represent his or her subject to outsiders (other teachers, advisers, governors, parents, etc.).

                                    (Campbell 1985, p. 53) [my emphasis in bold]

Since 1988 various aspects of legislation have added to, rather than diminished, the work expected of co-ordinators in both curriculum and interpersonal aspects of the role:

1 External accountability demands increase the pressure on curriculum co-ordinators to ensure that practice in their area conforms with statutory requirements and official school policy.
2 From a purely pragmatic point of view, it is co-ordinators who are expected to interpret and disseminate the greatly increased documentary information from a wide range of external, official sources.
3 Increases in the scope and complexity of the curriculum create huge demands in terms of keeping in touch with frequent developments and revisions. In addition, many co-ordinators have responsibility for more than one area of the curriculum.
4 Moderation of standards and professional judgement within and across schools in relation to portfolios of evidence, teacher assessment and records of achievement suggest that co-ordinators have to liaise more closely with colleagues in other institutions and as a result publicly defend policy and practice in their own school.
5 The rhetoric of school development planning suggests that the development and maintenance of curriculum areas should be linked to both whole school and individual teacher priorities.
6 The need to ensure effective curriculum coverage, continuity, progression and entitlement demands a greater use of collaborative approaches to the planning, delivery and assessment of the formal curriculum.

In terms of Little's comments above (p. 25), however, the most challenging, yet potentially the most rewarding, elements of the model remain those which attempt to get closer to classroom practice. Assessing the effectiveness of the curriculum and ensuring a match with pupils' needs are only possible by teaching alongside and observing colleagues at work, by linking planning and target setting to monitoring and evaluation. Yet, as suggested above, these more threatening aspects of the co-ordinator's role are governed by the openness of colleagues rather than the aspirations contained, for example, in a formal job description. In short, if teachers feel threatened by the prospect of having their performance observed and commented upon by co-ordinators then those important aspects of the co-ordinator's role will not take place to any meaningful degree.

Redefining the role

Whilst the Campbell model is helpful, it was developed at a time when primary schools enjoyed greater freedom to dictate the content and delivery of their chosen curriculum than they appear to do in the 1990s.

Alexander *et al.* (1992) question the applicability of the traditional co-ordinator model given the demands of the National Curriculum. They suggest that, in the same way that teachers need to reassess the appropriate balance between whole class, group and individual pupil approaches to teaching and learning in their own classroom, schools themselves need to question the assumption that class teachers can teach all aspects of the formal curriculum with appropriate support from curriculum co-ordinators. The authors argue that, particularly at Key Stage 2, schools need to adopt a more considered combination of teaching roles:

- The *Generalist* who teaches most or all of the curriculum, probably specialising in age-range rather than subject, and does not profess specialist subject knowledge for consultancy.
- The *Generalist/Consultant* who combines a generalist role in part of the curriculum with cross-school co-ordination, advice and support in one or more subjects.
- The *Semi-Specialist* who teaches his/her subject, but who also has a generalist and/or consultancy role.
- The *Specialist* who teaches his/her subject full-time (as in the case of music in some primary schools).

(Alexander *et al.* 1992, p. 43)

The difficulty with the Alexander *et al.* model is that, quite understandably given its origins, it focuses rather narrowly on delivery of the National Curriculum rather than development of the whole school curriculum. The distinction is important for, as Edwards (1993) argues, the co-ordinator role does present significant development opportunities for the curriculum, staff and the school as a whole. She suggests that the co-ordinator role is misunderstood and underdeveloped in schools rather than being an inherently inappropriate vehicle for curriculum management:

> To have failed to maximise the potential of the curriculum co-ordinator as **change agent** is maybe to have lost an opportunity to have kept what is commonly regarded as 'the best' about primary education (class teachers, family atmosphere, close contact with parents) while grasping important development opportunities (whole school development, careful evaluations, effective in-house in-service activities).
>
> (Edwards 1993, pp. 51–52) [my emphasis in bold]

Edwards' arguments reinforce the idea that curriculum management in primary schools is about both development and maintenance, organisation and delivery, planning and evaluation – in effect an organic process.

The idea of the co-ordinator as change agent is helpful. It returns us to the context of the school within which the co-ordinator works. As change agent, the co-ordinator has to be aware not only of the demands of curriculum delivery, but also of the anxieties and concerns of colleagues, and their readiness for change:

> It isn't that people resist change as much as they don't know how to cope with it.
>
> (Fullan 1991, p. xiv)

In this sense, the Campbell, the Alexander *et al.* and the Edwards models each have something to offer co-ordinators in schools. Together they set out the skills and knowledge required by co-ordinators and address some of the constraints facing schools in the area of curriculum management.

As suggested earlier, however, the context within which co-ordinators work is a major determinant of what they are likely to achieve. In the final section of this chapter, therefore, we explore some practical issues concerning role management which impact directly on the effectiveness of the curriculum co-ordinator in the primary school.

TENSIONS AND OPPORTUNITIES IN ROLE MANAGEMENT

Most primary school teachers have a full teaching commitment. The basic difficulty for curriculum co-ordinators is perceived to be that they lack the time to fulfil the role (Stow and Foxman 1988, p. 55). The point is also made that formula funding under local management of schools (LMS) schemes has done little to redress the comparative financial constraints historically faced by primary schools (Alexander *et al.* 1992, p. 44), and therefore primary schools have difficulty in releasing co-ordinators from timetable commitments. I wish to suggest, however, that these problems are symptoms of a more serious management malaise in primary schools.

The way forward lies, as Edwards (op. cit.) suggests, in a redefinition of the role of the co-ordinator, but one which is based on a clear understanding of what the school as a whole is attempting to achieve. Below I set out four practical suggestions for redefining the role and for moving towards a culture of collaboration.

Publish a policy for learning

Most primary schools devote large amounts of time to the production of policy documents for individual areas of the curriculum. A policy for learning specifies the sorts of approaches to teaching and learning which are *valued* by the school and which observers might legitimately expect to see in action in all curriculum areas. The policy sets out 'the way we teach and learn around here'. The point is that the staff of the school *together* agree the policy. As such they are making a public statement about their professional values, which they can then defend and be held accountable for. The policy will identify core values within the school and, at the same time, incorporate external statutory requirements. The policy also acts as a focus for classroom observation by co-ordinators and in teacher appraisal. More significantly, perhaps, it creates an agenda for staff development linked directly to classroom practice.

Establish priorities for curriculum development

Many primary schools attempt too much rather than using school development planning to prioritise areas for action. In any one school the majority of curriculum areas will be in maintenance mode, ticking over whilst one or more urgent areas are thoroughly overhauled. Schools need to create an agenda for curriculum development and stick to it. With a policy for learning in place schools are able to assimilate external demands for change by adapting them to fit in with the *school's* values. Change takes place but is driven by the longer-term priorities of the school itself.

Use resources to fund areas of development

The idea that non-contact time is for use by senior managers in primary schools (Alexander *et al.* 1992) and that available resources should be distributed evenly across the school is anachronistic in the 1990s. If schools have identified priorities for curriculum development, it makes sense that additional resources be devoted to those areas to support development. Traditionally, costing in primary schools has been limited to books, apparatus and materials. In planning for developing a given curriculum area, however, it is perfectly feasible for co-ordinators to attempt to cost the development fully in terms of, for example:

- INSET time and money to provide knowledge and skills training for staff;
- non-contact time to support changes in classroom practice; and
- meeting time for whole school monitoring and evaluation.

Empower co-ordinators

Each of the three points already discussed contributes substantially to a redefinition of the role of the co-ordinator. Nevertheless, the major change is about headteacher and classroom colleagues *wanting* co-ordinators to have a substantive role, and *trusting* them to carry it out. The former needs headteachers to delegate authority and responsibility to co-ordinators, and to endorse publicly the role. The latter requires co-ordinators to demonstrate that they can help individual colleagues to improve teaching and learning in the curriculum area. Co-ordinators are only able to do that, however, by observing practice in classrooms, as a matter of routine, throughout the school.

SUMMARY

The culture of the school is a major factor in determining expectations about the role of the co-ordinator. Traditional models of the role fail to acknowledge this. In this chapter I argue that individual schools need to redefine a role for the co-ordinator which builds on the values of the school, an awareness of what is desirable and attainable in terms of teaching and learning styles within classrooms, and a clearer understanding of the full costs of co-ordination. Co-ordinators can only change and develop classroom practice with the active consent of colleagues. In this sense, the success or failure of the co-ordinator is the responsibility of all teachers within the school.

Chapter 3

The role of the co-ordinator auditing for development

Tom Whiteside

INTRODUCTION

This chapter will provide a variety of approaches for the recently appointed co-ordinator or the co-ordinator who is beginning to re-evaluate his or her role or is engaged in constructing a plan for development. Co-ordinators engaged in this process may be undertaking the review as part of a formal school development planning process (see Hargreaves *et al.* 1989) or may be undertaking a broader, and more personal, review. Whichever style of review is being undertaken, the formal development planning process of

- audit;
- plan construction;
- implementation; and
- evaluation

is a valuable framework for use and is one with which co-ordinators in primary schools are likely to be familiar and comfortable. This chapter will focus on the *auditing* phase and provide material to allow the co-ordinator to review strengths and identify appropriate development areas whatever the reason for the review. This will require a consideration of the changing external context, the school's structures and cultures, the state of the curriculum area and the personal strengths and weaknesses of the co-ordinator.

SWOT ANALYSIS

A SWOT analysis is a useful tool to use at the start of an audit phase to carry out an external and internal appraisal of the current situation. SWOT analysis was devised to identify the extent to which the current strategy of an organisation and its more specific strengths and weaknesses are relevant to and capable of dealing with changes in the wider environment. SWOT stands for Strengths, Weaknesses, Opportunities and Threats and in its original form a structured analysis would be under-taken to yield findings. However, it is also possible for the technique to be used as a useful common-sense checklist. The co-ordinator should identify the Opportunities and Threats provided by the external environment and the Strengths and Weaknesses of the school as an institution.

Opportunities might include the appointment of a dynamic advisory teacher or subject inspector to the area, the setting up of a curriculum support group within the local family of schools, or the dissemination of a new collection of in-house teaching resources by the LEA.

Threats could include the loss of support networks such as those out-lined above, the prospect of another change in curriculum at a national level or, indeed, rumours that excellent and very different approaches to the curriculum are being offered at a neighbouring school which may attract pupils away from your school.

Strengths may include an established record of good, innovative teach-ing in one or more curriculum areas, good levels of support from the headteacher, a willingness amongst colleagues to be open about suc-cesses and failures, or a dynamic parent association which raises consider-able amounts of discretionary funding for the school.

Weaknesses might include the reluctance, fear or inability of one or more colleagues to take on board meaningful changes in classroom prac-tice, a tradition of formal teaching in the school which hinders the develop-ment of practical, problem-solving approaches to learning, or the lack of volunteer adult support in the classroom.

It is likely that different facets of the same issue will be represented as both threats and opportunities or as strengths and weaknesses. For exam-ple, a lack of young staff, i.e. an experienced staff may be viewed as both a strength and a weakness.

THE SCHOOL'S INTERNAL ENVIRONMENT

In analysing the internal environment of the school it is critical for the co-ordinator to focus on the institutional setting, its structures and cultures and in particular on senior management styles and practices. In Chapter 2 John O'Neill argues that given the wide variety of cultures to be found in primary schools it is critical that co-ordinators identify the structure and culture of their particular school. The traditional model of the pri-mary school emphasises the individual teachers working on their own maintaining their classroom privacy and curriculum autonomy. This is paralleled by the individual autonomy of the headteacher responsible for the management of the school (Pollard *et al.* 1994). Handy and Aitken (1986) have described the typical model of primary school organisation as one that revolves round a single authority figure using a very personal approach to management and a notion of 'his' or 'her' school. During the

1980s collegiality was advanced as the way forward for primary schools and Campbell (1985) argues this model has been promoted by the Inspectorate since as long ago as 1978. Writers have consistently advocated a model of good primary management practice: all professional staff participate actively in negotiating an agreed curriculum and contribute jointly to planning, implementing and evaluating its delivery (Wallace 1988). Used in this sense collegiality implies a high degree of consultation amongst staff, their collaboration in co-ordinating the curriculum and their participation in policy making.

However, recent studies have pointed to situations where the heads of schools remain central, powerful figures exercising controlling influence upon the school and its development. Nias *et al.*'s (1992) study distinguishes between 'whole schools' and collegial schools noting that in 'whole schools' it is acceptable to both the heads and the teachers that the head plays a powerful and pivotal role. The implementation of recent reforms appears to have supported such 'whole school' approaches to management. The heads in Pollard *et al.*'s (1994) study showed, between 1990 and 1992, a shift away from collegial and participative approaches towards more directive approaches although participation and collegiality still predominated. Webb (1994) has pointed out how the introduction into primary schools of teacher appraisal, school development plans within which targets are set for individual teachers and the new role for headteachers as resident inspectors have all encouraged 'the growth of top-down directive styles of management, albeit involving staff consultation, at the expense of more collegial approaches' (p. 20). Osborn and Black (1994) have found that the rhetoric of collaborative school development planning has proved problematic in practice with headteachers or senior management teams frequently producing development plans with limited consultation. Hargreaves (1994) has pointed out that the necessity to get together at prescribed times in order to tackle work imposed by external requirements often resulted merely in what he characterises as 'contrived collegiality' – 'a safe administrative simulation of collaboration'. Indeed Webb (1994) found evidence of teachers increasingly questioning the rationale and efficiency of whole school meetings and the value of spending time in this way.

Co-ordinators work therefore in schools with varying structures and cultures which may themselves be changing and adapting to changing external demands. Analysis of the co-ordinator's school in terms of these models is a crucial starting point. Moreover, it is crucial that the co-ordinator identifies prevalent attitudes to the National Curriculum in his or her school. Researchers have identified a range of school responses to externally imposed change. Evans *et al.*'s (1994) study identified four approaches they referred to as 'head-in-the-sand', 'paying lip-service', 'common sense' and 'by the book', while Pollard *et al.* (1994)

distinguished between the extent to which changes were being incorporated into previous practice (a form of mediation) or were superseding previous practice (compliance).

Within any individual school it is difficult for a teacher to challenge existing cultures. For the individual co-ordinator, therefore, difficult decisions have to be made as to how far he or she is willing to work within existing definitions of the co-ordinator role or whether they are going to attempt to act as an agent of change. The co-ordinator's ability to introduce change is severely limited by the need to 'promote policies and changes in practice that were congruent with the vision of the headteacher and also met with the approval of deputies and/or senior management teams' (Webb 1994, p. 61). However, with careful planning and preparation, identification of appropriate short-term targets and support from colleagues changes can be made.

SUPPORT FROM THE HEADTEACHER

In the analysis at the school level attention should be paid to the headteacher who plays the key role in shaping this culture and in determining the framework within which co-ordinators will operate. It is useful for the co-ordinator to identify, perhaps with the aid of another member of staff, the general management approach taken by the headteacher. Stow (1989) identifies a range of headteacher types:

- non-supportive;
- nominally supportive;
- indecisive;
- dictation, not delegation; and
- fully supportive.

Stow discusses useful strategies for the co-ordinator working with each of these different types. More specifically it is critical for the co-ordinator to identify the views that senior management hold of their role and their part within the school management culture. Moore's (1992b) study of headteachers' views of the role of the science co-ordinator showed that they placed little emphasis on the co-ordinator's subject knowledge and considerable emphasis on knowing how to help colleagues. The emphasis in this aspect of the co-ordinator's role was on talking to colleagues, explaining to them and answering their questions. The role was seen as one of 'helper' and 'fellow worker' rather than as 'school adviser' and 'decision maker'. Other studies (see, for example, Osborn and Black 1994) have shown that for heads, the key role of their co-ordinators is as distillers and disseminators. The widespread support by headteachers for these limited definitions of the co-ordinator's role contrasts with the wider definitions of the co-ordinator's role which place emphasis on curriculum leadership. Harwood (1992) has argued that the concentration on the training needs of co-ordinators has diverted attention away from the ways in which management styles and practices can create or exacerbate difficulties for the co-ordinator.

THE REALITIES OF THE CO-ORDINATOR'S ROLE

The role in practice of the curriculum co-ordinator varies across schools. Osborn and Black (1994, p. 27) identified a spectrum of practices which they classify as follows:

1 resource gatekeeper;
2 planning and resource facilitator;
3 subject consultant;
4 'critical friend' – working alongside other teachers in the classroom.

The least involved end of the spectrum was the resource gatekeeper role with 30 per cent of the teachers working in this relatively limited way. About 20 per cent of the teachers had a higher level of involvement typically making an input into the planning stage for their subject area with colleagues and playing a more active role in disseminating ideas from courses and suggesting resources. A further 30 per cent of the sample acted as 'subject consultant' but did not actually go into the classroom. Compared with the planning and resource facilitators they took a more active role in meeting regularly with groups of teachers to discuss their on-going teaching as well as their planning. Only 20 per cent of teachers went beyond this level of involvement as curriculum co-ordinators. In addition to acting as planning and resource facilitators and subject consultants, they spent time working alongside colleagues in their own classrooms, acting as a kind of 'critical friend' who was a catalyst in seeing things from a different viewpoint or trying to do things in a different way.

Co-ordinators will also have to examine teachers' views of their competence and confidence in their curriculum area. A recent study of 44 teachers in small rural primary schools by Hargreaves *et al.* (1996) has pointed to wide variations in teachers' views of their areas of confidence and competence across the curriculum. Only one in five teachers was very confident or confident in his or her ability to teach the music curriculum, approximately two in five the information technology and technology curriculum, yet four in five teachers were confident or very confident about delivering the English curriculum. Two out of five teachers considered their competence in delivering the music curriculum was such that they needed more training and support while no teachers considered they needed more training and support in delivering the English curriculum. Such research shows that care must be exercised when considering the potential role of the co-ordinator in different curriculum areas.

In an attempt to help co-ordinators review their own role, developments in their particular curriculum area and to identify priority areas for action the questionnaire presented below has been developed. It contains a series of statements structured around key aspects of the role of the co-ordinator identified by Campbell (1985). The statements contain within them notions of 'good practice' developed from a content analysis of HMI reports and other literature.

REVIEWING THE ROLE OF THE CO-ORDINATOR

General role

I have got a job description and I have been involved in the discussion of it.	I have got a job description but it was given to me.	I have not got a job description.
I have a very clear idea what my responsibilities as Co-ordinator are.	I have some idea what my responsibilities as Co-ordinator are.	I am not very clear what my responsibilities as Co-ordinator are.

Knowledge of subject

I am confident that I have sufficient grasp of my subject to lead developments.	I am fairly sure that I have sufficient grasp of my subject to lead developments.	I am not sure that I have sufficient grasp of my subject to lead developments.

Professional skills

I have identified the main priorities for development in my curriculum area, discussed them with my colleagues and they are included in the School Development Plan.	I have identified the main priorities for development in my curriculum area.	I have not as yet identified the main priorities for development in my curriculum area.
I have produced a policy statement with guidelines on planning, organisation and management.	I have produced a short policy statement.	I have not as yet produced a policy statement.

I have produced a policy statement taking into account the requirements of the National Curriculum.	I have produced a policy statement.	I have not as yet produced a policy statement.
I have a clear idea of the standards of achievement in my curriculum area and have a plan for improving it.	I have a clear idea of the standard of achievement in my curriculum area.	I am not clear about the standards of achievement in my curriculum area.
I have identified staff development needs and have a systematic programme.	We have a programme of staff development.	If staff ask me for help I provide it.
I am sure that the scheme of work provides a comprehensive cover of the National Curriculum.	The scheme of work does not as yet provide a comprehensive cover of the National Curriculum.	The scheme of work does not as yet cover the National Curriculum.

Professional judgement

I am very well informed about developments in other schools in this curriculum area.	I have some knowledge of developments in other schools in this curriculum area.	I have very little knowledge of developments in other schools in this curriculum area.
I have undertaken an audit of resources and identified priorities for future expenditure.	I have undertaken an audit of resources.	I have not as yet undertaken an audit of resources.
I am confident that planning in my school takes into account the differing abilities of pupils and their previous experience.	I am fairly sure that planning in my subject in my school takes into account the differing abilities of pupils and their previous experience.	I am unsure that planning in my subject in my school takes into account the differing abilities of pupils and their previous experience.
I am confident that the scheme of work provides for progression for the pupils.	The scheme of work considers progression but it is not sufficiently covered.	The scheme of work does not as yet address issues relating to progression for pupils.

Social skills

I regularly work alongside other teachers in their classrooms to help them in this curriculum area.	I have worked alongside other teachers in their classrooms to help them in this curriculum area.	I do not work alongside other teachers in their classrooms to help them in this curriculum area.
I feel I have considerable influence on the general teaching of the curriculum area for which I have responsibility.	I feel I have some influence on the general teaching of the curriculum area for which I have responsibility.	I feel I have very little influence on the general teaching of the curriculum area for which I have responsibility.
I have worked with staff so that they are familiar with and can use the resources available.	Staff are aware of the resources available.	Staff inform themselves of the resources available.

External representation

I am confident that the governors know about developments in this curriculum area.	I think that governors know about developments in this curriculum area.	I am not sure that governors know about developments in this curriculum area.
Opportunities exist within the school for me to share ideas with colleagues.	Some opportunities exist within the school for me to share ideas with colleagues.	Very few opportunities exist within the school for me to share ideas with colleagues.

Completion of the questionnaire by over 60 teachers undertaking GEST courses on Co-ordination in the Primary School indicates that many consider themselves to be working in school cultures with a relatively restricted view of the co-ordinator's role. Many were able to agree that they had met external requirements relating to DfE and Ofsted documentation but few felt they exerted considerable influence on the general teaching of the curriculum area for which they had direct responsibility. This was related to a perceived lack of clarity as to their specific responsibilities as Co-ordinator, the lack of opportunities they had to work alongside teachers in other classrooms, their limited opportunities to share ideas with colleagues and their lack of clarity as to standards of achievement in their curriculum area. Most felt uninformed about developments in other schools in their curriculum area and few were confident that governors were informed about developments in their own curriculum area.

This view of the limited power of the co-ordinator is supported by recent research which has pointed to co-ordinators feeling that there was an enormous discrepancy between the rhetoric surrounding their role and the reality of what they were able to achieve (Webb 1994, p. 58, Osborn and Black 1994, p. 27). Research indicates that with the onset of the National Curriculum more teachers feel they are co-operating with and working more closely with colleagues, with working together at the initial topic planning stage the most common form of collaboration. Much less frequent was sharing teaching or working alongside colleagues in the classroom.

SUMMARY – PLANNING FOR DEVELOPMENT OF THE CO-ORDINATOR'S ROLE

For the co-ordinator who has completed the audit it is important to recognise that any move in the direction of an extended definition of the co-ordinator role is going to require support from the head in creating the non-contact time which is crucial. Studies (e.g. Osborn and Black 1994) have shown that where co-ordinators undertook the wider role of curriculum leadership outlined by Edwards (1993) two key factors appeared to be present. The first was the existence of at least *some non-contact time*. The second was *support* whether from the head, or a deputy or someone who recognised the potential for more active involvement and took *action* to facilitate it. It will be difficult without such support to visit the classrooms of other colleagues and to audit, monitor and evaluate work in the curriculum area.

Chapter 4

An inspector calls

The role of the curriculum co-ordinator in inspection

Sally Featherstone

INTRODUCTION

The purpose of inspection is to identify strengths and weaknesses in schools so that they may improve the quality of education offered and raise the standards achieved by their pupils. The publication of the report and summary report of the inspection of a school is consistent with the requirements of the Parent's Charter.

(Ofsted 1993a)

Under the provisions of the Education (Schools) Act 1992 all maintained schools must be inspected on a regular basis, using a standard framework and teams of independent inspectors. This programme, a central element of the Parent's Charter, began its four yearly cycle with secondary schools in September 1993. September 1994 saw the programme extended to primary and special schools. The focus of inspection is the classroom, the quality of teaching and learning, the standards achieved by pupils, and the extent to which the school is fulfilling statutory requirements and its own stated aims.

A successful inspection depends on the professionalism of the participants (both the inspectors and the inspected), and the quality of the information provided by the school; the judgements of the team should reflect both the performance of the school and its unique nature. All members of the school community have a part to play in ensuring that the inspection process and the resulting report reflect the school as it really is, its achievements and its difficulties, its strengths as well as its weaknesses. This chapter outlines the issues for curriculum leaders in supporting the management of an inspection of their school. It covers their role before, during and after the inspection.

THE INSPECTION PROCESS

The discussion between curriculum leaders in primary schools and members of Ofsted inspection teams is an important component of the inspection, and provides an opportunity to amplify the documentary and classroom information available to the team. The quality of the discussion depends both on the skill of the inspector and the preparation undertaken by curriculum leaders in collecting and presenting information about the range of subjects and aspects which make up the whole curriculum experience for pupils. In small primary schools, one teacher may be responsible for several subjects or aspects of the curriculum; in larger schools, teams of teachers may work together to develop a related group of subjects and aspects. If the inspectors' time during a very pressured week is to result in the recognition of quality information about the successes and priorities of the curriculum area for which you are responsible, you need to do your homework!

Inspectors come to their judgements about your school from many different sources of evidence, collected in various ways. The majority of the inspection team will be primary specialists, and 60 per cent of each inspector's time during the inspection week will be spent in classrooms, observing teaching and learning, and coming to conclusions about standards of achievement. The remaining time will be spent examining children's work and talking to them, and observing the non-teaching elements of the day (playtime, lunchtime, after school, movement around the school). Inspectors will talk to support and clerical staff, parent helpers, governors, crossing patrols, caretaking and cleaning staff. They will join swimming, sports lessons and visits when you take the children out.

However, the central issue for all concerned, and the focus of the report, is the quality of teaching and learning within the classroom and the way this is supported and improved by the governors, the head and the teachers.

> Every aspect of the school listed in the schedule is to be evaluated in terms of its impact on the pupil's standards of achievement and quality of learning.
>
> (Ofsted 1993a)

PREPARATION FOR THE INSPECTION

In preparing for inspection, curriculum co-ordinators need to be clear about their role in the following areas:

* defining the school's purpose/recognising strengths and successes;
* defining your role in the management of the curriculum area;
* your part in whole school management and development;
* preparing the documentation;
* preparing for the discussions with the inspector(s);
* receiving and interpreting feedback.

Each aspect has its own tensions. I discuss these in more detail below, and suggest that you consider each one as you prepare for your conversations with the inspection team.

What is the purpose of the school?

The Vision or Mission Statement and the statement of aims for your school are key indicators against which your practice, the quality of teaching and learning, and the standards of achievement in the school will be judged.

> The (Inspection) report should include evaluation of the effectiveness of the school's stated aims and its success in meeting them.
>
> (Ofsted 1993a)

In a school with clear aims, the teachers, governors and parents are able to identify appropriate tasks and developments on the road to achieving those aims. Pressures to respond to inappropriate demands can easily be resisted. Priorities and responsibilities are clear, and achievements are recognised. The aims are used as a constant touchstone against which all achievements are evaluated. They reflect the unique nature of the school and its aspirations.

The following diagram (Figure 4.1) attempts to explain the way in which whole school aims and principles guide each curriculum subject and area. Curriculum policies should reflect the general aims of the school and should describe how the process, content and organisation of each curriculum area contributes to the achievement of these aims.

• Whole school aims and vision statement • Development plan • Management and staffing structures • Curriculum aims

• Individual curriculum policies (National and whole curriculum) • Schemes of work • Assessment, recording and reporting policies	• Governor policies (pay, SEN, Health and Safety etc.)

• Target setting and action plans • The curriculum in action • Monitoring, review, evaluation • Recognising success

Figure 4.1 How whole school areas guide each curriculum area

The best School Development Plans contain a set of clear school aims. These are the aspirations which drive the school, the essential values it

stands for. Publishing them prominently in the development plan reminds planners of the reasons underpinning what they are doing.
Schemes affecting separate departments as well as whole school issues
can thus be related to each other.

(Ofsted 1994a)

- How well publicised are the aims of your school?
- How could you as a co-ordinator use these aims as a measure of your
  success and a framework for your aspirations?

Recognising successes

Before the inspection there is time to take stock, to review the successes
of the whole school and the curriculum areas for which you hold responsibility. Some schools are beginning to amass 'curriculum records of
achievement' for curriculum areas or for the whole school, containing
photographs, children's work, newspaper articles, and other items
which demonstrate the successes of the school. Other schools are building an 'achievement' section into their development plan, prospectus or
newsletters to parents. However you decide to do this, the results may
surprise you by their sheer quantity, when you acknowledge everything
you have achieved and the breadth of the whole curriculum experienced
by children.

- How are things going in your school?
- What are the successes of the work you are doing and the curriculum
  area you are leading?
- How can you begin to collect evidence of the achievements of the
  school and in your curriculum area into a manageable format to
  present either verbally or in writing to the inspection team?

Your part in the management of the curriculum

Defining your role depends on the clarity with which you and others
distribute the tasks and responsibilities in the school. Schools need clear
lines of responsibility, flexible enough for task groups to be set up when
initiatives are identified but firm enough to give consistent support to
individuals and groups. Job descriptions describe the reality of tasks
undertaken, and the structure enables individuals to take responsibility
for managing their complex roles.

Clayton Middle School (9 to 13) was inspected by HMI in 1991 and
was visited again in 1993 when it reported as follows:

the senior management team supports teachers with ideas and guidance, heads of department receive sufficient supply cover to let them

work alongside colleagues. Thus teaching quality is developed across the board . . . and pupils' learning is enhanced.

(Ofsted 1994a)

- Do you have a clear job description, which helpfully outlines the different parts of your job? Does it reflect the balancing act you undertake between classroom teacher, curriculum co-ordinator and member of the school management team?
- Have you reviewed your job description recently, registering achievements and identifying gaps, areas of difficulty and training needs?
- How do you manage the complex role of class teacher, of identifying curriculum, development, resource and training needs and that most difficult task of monitoring the curriculum in action?

Your part in the school development planning process

Some recently inspected schools showed signs of quality planning:

All staff are expected to budget clearly for the resources they need in their various subject areas and to make a clear case to the senior management team for new items of expenditure . . . . The school arranges for separate action plans to be drawn up for each area identified as a priority in the Development Plan. The action plans are the responsibility of a named team leader, usually an incentive allowance holder, and are required to be set out according to a uniform format. This provides a clear and practical basis for planning, action, evaluation and review.

(Ofsted 1994a)

The School Development Plan is another vital component of the information requested before the inspection, and one of the first documents used by the inspection team in identifying the issues for inspection in your school. The school aims and the development plan together present a manageable overview of priorities within the school, balancing *development* tasks with vital *maintenance* activities.

In *Improving Schools*, Ofsted (1994a) praised the development planning process in a small primary school, describing it thus:

Little Snoring County Primary School (age 5–11, 74 on roll, scattered rural catchment). The school adopts a pragmatic approach. The first development plan was simple and direct. The areas for development are set out in the form of headings on a large matrix. Key targets are identified, and the tasks required to achieve these targets are set out along an agreed timescale in a specific chronological order. Simply worded criteria describe how each area will have changed when the desired improvement is achieved. Work under each heading is listed in detail over at least four terms while the plan itself extends to 1995 to indicate broad areas of development which lie ahead.

(Ofsted 1994a)

A manageable development plan usually has the components shown in Figure 4.2, and in many primary schools now appears as a strategic plan on staffroom notice boards, is discussed in staff meetings, adjusted throughout the year and reviewed at regular intervals.

THE SCHOOL'S AIMS AND MISSION	• where is the school going?
CONTEXTUAL STATEMENT	• what is the unique nature of the school?
RECENT ACHIEVEMENTS	• what does this school do well?
NEW PRIORITIES	• what do we need to do to make it even better?
MAINTENANCE TASKS	• what are the maintenance tasks in the curriculum and other areas that must be done in order to keep the school functioning in areas which are not major priorities?
FOR EACH PRIORITY: ACTION PLANS	• what are the responsibilities, resources, targets, timescales, success criteria, arrangements for monitoring, review and the identification of new priorities associated with current developments?
LONG TERM AND EMERGING PRIORITIES	• how does the plan move from short term targets to long term vision?

Figure 4.2 Components of a development plan

- What is your role in, and influence on, the development planning process, ensuring that your curriculum areas have a fair share of priority time and discussion?
- How are priorities for development identified at your school, how are resources allocated, how is curriculum development managed?
- How do you balance development and essential maintenance tasks within your curriculum area? What is the effect of this balance on the budget allocated to you?

Preparing the pre-inspection documentation

The May 1994 update to the *Handbook for Inspection* contains the following advice on pre-inspection documentation:

> The inspector should explain to the school that their documentation is needed for a pre-inspection review which will highlight issues for inspection and raise hypotheses about the school to be followed up during the course of the inspection. The Registered Inspector should be at pains to minimise the burden of work which this request places on the school. The wholesale revision of documents should be discouraged. The school should be asked to provide all **available** documentation in the following categories
>
> i   policies and written procedures;
> ii   details of curriculum and timetables;
> iii information for parents including the Prospectus;
> iv   management documents including the development plan, budget information, minutes of staff and governor meetings, staff handbook, job descriptions;
> v   any achievement data not included with the headteacher's form, access to schemes of work, forecasts, lesson plans, records. **It is not necessary or desirable to produce new documents just for the inspection; it is the school that is being inspected, not the policies**.
>
> (Ofsted 1994b)

As soon as the inspection date is known, the Registered Inspector leading the inspection team will notify the school of the documentation needed for the inspection. As emphasised above, the inspection team will want to see a real picture of your school, not a cosmetic exercise. Some schools already inspected felt that they should write policies and other documentation specially for the inspection. *This is not the case!* However, just as you would go through a child's records before sending them to a new school, you will want to ensure that the documentation you present is as up to date and complete as possible, and represents the reality of children's experiences in your school.

In most schools, the process of reviewing and updating documents is a continuous cycle, following priorities identified in the development plan. Some documents will be in draft form, following or awaiting whole staff or governor discussion, others will be newly written, and just about to be implemented. Some may have been written some time ago and are scheduled for development in future years. In this way, maintenance and development are both supported.

Successful schools are constantly developing, reviewing policy against practice and updating over a manageable programme, with targets identified in the development plan. Writing a curriculum area action plan can be very useful in preparation for an inspection.

- What are the priorities for documentation in your curriculum area?
- When did you last review policies, schemes of work and other guidance?
- How are you responding to the new National Curriculum?
- How can you manage any necessary review in a measured and benefic-ial way?

The blue section in the *Handbook for Inspection* contains useful information and checklists for each curriculum area. Co-ordinators might consider how they use this information in preparing for inspection.

In addition to policies and schemes of work, the school will be asked to produce *statistical information*. Some of this is of particular interest to the curriculum leader. Here are some pointers:

- *SAT/NCT results, where these are available*. By law, this information must be published in the Annual Report to Parents for each child, and in the prospectus. Inspectors will be interested in the use you make of such information in planning for developments, identifying training needs and monitoring curriculum provision. Have you looked at the aggregate information for your subject area?
- *Budget and resource management information*. How much information is available about the budget for your school? How well is the school using the allocated funds to enhance the learning of children?
- *In-service training and development*. How are staff development needs identified and met?

It is vital that everyone on the staff, particularly those people who will be asked to meet with inspectors, knows what the pre-inspection docu-mentation contains, has an opportunity to look at it and time to reflect on the issues it raises. Discussion at staff meetings will help this process.

Preparing for discussions with the inspection team

The main activity will be the inspection of work in the classrooms. Time will also be required for discussions with staff, especially those with management responsibilities. Time for discussion with staff will require negotiation between the inspector and the member(s) of staff concerned.

(Ofsted 1994b)

At the beginning of the inspection, members of the team will want to meet curriculum leaders or teams to discuss both the documentation and the curriculum in action. The timing of this discussion will be negotiable, and the inspector should tell you how long the discussion will take and what it will cover.

Your preparation will involve you in collecting your thoughts and some additional existing material to help you to talk through your achievements and the issues associated with your job. It is an opportunity for you to draw the inspector's attention to the good things that are happening and any difficulties associated with curriculum leadership. You may wish to prepare a folder or small collection of examples of work, projects, plans, training programmes, etc., but remember that you will only have a short time to talk – make sure you focus on the *real* strengths. The discussion will cover all or most of the following:

- Management of the curriculum area including your involvement in the development planning process and resource management.
- The documentation provided for the inspection, its status and evolution.
- National Curriculum implementation, including assessment, records and reporting.
- INSET – your own.
- INSET – for others.
- The curriculum throughout the school. Planning, continuity, progression, resources, monitoring the curriculum in action.

Many teachers lack opportunities to talk in detail about their responsibilities. This is one area of preparation where practice with a trusted colleague, appraiser or the head might be appropriate.

Receiving and interpreting feedback

Normally feedback would be to the subject/aspect coordinator, but the school may wish other staff to attend. The headteacher of a small primary school may wish the whole staff to be present. Feedback meetings should be seen as part of the inspection. They provide opportunities or the findings of the inspection to be discussed with those immediately involved and for factual issues to be clarified.

(Ofsted 1994b)

Curriculum co-ordinators may not be in a position to gain direct feedback from inspectors. The judgements of the team may all be gained via the head and deputy after the end of inspection feedback, and through the written report. It is sometimes hard to accept judgements (particularly those that imply criticism) without the right to reply. There is always a temptation to concentrate on negatives, even when there are many positive elements of the report. It is helpful to establish before the inspection the possible areas identified for development, and pre-empt any negative effect of the judgements by including these in your preparation and even the discussion with the inspector!

Most of this chapter has concentrated on the preparation for inspection. Undertaking the preparation in a measured way, while at the same time maintaining the equilibrium of the school, will take careful management. The following sections cover some relevant management issues for the inspection week and the activities after the inspection.

DURING THE INSPECTION

Teachers' work in the classroom will take many different forms, and it is important that the judgements about the effectiveness of teaching are based on its contribution to outcomes, and not on inspectors' preferences for particular methods.

(Ofsted 1994b)

An inspection report should reflect reality and your school should be instantly recognisable within it. Many teachers change their teaching and organisational styles dramatically during an inspection. This only serves to confuse the children, and provides false evidence for inspectors, rather than a true picture. You will see from the above advice to inspectors that there is no 'right method' for teaching. The inspectors should only judge *the effectiveness of the methods used, not the methods themselves*. Remember that children often respond badly to sudden changes in routine.

Support for colleagues during the inspection week is vital. Everyone will feel under pressure, and curriculum co-ordinators will often be able to locate other individuals who need support.

Managing contacts with inspectors is important too. In addition to the more formal meetings with individual inspectors, there will be opportunities to talk to them at the beginning and end of lessons, and at other times during the day. You will want to ensure that inspectors have all the information they need in order to understand what they are seeing. You may also like to familiarise yourself with the proformas used during the inspection (e.g. lesson observation forms and judgement recording forms). There are copies of all the inspection forms in the *Handbook for Inspection*. You may also decide as a staff to monitor the activities of the team, making notes of any feedback given, classes visited and documents examined. This can help in plotting the general direction of the inspection as it progresses, and in identifying the main issues to be addressed.

Planning for the formal senior management feedback described above is another area to consider. Making detailed notes of this meeting will help you to plan future developments.

AFTER THE INSPECTION

The inspection team will make a formal verbal feedback to the headteacher and senior management team immediately after the inspection, and to the governors a little later. You may be involved in one or both of these. Nothing in the ensuing report should come as a surprise to the school.

The report must be completed and returned to the school within five weeks. It will be made public, both to parents and the media. You can help the head and other senior managers to analyse, interpret and present the judgements contained in the report in the following ways:

- By reading the report carefully, concentrating on the areas for which you are leader and listing both the successes and the needs. You may have already identified many of the issues, and they may even be included in the current School Development Plan.
- By suggesting the priority order for such developments, remembering that maintenance tasks will still be necessary.
- By assessing the scale and scope of the development needs, and how long-term tasks can be balanced with more immediate and short-term goals.
- By identifying the training and other staff development issues.
- By identifying resource issues and beginning to explore the costs of developments and improvements in resources and training.

This will all help in the preparation for the governors' action plan.

The governors must prepare an action plan, demonstrating how they will address the issues raised in the report, and they will need the assistance of the head and the curriculum co-ordinators in constructing and implementing the plan, which will influence the development plan for the next four years. You will need to define the role of the curriculum co-ordinator in supporting the outcomes and priorities identified.

SUMMARY

Inspection has been described by an inspector as 'two groups of professionals looking at the work of the school together', and by a head as 'the greatest INSET opportunity this school will ever have'. The experience may not feel so to those being inspected, but the better the preparation, the more comfortable and in control you will feel, both during and after the inspection. As curriculum co-ordinator, you have a vital role in informing and demonstrating to the inspection team the quality of educational experiences provided for the children in your school.

Chapter 5

Quality and the primary school curriculum

John West-Burnham

INTRODUCTION

The purpose of this chapter is to explore the contribution that an understanding of total quality principles can make to the management of the
curriculum in the primary school. A central thesis of the chapter is
the need for an integrated and holistic view of learning and managing.
Previous chapters in this volume have drawn attention to some of the
tensions in developing and implementing the relationship between the
role of the co-ordinator and the actual experience of children as learners.
Total quality is offered as a means of integrating the traditional components of managing with the requirements of effective learning.

One of the most significant issues in discussing management in the
primary school is the extent to which it is perceived as an essentially
alien construct – bearing little relationship to what is understood as the
'character' of the primary school. The increase in bureaucracy associated
with LMS and the more formal demands for accountability emerging
from the requirements of the National Curriculum appear to deny the
possibility of retaining traditional modes of operating in the primary
school.

There are, therefore, two tensions to be reconciled – the imperative for a
learning focused approach to school management and the development
of ways of managing which are consistent with the changing demands
on schools. The aims of most primary schools will usually stress the
importance of contextualising learning by reference to social, emotional,
physical and spiritual dimensions. What is needed is an approach to
management which has the same holistic integrity, i.e. it gives equal
significance to all components of organisational life.

Since its introduction to Britain, total quality (TQ) has been seen as one
approach which offers the potential of achieving a value driven, integrat-
ive and client focused strategy. It is still widely referred to as total
quality management but the latter word is increasingly being dropped as
too constraining – it is argued that quality is about more than managing
and that what gives total quality its distinctiveness is its emphasis on the

profound aspects of organisational behaviour – values, relationships and the integrity of the commitment to those for whom it exists.

It is in this context that the work of the co-ordinator needs to be placed if the related dangers of bureaucracy and hierarchy are to be avoided. Curriculum co-ordinators can only function effectively if they are operating within an explicit moral framework which informs every aspect of organisational life – total quality might provide such a framework.

For most people involved in primary school management the intellectual antecedents of total quality are decidedly unprepossessing. It is generally attributed to the use of statistical techniques in the munitions factories of the Second World War and was based on the principle of consistency and conformity and the elimination of variation. Ethically and practically this seems far removed from what we know of successful classroom practice in the primary school and the jury is still out as to whether a technique originating in quantitative methods for engineering and developed by multinational organisations has anything to say to the overworked and harassed curriculum co-ordinator in the primary school. The rest of this chapter seeks to define and apply the principles of total quality in order to allow the reader to make an informed judgement.

THE COMPONENTS OF TOTAL QUALITY

There is no one authoritative definition of total quality. The works of Deming are highly influential but require interpretation and elucidation to be applied to schools. Most organisations that have considered total quality have done so through a process of adaption and assimilation. It may be that total quality has made relatively slow progress in education because no one has had the time to adapt and assimilate.

Most descriptions of total quality can be reduced to one main proposition:

• Organisations should keep their promises.

From this simple statement it is possible to develop a number of subordinate propositions. Quality organisations:

1 Should be clear about what they are promising.
2 Need to ensure that everybody keeps their promises all the time.
3 Need to be confident about their ability to keep promises.
4 Have to remember that they only exist for those to whom they make promises.

In the language of total quality these statements can be expressed as

value driven leadership;
people management;

quality assurance; and
a customer focus.

Although the terminology may be problematic it is contended that these four elements are at the heart of the work of the curriculum co-ordinator. The school makes promises about learning to children and their parents, these promises can only be kept by the staff, there has to be confidence that promises are being kept and the criterion for success is the learning of the individual child. If this is not a description of the role of the co-ordinator (accepting that it might need translation) then it is difficult to see what else it might consist of – other than the circulation of documents. The four components of total quality will now be examined to establish their relevance to the work of the curriculum co-ordinator.

Value driven leadership

Imagine a long and complex journey. It is the role of *leaders* to secure agreement on the destination, to ensure that the purpose of the journey is kept firmly in mind and provide guidance and support. *Managers* ensure that all the resources are available in the right place at the right time, to sort out any detours and obstructions and to ensure that timetables are adhered to. *Administrators* keep track of the fuel consumption, check that appropriate documentation is available and ensure that managers and leaders can do their job. All three functions are essential but without leadership the journey is, literally, pointless.

It is easy to caricature roles in schools but it does not require a great leap of imagination to see the implications of the curriculum co-ordinator who functions primarily as manager and/or administrator. One of the fundamental contributions that total quality offers to the debate about leadership is the notion that it is not the monopoly of one person. Every function within the school has the potential to display the qualities of leadership – each stage of the journey is a microcosm. So while long-term curriculum development is the responsibility of the headteacher, the development of specific areas of the curriculum can only be the responsibility of the co-ordinator. Leadership is differentiated in terms of four key functions: vision, sensitivity, empowerment and creativity.

Vision is concern for the destination. It is closely associated with values and these two may be combined in practical and specific terms into mission and strategy. Leadership is expressed through the demonstration of clarity of vision and values in the School Development Plan, policy statements (e.g. special needs, learning), INSET activities and the clear linkage between the allocation of resources and the school's aims.

Sensitivity describes the nature of the relationship between leaders and followers. This has two significant components. First, aims and values are not self-legitimating; they have to be explained, understood and accepted. A crucial element of the co-ordinator's role is therefore communicating, bearing in mind that the way in which a message is communicated is often more significant than what is actually communicated. Second, the relationship between adults can often have a significant influence on the relationship between adults and children. Co-ordinators can influence the culture of a school if they use their behaviour towards colleagues as a model of the desired relationship between adults and children. I am much more likely to be positive and supportive if that is the way I am treated.

The actual behaviour that characterises sensitivity may be described as empathic listening, giving feedback and the use of appropriate questioning styles. In all cases the emphasis is on the notion of 'win–win', i.e. the problem is resolved or the decision is taken and personal relationships are enhanced. Thus the role of the teacher is to allow others to communicate effectively and to enhance self-esteem in the process. As the management of learning is founded on communication it does seem appropriate for co-ordinators to exemplify the desired qualities.

Empowerment is dealt with more fully in the section on people management. However, in the context of leadership it is important to stress the importance of trust as an enabling force. Although trust is frequently cited as one of the most important attributes of leadership it is more frequently exhorted than practised. What real trust means is the ending of a dependency culture – the need to ask permission. Schools are usually good at delegating responsibility but do not always devolve the concomitant authority. This is often exemplified in the work of deputy heads and co-ordinators who are often not given a budget to complete a project but have to obtain approval for each item of expenditure on a piecemeal basis. Trust is often the area of school management where rhetoric and reality are most widely divergent.

Creativity refers to the capacity of leaders to make the most effective decisions and to solve problems. We know that the enhancement of cognitive skills in children can significantly improve their academic performance. The same is also true of adults in terms of their capacity to act. There are numerous techniques available which can help in the process of diagnosis, analysis, generation of solutions, prioritisation of optimum options and the involvement of others in these stages of problem solving. Equally there are skills which can facilitate group processes in meetings. Just as no teacher would ask a child to engage in a piece of work without ensuring that the child had the appropriate skills, so co-ordinators might consider the extent to which they have relevant skills and ensure that these are also available to colleagues.

People management

Total quality organisations are overwhelmingly people centred. Schools often claim this but the extent to which it is true might be understood in terms of the responses to the following questions:

1 How often are adults engaged in a significant one-to-one conversation about their work: weekly, termly, annually?
2 Is all information available on demand?
3 Does everybody feel as if they own the place?
4 Does INSET make a real difference?
5 Are staff meetings fun?

Total quality organisations manifest their commitment to people in three crucial respects: a lack of *hierarchy*, *teamwork* and an emphasis on *training and development*.

Formal hierarchy is rarely an issue in the primary school; informal (hidden) hierarchies are often pervasive. One of the manifestations of the co-ordinator's role is the access to specialised knowledge; if combined with hierarchical status this can lead to a control model where the relationship is transactional rather than transformational. This means that it is characterised by bargaining, exchange and reward, which reinforces relative status and control. A transactional relationship serves to reinforce the status quo and can minimise the potential for growth and improvement. By contrast a transformational relationship will be concerned with development and enhancement in terms of outcomes and relationships. Hierarchy engenders a culture of 'asking permission' – this is alien to most models of learning for understanding.

The designation 'team' is widely used in schools, but in reality is usually an aspirational rather than descriptive statement. The difference between a real team and a pseudo-team can be found in the extent to which the following criteria are met:

- there are explicit, understood and accepted values and vision;
- the core purpose of the team is clear and unambiguous;
- leadership is situational, i.e. based on expertise rather than status;
- there is an emphasis on interpersonal relationships;
- use is made of problem-solving and decision-making techniques;
- team processes are constantly reviewed;
- there is an emphasis on action.

In essence the effective team *learns* how to function in terms of completing the task and working together.

If the staff are perceived as a team led by the co-ordinator to deal with a specific curriculum issue, e.g. language, maths, science, etc., then the potential for implementation is significantly enhanced. This is because of the greater potential to establish a linkage between the co-ordinator's position as expert leader, involvement leading to collaborative decision making and consistency of purpose. Perhaps the most important outcome of a team based approach is the level of openness and trust that can be achieved – this can help to open up discussions of problems in classroom practice, anxieties, concerns, etc. The more sophisticated a team is the more likely it is that members will feel able to share perceptions and problems *and to contribute solutions*.

The effectiveness of a team, and of its individual members, is a direct correlation of the investment in training. Total quality organisations regard training as the critical factor in bringing about improvement. The issue is not so much the volume of training as the extent to which it pervades organisational practice. Thus, in the quality organisation, leadership and management are perceived as being fundamentally concerned with training and development.

A quick way to establish how far this is the case in a school is to look at the job descriptions of head, deputy and co-ordinators. To what extent do they define and prioritise a responsibility for personal learning and development and a responsibility for the growth of others? This is often manifested in terms of mentoring and coaching. It might also be covered in appraisal if that is seen as a continuous developmental relationship rather than an occasional bureaucratic procedure.

The contribution of courses and training days to real professional learning is probably minimal in that it might lead to an increase in knowledge, but what makes a difference to classroom practice is understanding which leads to the capacity to act, i.e. the ability to change behaviour. This can only come about through the capacity to reflect on existing practice and to identify strategies to bring about change. This requires skilled, expert and credible help and it is difficult to envisage a more significant role for the co-ordinator than the provision of this practical and specific support.

This in turn implies a strategy for the development of post holders both in terms of specific subject knowledge and expertise and in the capacity to transmit that expertise.

The obvious constraint on this approach in the primary school is time – post holders rarely have an allocation of time which is sufficient to meet a minimalist view of the components of the job. Constraints on staffing make it unlikely that schools will be able to create 'management time' in the current situation. At the same time the demands of accountability make a systematic approach to improvement all the more necessary. Some strategies are available:

• the incorporation of training days into a systematic approach to development derived from the School Development Plan;

- making all meetings team events focused on developmental issues;
- the enhancement of ancillary staff;
- reconceptualising appraisal so that it becomes a mentoring/coaching process;
- enhancing the role of the deputy or eliminating it, creating team leaders and thus buying time;
- reviewing how the head uses non-contact time;
- encouraging peer review and support;
- removing controls on access to resources.

Quality assurance

We all know in our daily lives that prevention is better than cure. Putting things right wastes time, money and energy and has an opportunity cost in that something else is not being done. The concept of quality assurance is based on the principle of prevention through definition which can then be assessed. The principle is derived from manufacturing industry where it is relatively simple to produce a highly detailed and specific definition of a product or process.

It is clearly not possible to produce a detailed specification for every process that occurs in a school. What is disturbing is that schools are often very adept at producing specifications for significant but rare events, e.g. a fire drill, and for relatively trivial activities, e.g. marking the register. What they are not always as comfortable with is producing definitions and specifications of the crucial educational processes which can then be used to manage those processes. In essence if I am regarded as being an ineffective teacher then it may be because nobody has ever defined what being an effective teacher actually comprises. It is often assumed, understood and may only be defined as a last resort as part of a competency procedure. This lack of definition can also explain the ineffectiveness of much INSET – the outcomes are not clearly defined or understood. It is almost impossible to train, to reflect on practice and to ensure consistent effectiveness if there is no clear statement as to what is required in any given process.

To some extent this gap has been filled by the documentation associated with the National Curriculum and many schools have used the Ofsted 'Handbook' as a source of criteria for effectiveness. However, both these sources have the problem that they are 'alien' to the school in that they, probably, use inappropriate language and do not reflect the values and vision of the school – they need to be translated.

The problem remains for the co-ordinator as to how effective learning and teaching can be guaranteed. In the current climate of accountability and parental choice it is not enough to say that a problem will be rectified for next year. My child will never be 5, 7 or 10 again. The issue is one of the school keeping its promises to each child in terms of the child's time-scale – 'all children are on short-term contracts'. The school will be working to improve over time but one generation of children cannot be regarded as the 'test-cases' for their successors. The issue is therefore a moral one: how are a school's promises expressed in its aims or mission to be translated into the actual experience of every child all the time?

There is a very real problem if some classes are being taught science, the humanities or music in a highly stimulating and effective way and others are not. There are implications for progression, differentiation and equal opportunities if provision is inconsistent. The co-ordinator therefore has to manage a tension between control and prescription and a *laissez-faire* approach. Total quality suggests an approach which reconciles confidence with trust.

First, there has to be absolute clarity about values, vision, core purpose and outcomes. If these are not understood and accepted then any attempt to ensure consistency is doomed. This can only be achieved by heads, deputies and co-ordinators talking about the key elements of what the school is about.

The second element is the translation of principles into practice usually in the form of policy statements. For example, schools will usually have a curriculum policy but they will not always have a policy on learning and teaching. A key function of the co-ordinator must be to contribute to the debate on how learning should take place as well as defining what has to be learned.

A number of schools have found it helpful to develop a third component which might be described as criteria for effectiveness. These can help to specify what good practice actually comprises, e.g. what are the manifestations of differentiation, what are the characteristics of an effective taught session, how effective group work can be defined. Very often such criteria exist in school but have never been made explicit, clarified and codified. Such criteria might well be published as they can then be used to inform the design of INSET, reflection and data collection as part of appraisal, induction of new teachers and school review and planning procedures. If managing a school is about a journey then these criteria are important milestones which can help to indicate that progress is being made.

The final element of quality assurance is concerned with the behaviour of managers. It can be summed up as celebrating good practice and this might well be a pivotal role for the co-ordinator. It is axiomatic that the reinforcement of success is central to good practice in the classroom. The same principle applies to the management of adults. The best way to assure quality is to capture good practice, reinforce, celebrate and even enthuse about it. This can then be extended into a common language – a shared conceptualisation – in the same way that the members of an orchestra will play the score but will also learn a common interpretation. Such harmonisation is only possible with clear roles, defined levels of performance, proactive leadership inspiring a great performance and a love of the music. Managing learning is not so different.

Customer focus

For many educational professionals this is the most problematical concept to be taken from the quality movement. The argument is simply that children are not customers. Some argue that the term 'client' is more appropriate as it denotes a professional relationship; however, both terms imply a cash transaction. Of course children do not pay but their parents do make a choice and have legal rights and entitlements. It is in this sense that customers may be a helpful term. The semantic debate can be somewhat sterile; the terminology is less important than the underlying concept which is that quality is defined by customer needs rather than by the supplier's intentions.

What this means is that the criteria for a successful lesson are derived from the needs of children and the extent to which they are met in practice rather than the perceptions of the teacher.

Quality is defined as 'fitness for purpose', i.e. the extent to which the needs, motivation and ability levels of individual children are actually met. This same principle can be extended to the way in which a co-ordinator works with colleagues; they are the co-ordinator's customers and the extent to which he or she is 'successful' is determined by them rather than personal, subjective criteria. I might imagine that this chapter is erudite, witty and enlightening, but if it has not met your needs as a reader than it is not a quality piece of work.

Total quality offers the co-ordinator an important and fundamental question to guide discussions about quality: to what extent is what I am doing meeting the actual needs of children and colleagues? The maths co-ordinator in a large primary school will have to deal with a wide range of ability, experience and levels of confidence in his or her colleagues. A generic approach may be appropriate for certain aspects of the job but real support has to be on an individual basis. None of us would be satisfied with the supermarket that gave us a shopping list when we arrived on the basis that it made the job of stock control so much easier.

Quality is the result of the experience of the individual – not the aspiration for the many. The way in which we perceive any service is based upon 'moments of truth' – individual transactions which meet or fail to meet our needs. It is the function of the suppliers – teacher, co-ordinator, headteacher – to manage the service they provide in terms of individual moments of truth. This may sound intimidating but most schools express this as the core purpose in their aims which are usually written in terms of the individual child and not of the class or key stage. There is no real difference between customer focused and child centred approaches – total quality may offer some insights on what it might mean.

SUMMARY

This chapter has sought to show how the elements of total quality might offer leaders and managers in primary schools an integrated and holistic model which is consistent with the best of primary practice and practically orientated. What is important in the work of the co-ordinator is the notion of totality – every lesson, every child, every colleague – all the time. To manage with any less of an aspiration is to deny individuals their entitlement to the most appropriate and effective mode of learning.

Total quality also offers an end to the artificial dichotomy between managing and learning – to manage others is to help them to learn and the application of total quality principles might help schools become genuinely learning organisations.

Much of what has been written will be recognised by readers as either already happening in their school or what should be happening. However, it is the totality that makes for effective learning in the effective school.

FURTHER READING

Bowring-Carr, C. and West-Burnham, J. (1994) *Managing Quality in Schools – A Training Manual*, Harlow: Longman.
Covey, S. (1990) *Principle Centred Leadership*, Simon & Schuster.
Murgatroyd, S. and Morgan, C. (1993), *Total Quality Management and the School*, Milton Keynes: Open University Press.
West-Burnham, J. (1992) *Managing Quality in Schools*, Harlow: Longman.

Chapter 6

Supporting new teachers

Roger Merry

INTRODUCTION

This final chapter in Part I considers some of the major issues which co-ordinators need to bear in mind when they are working with three groups of 'new teachers':

- students on initial training courses;
- newly-qualified teachers;
- those returning to teaching after a gap of some years.

Against a background of general trends such as the National Curriculum, local management of schools (LMS) and school-based initial training, supporting new teachers may simply seem like an added burden, and many schools now have a co-ordinator responsible for this work. This chapter therefore tries to offer some suggestions and points for them and for curriculum co-ordinators to consider. We begin by examining the needs of those just entering the profession as students.

INITIAL TEACHER TRAINEES

Understandably, many students going into schools for the first time find the transition from being on the 'receiving' end to being on the 'giving' end difficult. Many also feel aware of their lowly status even if they are not actually introduced to the class, as I was on my own teaching practice, as 'the student'.

From the student's point of view, two priorities seem to be very common. One is the dreaded class control or discipline which springs, understandably, from anxieties about taking on the role of teacher rather than student. Basically, the worry is 'will the children listen to me?', and the mentor will need to offer support sensitively here, without further undermining the student's confidence. For primary student teachers in particular, the other major concern is about the sheer amount of subject knowledge, since very few will have what they see as sufficient understanding across the whole primary curriculum. Once such areas of weakness or anxiety have been identified, preferably by the students themselves, curriculum co-ordinators obviously have a crucial role, not only in supplying particular expertise but also in boosting students' confidence. In many schools, arrangements are kept flexible enough to allow students to visit other classes to work more closely with curriculum co-ordinators, for example.

Significantly, both these concerns focus on the self as teacher, and it usually takes some time for students to develop enough confidence in themselves to begin to focus instead on the children as learners. The role of the mentor is therefore vital, though a detailed discussion of mentoring is clearly beyond the scope of this chapter (see, for example, McIntyre and Hagger 1993, or Wilkin 1992, for such discussion). Most writers recognise that the role of the mentor is not clearly defined: student and teacher may therefore have different perceptions of what is involved, or may find that the different roles conflict with each other. Thus Jenkins *et al.* (1991) describe four common mentor roles as the 'enabler' or facilitator, helping to resolve issues, the 'coach', offering a lead through experience, the 'counsellor', giving sympathy and support, and the 'model', setting an example. While these different roles would apply to all mentors, whether working with student teachers, NQTs or returners, there is another major role which applies particularly and increasingly to teachers helping to train students – the assessment role. It is here that perhaps the greatest potential for conflict arises:

> One problem of teacher training as it exists at the moment is that the mentorship role, on which so much emphasis is currently placed, has been constructed without regard for the separable trainee needs for friendship, counselling, tutoring and assessment. One result of this construction appears to be that trainees carry a burden of things they cannot tell their mentors, which becomes a burden that inhibits their classroom performance.
>
> (Pateman 1994)

Regular meetings with another teacher, probably the co-ordinator responsible for all students, could help relieve this burden, though it would need to be made clear from the start how far such discussions were confidential, to avoid the co-ordinator being put in a difficult position. If there are several students in a school, group meetings not only save the co-ordinator time, but usually allow students to compare notes and realise that they are not alone in their problems. However, assessment can still be difficult in a profession where this has traditionally been done by college tutors, where teaching has often been a solitary act carried on behind closed doors and relying heavily on the teacher's individual decisions, and where to criticise a colleague's performance seems almost unprofessional. In their different ways, the shift towards school based training, the National Curriculum, and the advent of staff appraisal and accountability have all helped to produce a climate where mentors are expected to offer constructive criticism, but it can still sometimes be difficult on a personal level. Conversely, some students, comparing themselves with experienced and successful teachers, may be much harder on themselves than the teachers would be, so that the assessment and support roles again become entangled. Of course this can occasionally become a habit – one teacher couldn't understand why her quite capable student was so destructively self-critical, until she realised that the student enjoyed the constant praise and reassurance of being told how good she was.

Given such complexities, the development of teacher competencies could be seen as an attempt to introduce more objective, consistent and open forms of assessment which co-ordinators working with several students and teachers should find useful. The DfE have been keen to promote such developments, and examples range from relatively straightforward checklists to rather daunting documents with numerous rows and columns. Berril (1992), for example, describes a system based on twelve competencies, grouped in four areas, and each assessed at five levels:

- 'Preparatory areas' (planning, environment, resources);
- 'Relationship areas' (control, teacher performance, rapport);
- 'Management of learning areas' (organisation, promotion of learning, flexibility);
- 'Professional areas' (subject competence, pastoral, professional approach).

In keeping with trends in other areas of assessment, students should be involved in self-appraisal of their competencies. For the Leicester University Primary PGCE course, for example, local teachers drew up a set of competency statements under seven headings.

- Planning and preparation
- Management and organisation of classroom
- Presentation and management of activities
- Children's progress and achievements
- Reflection, analysis and evaluation
- Professional relationships
- Further professional development

Students have regular 'Individual Action Plan' tutorials where they discuss their own progress, rather than having an assessment imposed on them. Although such lists of competencies can be helpful to co-ordinators, mentors and students by making expectations and progress more explicit, their limitations do also need to be recognised. McIntyre and Hagger (1993), for example, point out the dangers of seeing mentoring as a single, consistent process which makes for easy management but which does not offer much help to individual trainees and can even result in class teachers feeling de-skilled because the checklists apparently contain all the expertise. Smith and Alred (1993) in the same volume make a similar point in their comment that 'increasingly the "busy teacher" becomes reluctant to do more than scan lists and glance at diagrams'. Others have argued that an approach emphasising competencies fails to acknowledge the importance of coming to terms with one's incompetencies and that coping with failure is at least as important in learning as achieving success (e.g. Claxton 1984).

Making the shift from student to teacher is not easy and most teachers have vivid memories, if not recurrent nightmares, of their own teaching practices. However, the development from 'novice' to 'expert' clearly does not come to a halt with the celebration parties at the end of the initial training course, and the next section therefore looks at some approaches to working with new entrants to the profession.

NEWLY QUALIFIED TEACHERS

One change which has had a particular effect on NQTs occurred in 1992 when Kenneth Clarke, the Education Secretary, announced the ending of the statutory probationary year, claiming that it had become widely regarded as the weakest link in our system of teacher training. This decision was based in part on the findings of an HMI report, which described wide variations in the quality of induction arrangements between LEAs and even within the same LEA (HMI 1992).

A DfE memorandum (2/92) provided details of posts considered unsuitable for NQTs and a list of information which NQTs should receive before they took up a post. It then went on to outline what should be available once the NQTs had taken up their posts, and the details are worth quoting in full, if only as a basic checklist for co-ordinators to consider:

> After taking up appointment the NQT should be able, so far as practicable:
> * to seek help and guidance from a nominated member of staff who has been adequately prepared for the role, and from the head of department where appropriate;
> * to observe experienced colleagues teaching;
> * to visit and observe teaching in other schools;
> * to become aware of the role of their school in the local community;
> * to have some of their teaching observed by experienced colleagues and/or LEA advisers; to receive prompt written as well as oral

feedback on the teaching observed; and to receive advice as necessary;

- to have regular discussions and opportunities to share experiences with other NQTs;
- in the case of teachers in LEA maintained schools, to attend any meetings of NQTs organised by the LEA.

(DfE 1992c)

Clearly, many of the issues discussed in the previous section would therefore be equally relevant for NQTs. The change in role and status, while appearing less extreme than that for student teachers, can still be daunting. As one NQT put it:

It began well – the bliss of ignorance! As guilt and self-doubt set in, it was probably one of the most testing and upsetting experiences I have had.

Another NQT, reflecting on the transition to being a real teacher said:

It all happened amazingly quickly: one minute I was 'the student', the next I'm the new teacher – the word 'student' disappears, leaving one feeling professional but somehow defenceless – a 'fledgling'.

Although there is considerable overlap with the needs of student teachers, some of the needs and priorities of these 'fledgling' teachers are therefore rather different. For example, problems with parents are often mentioned by NQTs, but less so by students, presumably because the latter are partly shielded from them during teacher training. The previous section mentioned a change in emphasis for many students as they become more confident and shift their focus from themselves as teachers to the children as learners. For many NQTs another shift takes place as they take on the wider responsibilities of being professionals with their own classes, working alongside other teachers. Most comment on the pleasures of having your own class for a whole year, rather than borrowing somebody else's for a few weeks, but some of the most negative comments from NQTs concern their colleagues rather than their pupils. One began

I love seeing the children make progress – you don't have time to see that on 6 week teaching practices

but went on to say

staff politics are very hard to get to grips with. We behave worse than the children sometimes!

Another said:

I love the children and the creativity in teaching – it's the pressure and staff tensions I could do without.

Such problems are perhaps made worse for some NQTs because they may feel that they still have rather low status and yet are expected to cope just as well as experienced teachers. As one put it 'you are treated as a real teacher and resented if you can't cope', while another said 'although it has been acknowledged that I was an NQT, I have felt under pressure to know exactly what I should be doing and at times have felt too embarrassed to ask'.

It is clear, then, that NQTs still do need considerable support, even if their circumstances are rather different from those of student teachers, and it does seem appropriate that the first item on the DfE list implies that there should be a mentor for each NQT, or a co-ordinator to whom all NQTs can turn, or both. For NQTs assessment is still going on and though it may be less explicit, it can be just as important, especially given the dramatic increase in one-year temporary jobs thanks largely to LMS. In secondary schools, an obvious choice for mentor would be the Head of Department, but the choice is less clear in primary schools, lacking a departmental structure. In many ways, the mentor will be seen more as an equal and Cole (1991) actually proposes that a 'natural' personal relationship in which NQTs choose their own mentors is much more effective than an imposed system. Similarly, some larger primary schools are able to use a 'year partner' system in which the NQT is paired with an experienced colleague teaching the same year group, enabling them to plan together and perhaps to team-teach, thus meeting several of the objectives of the DfE list. In other cases, the co-ordinator is expected to take on the close, personal one-to-one role of the mentor as well as the administrative 'whole school' co-ordination role.

In practice of course the everyday pressures of teaching can make it difficult for good mentoring to succeed. The HMI report *The New Teacher in School*, for example, noted that

> Although most schools saw a need for a system of support and guidance involving a designated colleague or colleagues, regular meetings, observation of the probationer while teaching, open and frank evaluation, the opportunity to see experienced colleagues teaching, and time for discussion, preparation and thinking, not all were able to operate the system as they might have wished.
>
> (HMI 1987)

Similarly, the 1992 HMI report on the induction of new teachers found wide variations in practice. What often seems to happen is that help may be available to begin with, but the level of explicit support may well decline as time goes on. One NQT said:

> I have an excellent, supportive mentor who I work closely with, as she teaches the same year group. In my first term I had one hour a week

(approximately) contact time, but this declined in the second term and vanished by the end of the spring term.

This decrease in support is probably not due to a decline in interest or commitment on the part of the mentor, however. What often happens is that, once the NQT can cope (or seems to cope), pressures of time mean that the mentor is less and less likely to offer support unless it is asked for, especially if the mentor is also the co-ordinator with other responsibilities. One NQT, in a large primary school with three others, commented:

> we have a mentor (the deputy head) in school, and that was fairly useful early on – but she is very busy and as long as we are coping, we don't like to bother her.

One partial solution could be to make the network of support extend beyond a single mentor, and curriculum co-ordinators could obviously have a role here. For example, as with student teachers, a meeting with their mentor might enable NQTs to discuss particular curriculum areas where they felt less confident, enabling the mentor to approach the appropriate co-ordinators for help rather than leaving it to the NQTs to pluck up courage and make their approach themselves. Similarly, Smith and Alred (1993) propose that the whole school should be involved, not just the teachers 'deemed worthy to be mentors', though such a support network will usually need a system of liaison between the mentor and the curriculum co-ordinators, rather than being left to chance or depending on staffroom friendships.

As far as co-ordinators are concerned, organising support for NQTs, while having many overlaps with provision for student teachers, does also require an awareness of their particular problems. NQTs may be seen as beginners, straight out of college, but they are often expected to cope, or at least to look as if they are coping. Student teachers will usually have a particular teacher, whose class they are taking over, assigned to them, but sources of support for NQTs may be less obvious and may need to be managed with considerable sensitivity by co-ordinators.

RETURNERS

Significantly, far less research has been done on returners as compared with student teachers and NQTs, yet they clearly do have their own particular needs and priorities. They also represent a substantial group – Buzzing (1990) claims that, of all the 'new entrants' to teaching in 1989, 53 per cent could be classified as returners. Moreover, changing career patterns mean that an increasing number of student teachers qualify as 'mature students' because they have brought up a family or had other jobs before training to teach, making them similar to returners in some ways. On many PGCE courses, the average age is now 25 or 26, and some students are even older than their tutors! Conversely, some 'returners' may never have actually taught once they had qualified, so that they will have a lot in common with NQTs. Bearing these similarities in mind, this section will look particularly at those returning to the profession who actually qualified and first taught some time ago.

In a period of dramatic change in education, when the goalposts for teachers may appear to be little more than a rapidly moving blur on the horizon, it is hardly surprising that many returners are particularly concerned about the changes that have occurred, even if it is only a few years since they left teaching. Students and NQTs should at least have an up-to-date knowledge of the latest version of the National Curriculum, and the vast majority of them accept it as what they must provide, but for returners it may represent a major source of anxiety. As one put it:

> I was reasonably confident about being able to control the class, especially after having had two children of my own. What really worried me was all those National Curriculum documents.

Once they have got over their initial anxieties about coming back to teaching, most returners find that they have not 'lost their touch', especially since they now have more experience behind them. What they do need is the support of curriculum co-ordinators in getting to grips with the changes in subject content, organisation and assessment. Moreover, it is likely that such support will be needed initially from all subject co-ordinators and not just from those where the new teacher feels particularly weak, as is more likely with students and NQTs.

Apart from their previous teaching, many returners also bring with them other valuable experiences which can enrich not only their own teaching but also the life of the school. A large number, of course, have brought up their own children and are therefore very used to dealing with everything from runny noses to temper tantrums, though the parallels between looking after your own children and teaching a class should not be extended too far. Having had their own children should also help teachers in their dealings with parents, even if only because it gives them more credibility. On the other hand, one returner actually said, 'If I'd had my own children before I taught, I'd never have had the confidence to teach!' In many cases, these parents have helped out at their own child's primary school, not only 'keeping their hand in' but also possibly giving them insights into working as teachers alongside other adults. Interestingly, some returners have trained and worked as secondary teachers, and decided to move into primary teaching only after having had their own children or helped in their local primary school. These returners will frequently themselves be expected to take on curriculum co-ordinator roles very quickly, in spite of their lack of primary experience.

On the other hand, returners may well also have other problems or responsibilities. Family commitments are an obvious example, and many returners acknowledge that they could not have managed without support at home. One typical comment was 'without such an understanding family I couldn't have put in the hours and hours at home that I have done'. Another problem is that, as older, experienced, fully qualified teachers, returners are probably *expected* to cope, even more than NQTs are, and there may be no special arrangements made for them at all – a returner could, after all, have more years' teaching experience than anybody else in the school!

Apart from being aware of such potential problems, what can co-ordinators do to help? As with other 'new entrants' having a mentor can be very useful – Jayne and Stokes (1992), for example, describe a mentor scheme for returners, which they found worked best when the mentors were open about their own teaching, including their weaknesses, rather than posing as 'models'. These findings are particularly interesting in the light of the earlier references to Claxton (1984) and Jenkins *et al.*'s (1991) 'model' mentor.

Jayne and Stokes also found that the returners' mentors were good at counselling and befriending but found criticisms difficult to make. This perhaps reflects mentors' perception of returners as being more of equal status, though a similar finding was made by Terrel (1990) who noted that tutors of student teachers also found it much easier to be supportive rather than critical. The returners may not always object to this, of course – one described her mentor as 'really wonderful, giving me help and advice without ever seeming to be critical in any way'.

Mentors and co-ordinators may therefore find themselves taking on complementary roles, with the mentor having a more personal and 'equal' relationship and perhaps acting as a link between the new teacher and the subject co-ordinators. In most primary schools, such a network will clearly involve just about all the staff in practice, and Buzzing (1990) for example discusses whole school approaches in the creation of 'returner-positive schools'. Apart from practical suggestions like help with child care and a 're-entry programme', she notes the danger of seeing returners as somehow rather inferior, and of therefore having low expectations of them, in contrast to the other danger of seeing them as experienced teachers and expecting them to cope without support.

Overall, returners do therefore have a lot in common with the other groups of new entrants, and some of the same support mechanisms will be very helpful to them. In other ways, their particular strengths in terms of experience may mask the particular anxieties that many have and may also cause heads, co-ordinators and other colleagues simply to assume that there are no problems.

SUMMARY

Though student teachers, NQTs and returners have a lot in common, co-ordinators need to be aware of the particular needs of each. Student teachers, for example, are often understandably anxious about class management, while NQTs tend to be more concerned about wider professional relationships and responsibilities, and returners often feel least confident about curriculum changes. Explicit lists of competencies may help, and co-ordinators may want to set up a system in which they or other teachers take on the role of mentors.

It is clear from talking to teachers who have taken on the role of mentor, or who have been involved in other ways with students, NQTs or returners, that it can be a rewarding and even enjoyable experience. Many mentors and co-ordinators, for example, feel that they too have learned, partly from having to make their own aims, values and ideas more explicit and reflect on them through discussion. Some have gained from the skills which their student or new teacher has been able to bring, or even from the all too rare opportunity to observe someone else teaching. Given the danger that teachers could come to feel de-skilled, having a beginner to support can actually help teachers recognise that they *do* have expertise and skills to offer, and that teaching is definitely not something that anyone can do at the drop of a hat; the old adage that you never really understand something until you teach it applies equally well to teaching itself.

Part II

Promoting a quality curriculum

Chapter 7

Co-ordinating the English curriculum

Neil Kitson

INTRODUCTION

Over recent years we have witnessed mounting pressure upon primary teachers to improve the quality of English teaching (Wray and Medwell 1994, Peel and Bell 1994). Increasingly, the development of English teaching within the school has fallen to co-ordinators, who Ofsted (1994c) indicate have insufficient time to do this effectively. In the face of external pressures to deliver the National Curriculum there is a grave danger of 'playing safe', with English teaching becoming stolid and unchallenging, the enthusiasm and thrill burned out of it for fear of not getting it right. Despite this, the fundamental job of the English co-ordinator is to raise the profile and quality of language work within the school. This chapter will explore the ways in which the co-ordinator can support and develop colleagues so that their teaching of English can be exciting and challenging. It will do so by looking first at the general issues of co-ordination of language throughout the school with specific reference to:

- marking policy;
- study skills; and
- books.

Then we consider the specific curriculum areas of:

- speaking and listening;
- writing – handwriting and spelling; and
- reading.

GENERAL ISSUES

The first thing that newly appointed co-ordinators need to do is empower themselves with knowledge; to find out what is going on in the school. One can start with a look at the existing resources, auditing what's there and where it is. This analysis will begin to create an overall picture of how the subject is viewed by the school. The level of access to shared resources and the degree of flexibility allowed in teaching aspects of the English curriculum within year groups will indicate the way that the subject is perceived. It will show you existing areas of strength and where help might be needed in the development of skills and knowledge of staff.

Having undertaken an audit the co-ordinator, in collaboration with colleagues, can begin to develop an action plan. This will take time to implement and often it will have to take its turn in the curriculum develop-ment cycle of the school. However, if a plan for English has been agreed then the co-ordinator will be in a much stronger position to lead change through enthusiasm and good practice in his or her classroom, through opportune intervention in staff meetings as well as structured policy review and development.

> In the immediate future, schools need to help primary English co-
> ordinators ... to monitor and improve work for which they have
> responsibility.
>
> (Ofsted 1994c)

So how does one go about finding out what is the existing practice within a school and where development might be needed? Paper docu-mentation plays a significant role in understanding existing thinking and philosophies. Documentation can take a number of forms ranging from formal policy statements through to individual teachers' plans. Much can be inferred from whether the teacher has identified individual lesson plans with specific learning areas within English or whether it is seen as 'a part of everything that children do'. One can also consider wider whole school language issues which will again give an indication as to the level of curriculum development that has been undertaken by the staff. Look, for example, at the marking policy for your school (if it has one) and see how it is used. Look at the development of study skills and how this is reinforced in other areas of the curriculum. Look at the school's book policy. Below we consider how each of these issues can be influenced by the co-ordinator.

Marking policy for writing

Although often overlooked, the marking policy of a school is crucial in the development of young writers. All too often there is little consistency between teachers within a school. Yet marking is the single most signifi-cant way that teachers respond to children's writing. The aim is to encour-age children to become independent, confident and flexible writers. The marking policy adopted by a school needs to reflect this. Ofsted noted that effective teaching of English at Key Stages 1 and 2 shared a number of characteristics of which one was the

> systematic and rigorous appraisal of written work, which addressed not only the surface features of spelling, layout, etc. but also structural features and quality of content and organisation.
>
> (Ofsted 1994c)

By too stringently marking children's work it is possible to inhibit them, making them dependent and imitative of the teacher's style. We need to encourage the development richness of content whilst maintaining levels of spelling, grammar and punctuation within children's writing. One must encourage staff to consider marking for a purpose as well as getting the children to write for one. Marking needs to be consistent across teachers and there needs to be a sense of continuity and progress throughout the school. Also, there needs to be a realisation that drafting and redrafting of work is very important and, in this respect, that different emphases within marking are appropriate for different occasions. Frequently, the majority of pupils never get further than the second draft which tends to be seen as the 'fair copy'. As a result, marking may only focus on surface features of layout, or gross spelling errors (Ofsted 1994c). It is imperative, however, that marking also takes into account composition, structure and content.

Study skills

Another area that can be looked at relatively simply is that of study skills. This is significant not only in its own right but also for the way that it informs other English processes. Here, a very simple comparison can be made between the use of worksheets and reference books. Whilst there is nothing intrinsically wrong with worksheets, an overdependency upon them means that the children will tend to become restricted in their ability to handle a wider range of source materials. In many schools, the notion of study skills may not have been addressed and if it has it may well have been separated from the general English curriculum. Together with study skills the co-ordinator should also consider how the library resources are used. Are the children encouraged to develop independent study skills through their use of the library? Are project collections taken out of the library for them to use in the classroom? Schools may have attempted to tackle the issue of study skills by purchasing resource packs or books of exercises which the children are able to do in isolation. What is important is the extent to which the skills learnt are carried over into other written work. A good guide to the effective carry-over of study skills is evidence of the extent of differentiation in the work of the class. By looking at a range of children's writing one can analyse the type of activities that the children have been involved in and the types of source materials that have been used. If there is little evidence of the development of study skills, a re-evaluation of how the library is used might be useful. You may consider:

- Introducing and familiarising children and staff with a colour coding scheme or Dewey classification.
- Making the cataloguing system of books and posters more accessible to children.
- Setting up library quizzes of authors or subjects.
- Developing sheets of questions on a theme which relate to events in a particular month, e.g. Florence Nightingale's birthday, Gunpowder Plot or Autumn.
- Devising sheets which require children to gather information through scanning of text and then completing grids of questions (true or false grids) thus (a) avoiding copying out and (b) encouraging reading for information.

Books

It is incumbent upon the co-ordinator to raise the profile of literature within the school to raise the excitement level created by books. This can be done by simply being an enthusiast and producing lists for colleagues of good stories relating to specific topics or themes as they arise. Frequently, there are lots of books in a school but they are situated in inappropriate classrooms. A simple way to revitalise the literature stock within a school is to have a book exchange where the books within the school are rearranged into a simple structure to meet the needs of the classes as they are at present.

Above all, there needs to be a wide variety of books in school 'including but not limited to reading schemes, and offering a good choice of poetry, novels, and non-fiction' (Ofsted 1994c). Peel and Bell (1994) suggest these should be in both the central school library and in individual classes. One strategy that creates interest and income for additional resources is the running of a book fair. Inviting a commercial company in to sell the books can be the focus for a range of book related activities such as readings, designing jackets and authors' visits.

A simple audit of the books that have been read to the children is useful. With the early years, is selection on the basis of whatever comes to hand or is there evidence of progression and range? With Key Stage 2, does the pattern take the form of 'a Roald Dahl, they always go down well, a book loosely related to the topic, something related to science, *The Lion, the Witch and the Wardrobe*, an old favourite, and then another Roald Dahl'? There is nothing wrong with such a selection in itself but, if the pattern is repeated across all the years, then one must consider the value of the reading models we are presenting to the children and how an appropriate range of materials can best be presented.

The way staff approach literature is also crucial to the way books are viewed in school. As co-ordinator, you can encourage the staff to become interested in books. They should begin to see themselves as role models for the children, perhaps by each teacher reading a favourite story and allowing the children to choose which of these they wish to listen to.

CURRICULUM ISSUES

We turn now to consider in detail the areas of speaking and listening, writing and reading.

Speaking and listening

Often taken for granted by teachers, speaking and listening also needs to be planned for and developed. A number of studies have shown that children have greater fluency of language at home than they do at school (Tizard and Hughes 1984, Wells 1986). Teachers therefore need to structure activities to promote the use of language rather than simply hope that it will occur naturally in the school environment. Activities range from story telling and structured play through to information giving. Whatever you do it is useful to consider the following points suggested by Peel and Bell (1994):

- What is the purpose of the activity?
- What aspects of the discussion will be passed on to others?
- How will the activity be introduced?
- How will the classroom space be arranged?
- What are the roles of the children and the teacher?
- How will reluctant speakers be encouraged?
- What form of classroom contract has been established?

One very effective strategy for developing speaking and listening which takes account of the points raised above is drama. There are, however, a great number of so-called 'drama' activities that take place within the classroom, so it is important to find out from colleagues what they mean by the term. Do they mean music and movement, assemblies or teacher-in-role (where the teacher take a role within the story)? Whilst not all *teachers* feel comfortable using drama, all *children* should have access to this very valuable form of learning. It may be necessary for the co-ordinator to introduce a range of simple activities for colleagues to try out.

- Link the drama to a children's story. Don't just act it out but bring the story to life. Ask children to take on the role of the other villagers who have suddenly noticed the beanstalk grown by Jack or the people trying to persuade Burglar Bill not to steal any more.
- Demonstrate how teachers at Key Stage 1 can use the pretend corner as the basis of drama work by working alongside the children and introducing problems within their play for them to overcome.
- Introduce drama structures through history and geography. Offer advice as to the use of such techniques as hot-seating, e.g. the teacher taking on the role of a Roman soldier being questioned by the children.
- Bring to life a still picture of the Earl of Catesby planning the Gunpowder Plot.
- If the only drama that goes on is the class assembly then it may be possible to use classroom drama activities as part of the assembly.

The co-ordinator needs to convey the effectiveness of this way of working and help colleagues to set attainable goals for themselves so that they and the children can experience the excitement and vitality of drama. Above all, help colleagues see that drama is not about 'knickers and vest in the hall', nor playing in the 'Wendy house', nor 'making up plays in the corner'. It is about 'real people' sorting out real problems.

Writing

It is important to try and establish progression throughout the school so that the developments made by individual teachers can be built upon enabling children to experience consistency. It is useful, for instance, to look at the fiction/story writing of the children not just within a year group but across the whole school. An explicit aim of their English experience must be to help them develop as confident, flexible writers. Having established good practice in the early years, often the only real subsequent development in a child's work is in the length of the children's writing. Children need to consider structure and form, be it in prose or poetry. They need to be aware of the use of paragraphs and the importance of style. For example, children using what they consider to be a journalistic form frequently write a simple narrative composition, fictional or otherwise, above which they put a large headline, all of which is beautifully presented on the computer. However, not only could they explore the medium by addressing the issues of style and content, through looking at different articles and newspapers, but the process of working with real evidence and real material can also be enjoyable. Similarly, it is important that poetry is introduced to and studied by the children so that they begin to appreciate and gain experience of the wide variety of styles.

Handwriting

As with other areas of the English curriculum, a consistent policy for handwriting is most important within the school if children's work is to develop. One must not leave handwriting solely to Key Stage 1, as is sometimes the case. The good practice that has been laid down needs to be maintained throughout Key Stage 2. Whilst the children may well have the basics necessary for good handwriting, such factors as writing equipment, furniture and physical maturation of the children should be considered. Teachers need to observe the children whilst in the process of writing, so that judgements can be made as to how they can best be helped to develop, rather than base their evaluation on the finished piece of work. For example, it may be that, having observed the children at Key Stage 1, you feel they need more experience of drawing in order to develop pencil control, in which case it might be necessary to liaise with the art co-ordinator.

By careful observation teachers can begin to think about task differentiation and readiness for progression. There are a number of schools where progression from print to joined letter formation and from pencil to pen is fixed and almost becomes a rite of passage. It is important that progression is discussed so that the children can be helped to develop specific handwriting skills when they are ready. Children need to be given an opportunity to experience different types of writing implements reflecting those that they will find outside school. They need to be made aware of a wide range of writing styles from formal presentational through to 'quick writing' and the school needs to value all of these. There needs to be an overall scheme for writing within the school that promotes the introduction of joined up script as early as possible.

> Handwriting could be better developed if schools taught a cursive hand earlier . . . pupils responded to early and systematic teaching of handwriting with work of a higher standard.
>
> (Ofsted 1994c)

This is the most economic style to use when under pressure rather than the 'fast print' style which involves much greater hand pressure and tension. Children need to be encouraged to move towards joined exit strokes. Once the flow is achieved, correct movement to shape the letters is far more likely. The earlier a cursive style is used the stronger it will become embedded in the child's motor memory and the more it will be sustained under stress.

Spelling

As co-ordinator, it is important to stress the joy of words so that language becomes fun. Spelling needs to be more than a test of children's short-term memory. Teachers need to be helped to set sensible, manageable targets and to build on success. To develop confident and independent spellers, teachers need to consider how the classroom is to be set up so that they can avoid falling victim to the 'spelling conga'. They need to consider also how word banks and dictionaries are sited and used. We frequently judge children's spelling after adult intervention when the work is completed but to gain any true perspective on the child's ability we need to assess unaided spelling as well.

Aim to develop a consistency of approach throughout the school. Some useful points to consider are:

- What do we see as the stages of spelling development?
- What are the skills required to spell?
- How are strategies such as visualisation and look/cover/write techniques employed?

Foster an interest in words by moving away from learning lists and exploring:

- word origins and place names;
- the history of English, e.g. monks got paid by the inch so they added 'e's on to words that didn't need them to make them longer; Caxton was the first to use the 'gh' from the Dutch language.

Introduce:

- spelling games;
- crosswords; and
- word lists linked to language study that consider derivatives, root words, prefixes and suffixes, letter patterns and letter strings.

Whatever is presented to the children, it needs to be planned so as to encourage depth of understanding rather than simply increasing word length.

Reading

There is always the danger that reading simply becomes the service industry to the rest of the curriculum. With increasing pressure on curriculum time it is clear that teachers do not feel that they have sufficient time to hear readers. Yet reading is seen as being increasingly important. This dilemma causes understandable tension for teachers. Irrespective of how individual schools resolve the issue it is important to appraise the position of reading and literature within the school and, if necessary, raise its profile. This can be addressed in two ways:

- by looking at the reading policy of the school;
- by examining the way that books are being valued and used within the school.

The role of the co-ordinator is to elevate the *profile* of literature by raising the *excitement* level for books with both teachers and pupils alike.

It is important to work with colleagues and to consider a structure for reading possibly using the criteria suggested by Wray and Medwell (1994):

- Reading is a complex process so that simple approaches will have little chance of success.
- Teaching reading needs to be built upon what the children do well before including aspects that they find difficult.
- Children do need the technicalities of reading but these need to be set in the context of meaning.

The questions that might usefully be addressed are:

- Why do we hear children read?
- What do we do when we hear children read?
- When we hear children read what are we recording?

There are no definitive answers to these questions but by giving colleagues a chance to question and reaffirm what it is that they are trying to achieve, you will bring reading to the foreground. With the first of these questions it is important to consider whether or not we are target setting effectively for the children (e.g. teaching specific phonic skills where appropriate) or whether the children are simply progressing through the designated reading scheme (as reported by Ofsted 1994c). You may find it useful to begin by looking at the reading resources within school and asking the following questions:

- Is there sufficient balance between structure and choice?
- Is there a lot of material at the same level?
- Is the core scheme simply a ladder by which reading success is measured?

It may be that as a staff you have decided on a 'free choice' approach to reading along the line of 'real books'. Although the teachers may well be given free choice regarding the books that they can choose for the children in the class, in reality they themselves may limit the choice for the children and, by so doing, limit the child's reading experience. It is important for the co-ordinator to establish what is really happening so that a meaningful structure can be introduced.

As co-ordinator you need to be aware of what teachers are actually doing. with regard to the recording of reading progress:

* Are they recording frequency of reading activity?
* Is there any sense of diagnostic interpretation?

The latter form of recording is the more beneficial of the two yet teachers may become concerned predominantly with 'when and how much' rather than 'what and how' children read.

Having considered the issue of recording reading progress the vexed question of resources will again be important. Diagnosing the need of a child is one thing; having the requisite material to help that child is something else. As you begin to look for the development of fluency in reading, of comprehension, of sight vocabulary or of phonics you will need to consider the materials that will be needed to support the children. These have to be identified, introduced into the reading scheme and then made available to all members of staff. If the whole process can be done collectively by the staff, the task will be that much easier and colleagues will feel that they have ownership of the developing scheme.

SUMMARY

The most important role that the co-ordinator of English has is to raise the quality of language throught the school. The more that the children are exposed to language, the more able they will be to produce it. Explore with staff how consistency of approach and a planned progression can be introduced in the areas of speaking and listening, reading and writing, and examine the marking policy, book policy and study skills across the curriculum.

Give yourself time to establish a good model of English teaching in your own classroom before moving on to the wider school issues. Once you have a picture of what is happening and have discussed what changes could be implemented develop a strategy which enables those people concerned to feel part of the process of change. All of the staff will be involved in the teaching of English so they must all be part of the developments if they are to succeed.

Above all the English co-ordinator's role is to be an enthusiast who makes English exciting, to demonstrate this through good classroom practice, to support colleagues and to enable them to develop their own knowledge and skills.

Chapter 8

Mathematics

Mike Price and Rose Griffiths

INTRODUCTION

The mathematics co-ordinator in a primary school starts with the advantage that every teacher and parent is likely to see this subject as being important, even if they are lacking in confidence in it themselves. This chapter examines attitudes to mathematics, and the breadth of mathematical content necessary in a changing world. We look at the repertoire of teaching and learning styles and methods which a co-ordinator should encourage in order to make mathematics teaching both effective and enjoyable. Lastly, some brief case studies illustrate our conclusions about some of the characteristics of successful maths co-ordinating.

ATTITUDES TO MATHEMATICS

Mathematics enjoys high status as a subject in both schools and society. But the widely recognised importance of this subject brings with it pressures for success and strong feelings in relation to failure. Adults, including parents and primary teachers, have normally been exposed to a relatively large amount of mathematics compared with other subjects in their compulsory education. The quality and quantity of this exposure fundamentally affects both attainment and attitude. Relatively few primary teachers have specialised in mathematics, beyond the compulsory stage. The Cockcroft Committee commissioned a study into the use of mathematics by adults in daily life. A disturbing picture was reported in which 'the extent to which the need to undertake even an apparently simple piece of mathematics could induce in some people feelings of anxiety, helplessness, fear and even guilt was perhaps the most striking feature' (DES, 1983, p. 1). Such feelings were not confined to the less academically qualified, and the study also found many people who had unhappy recollections of their mathematics lessons.

In every mathematics lesson, children's learning or failure to learn is accompanied by the development of their attitudes to the subject, and teachers convey, consciously or unconsciously, messages about the subject which affect the children's attitudes. Furthermore, once attitudes have been formed they can have a long-term influence, for good or ill, on subsequent learning. Co-ordinators need to recognise and be honest about their own feelings in mathematics and aim to encourage openness among their colleagues who will typically embrace a wide range of mathematical attainments and attitudes. Providing opportunities for children to communicate their feelings about what they are experiencing in mathematics should also be encouraged.

PUBLISHERS AND SCHEMES

The choice or at least the management of a commercially produced mathematics scheme is commonly a major part of the co-ordinator's role. The range of choice in mathematics is very wide, and the ways in which published materials are used to support, or inhibit, children's learning vary considerably from school to school.

HMI surveys in both the 1970s and 1980s pointed to *two* major weaknesses resulting from the excessive reliance on the use of commercial schemes, driven by pupil materials:

- too much practice of skills which have already been mastered;
- insufficient time given to direct teaching and to discussion.

(DES 1989, p. 13)

HMI pointed to the benefits, in terms of both efficiency and quality of communication, of a blend of whole-class and small group teaching, to deal with particular topics or processes. HMI's conclusion concerning the centrality of the teacher's role in developing children's learning was unequivocal:

> No matter how good the mathematical resources, such as published schemes and practical materials, it was the quality of the exposition and dialogue with the teacher that enabled the children to reflect upon and think through mathematical problems and ideas. This factor more than any other marked the difference between good and mediocre work.
>
> (DES 1989, p. 27)

Given the demands of mathematics in the National Curriculum era, primary teachers' understandable need for published mathematics schemes, at least to support their work in mathematics, remains undiminished. A recent survey of 25 Leicestershire primary schools (Price 1994) revealed only one school, for infants, which did not use any published scheme. The schools as a whole referred to over ten different published schemes in use to some extent, singly or in some combination. The potential of published schemes as mediators of the National Curriculum may be problematic, as a recent evaluation report published by SCAA (1993) has pointed out.

Co-ordinators should keep under review the ways in which their school uses a commercial mathematics scheme or schemes. Such a review will need to consider classroom organisation and management strategies which both address the criticisms of HMI and serve to maximise the potential benefits of the commercial materials which are currently available in the school. Changing to a new commercial scheme is a very large and potentially expensive undertaking.

What is remarkable about post-war developments in primary mathematics, particularly over the last fifteen years, is the extent to which a professional consensus has emerged about the nature of the subject, the ways in which children learn and the implications for classroom practice. We will aim to identify the main characteristics of this vision for primary mathematics, a vision which transcends both the various 'tinkerings' with the statutory framework of attainment targets and programmes of study, and all the difficulties associated with 'implementation' linked to a national system for assessment.

CHILDREN'S LEARNING

The post-war influence of psychological perspectives and research into children's learning of mathematics has been considerable. Such influences first came to prominence in a seminal report from the Mathematical Association, which was published as early as 1955:

> children, developing at their own rates, learn through their active response to the experiences that come to them; through constructive play, experiment and discussion children become aware of relationships and develop mental structures which are mathematical in form and are in fact the only sound basis of mathematical techniques.
>
> (Mathematical Association 1955, p.v)

This view of children as active agents in their own learning is very well developed in the exemplary guidelines produced by the ILEA, before its demise. A number of pointers for good practice are identified in relation to each of the following four assumptions about children's learning.

- Children learn best when they are motivated.
- Each child learns in a way that is unique for that child.
- Children learn both independently and through collaboration.
- Children consolidate their learning by meeting the same idea in different contexts.

(ILEA 1988a, pp. 6–7)

Central to such views of the learning process is the following fundamental proposition:

> What children learn is fundamentally connected with how they learn it.

(Lindquist 1994, p. 134)

The 'what' and 'how' of children's learning have been well analysed in an important HMI publication, *Mathematics from 5 to 16* (DES 1985). Five categories of objective are distinguished:

- mathematical facts;
- mathematical skills;
- conceptual structures;
- general strategies;
- personal qualities.

Mathematical facts and skills

Factual knowledge includes remembering terms (e.g. multiples of two are *even* numbers), remembering symbolism (e.g. ÷ means division), remembering conventions (e.g. tens on the left, units on the right) and remembering results (e.g. number bonds). Skills include written computational skills, keyboard skills involving calculators and microcomputers, and practical skills in measurement and construction.

Conceptual structures

'Understanding' is closely linked with the ability to select, apply, relate and interpret the mathematics connected with particular contexts. A considerable body of knowledge has accumulated concerning the ways in which children's understanding of mathematics develops (Dickson *et al.* 1984). Research clearly shows that learning does not proceed in a straightforward linear fashion, along parallel tracks, but involves the gradual build-up of a complex network of interrelated parts. This complexity may not be widely appreciated but the importance of the abilities to 'know, understand and do' mathematics is widely accepted, both within and outside the profession. However, HMI's fourth and fifth categories point towards a broader and less widely understood agenda for primary mathematics.

Personal qualities

We have already highlighted attitude formation as an important consideration in working with children, other teachers or parents. HMI identified several features of a positive attitude to mathematics including:

- appreciation of the purpose, power and relevance of mathematics;
- satisfaction derived from a sense of achievement;
- confidence in an ability to do mathematics at an appropriate level.

(DES 1985, p. 25)

HMI also identified a second aspect of personal qualities: the development of 'good work habits'. Such habits involve being:

- imaginative, creative, flexible;
- systematic;
- independent in thought and action;
- co-operative;
- persistent.

(DES 1985, p. 24)

Personal qualities are not mathematical *per se* but the importance of their development through appropriate mathematical activity from the earliest stages should not be overlooked. HMI's fourth category of objective – general strategies – shifts the focus from the child to the nature of mathematics itself.

THE NATURE OF MATHEMATICS

The Cockcroft Report (1982, p. 83) welcomed the broadening of the curriculum beyond arithmetic for its 'beneficial effect in improving children's attitudes to mathematics and also in laying the foundations of better understanding'.

Since the Cockcroft Report there has been some further widening of the content of primary mathematics and some new interpretations in established areas. These developments have been driven by a desire to relate mathematics as widely as possible to contexts for its use and to the ways in which it is actually used and applied. In number, the potential of electronic calculators has also forced a reappraisal of the skills of calculating in three modes: in the head ('mental arithmetic'), on paper or using a calculating aid (from fingers to a calculator). Work on estimation, in number and measurement, has assumed greater importance. Number is also linked with the roots of algebra, through work on patterns, relationships, missing number problems, functions and simple graphs.

Shape and space – in both two and three dimensions – involves the classification and properties of shapes, their relationships and uses, and the study of location and movement in space, including links with design and pattern making. Floor robots and microcomputer screen displays provide stimulating new contexts for such work. Handling data has been a major area for development in recent years. The work now involves a wide range of forms of visual communication for classifications, relationships and quantitative information. Skills of data collection, recording, processing, representing and interpreting are emphasised, including the potential of microcomputers. Most ambitiously, the introduction of the language of uncertainty and simple ideas of probability has also formed a strand in the National Curriculum, following the lines of the ILEA specification (1988a, pp. 100–102).

The content of primary mathematics now makes considerably greater demands on general classroom teachers, and colleagues will need material or human support in particular areas. However, a co-ordinator cannot reasonably be expected to act as the fount of all knowledge in this respect.

We have been discussing mathematical content, but there is more to consider in relation to the question 'What is mathematics?'

General strategies

HMI (1985, pp. 18–24) identified the following range of strategies involved in doing or using mathematics:

- ability to estimate;
- ability to approximate;
- trial and error methods;
- simplifying difficult tasks;
- looking for patterns;
- reasoning;
- making and testing hypotheses;
- proving and disproving.

Such strategies have become firmly established in the National Curriculum as Attainment Target 1: **Using and Applying Mathematics**. This target involves three main 'strands' of development: making and monitoring choices; mathematical communication; and reasoning, logic and proof. It has not proved easy to build progression into these strands at ten levels, but the separate existence of this target, alongside those covering the main content areas, represents a major victory for professional judgement in determining a very broad view of primary mathematics in the National Curriculum. This view (Figure 8.1) of mathematics in *three* dimensions – content, process and context – is well captured in the model of a cuboid (Curriculum Council for Wales 1992, p. 12).

What then are the implications of all this for classroom practice?

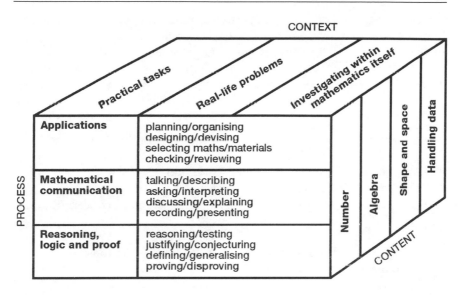

Figure 8.1 The process, content and context dimensions of *Using and Applying Mathematics*
Source: From *Mathematics in the National Curriculum: Non-statutory Guidance for Teachers* (1992), Curriculum Council for Wales

TEACHING AND LEARNING STYLES

It was the Cockcroft Report (1982, p. 71) which sharply focused on the need for teachers to provide a broad range of learning experiences at *all* levels of mathematics education, including opportunities for:

- exposition by the teacher;
- discussion between teacher and pupils and between pupils themselves;
- appropriate practical work;
- consolidation and practice of fundamental skills and routines;
- problem solving, including the application of mathematics to every-day situations;
- investigational work.

Over the last ten years, LEA advisory teachers have done much to help classroom teachers in developing all aspects of the Cockcroft list. Since 1990, further opportunities for development on a national scale have come from GEST courses for both co-ordinators and other interested teachers. The importance of the Cockcroft list and the need for further national support in helping teachers to develop children's strategies for using and applying mathematics (Attainment Target 1) continues in the 1990s (SCAA 1993, p. 29). Further impetus for working along such lines has also come from the Ofsted schedule for school inspections. Inspectors are looking for a range of approaches, breadth and balance of content, links between topics, provision for individual differences, and evidence that all aspects of the Cockcroft list are being addressed.

In evaluating 'quality of learning', the schedule includes a checklist of personal qualities and general strategies, covering children's capacity:

- to show curiosity, to question and to probe persistently for meaning;
- to recognise patterns in their work and to make generalisations based on what has been learned earlier;
- to communicate what they have learned showing concern for clarity and accuracy of meaning;
- to evaluate their progress and be self-critical;
- to apply what has been learned to unfamiliar situations;
- to work independently or co-operatively as appropriate.

(Ofsted 1993a, pt 4, p. 28)

We have surveyed the development of a vision for primary mathematics which we hope will help to inform the production of school policy statements. It is part of the co-ordinator's role to develop such a statement and to work upon its implications with colleagues. Since 1990 we have had the good fortune to work with around 150 Leicestershire primary teachers, including many mathematics co-ordinators, on centrally funded in-service courses based at the University of Leicester. The related school based work of these teachers has involved a wide range of foci for development, levels of responsibility and strategies for working with children, colleagues and parents. Their learning has contributed to our learning, which we would like to share through a small number of case studies.

PUTTING THEORY INTO PRACTICE

Each co-ordinator's working situation is different, and the following descriptions have been chosen to show the range of initial methods you might use. Changing or improving your *own* way of working within the classroom is difficult enough, and it is important not to underestimate the task of helping colleagues to work with you to improve mathematics teaching throughout your school, and not to be discouraged if you feel progress is slow.

The first case study (Lynn's school) was chosen to show how progress was made in a school where the co-ordinator, and patterns of work in maths, were well established, and where many staff felt there was little need for review or change.

The second case study (Anne's school) illustrates the issue of teacher confidence, and lack of familiarity with parts of the maths curriculum.

The last (Tony's school) describes how a co-ordinator can work alongside colleagues to introduce new areas of mathematics.

All three examples show how important it is to focus teachers' attention on the mathematics which individual children are actually learning and using.

Writing a mathematics policy

Lynn was well established as maths co-ordinator in her school, and had produced a comprehensive document which staff obviously valued as a practical aid when they were planning for maths. It included a scheme of work for each key stage, and references to all the maths scheme materials (both commercial and teacher written ones) and other resources which were available within the school. However, Lynn felt there were some areas of maths which were rather poorly covered in her scheme, and she was concerned that there was not sufficient provision for children with special needs.

Lynn began her review by talking to the head, who made time for her to outline her concerns at a staff meeting. She then invited any members of staff who were interested to join her for an after-school meeting about reviewing maths, and suggested that if they had time beforehand they could think of a particular issue or problem which had arisen in their classes recently, as a possible 'starter' for discussion.

Lynn's school has a staff of over 20, but only two came to the meeting. She felt it was interesting, though, as Celia raised the problem of 'Tom in my class, who still can't do taking away on paper and he'll be going to secondary school next year.' They looked at some of Tom's written work, talked about the difference between what he seemed to be able to do successfully in his head and his poor performance on paper, and realised that they actually did not know whether there were similar disparities for other children in their classes, since they usually only assessed written work. Lynn abandoned her plan to work through copies of the existing school maths document with her colleagues, and instead they agreed to try out some subtraction with individual children in their classes during the next week, and to report back at a second meeting.

Lynn put up a notice inviting all staff to the second meeting and talked to as many individual staff as she could in the next few days about what she, Celia and Jane were trying to find out. Nine staff came, and the meeting resulted in a succession of other voluntary sessions looking in detail at what children were able to do (and how they did it) in number work across the age range.

Lynn felt that the term's meetings had changed her view of what needed reviewing, and that they had raised staff awareness of the importance of using a variety of teaching styles, and of valuing children's own methods in number work. The subsequent review of the school's maths documents was undertaken by a small group of staff working with Lynn, and concentrated on augmenting the information already available about mathematical content and resources with agreements about whole school commitment to principles concerning the ways in which maths would be taught.

Showing that maths can be enjoyable

When Anne moved schools and took up her post as maths co-ordinator, the head asked her to write a policy document and scheme of work as her first priority. She managed to persuade him, however, that it would be better to wait until she had had time to get to know people, so that she could involve the whole staff in some way with writing a policy which would reflect what people would do in their classrooms rather than just her view of what should be happening.

Nearly a year later, Anne was feeling very dispirited, as she felt the views of staff were so disparate that she was unlikely to find any common ground. The majority of staff had said they disliked the commercial maths scheme upon which work had hitherto been based, but were unable to agree on a replacement. Anne's scheduled meetings after school, which she had hoped would result in some agreement about their aims and principles in teaching maths, had degenerated into sessions of complaints about poor resources, lack of time, and naughty children.

Anne was so depressed at her lack of progress as co-ordinator that she decided to retreat into her own classroom and concentrate for a while on providing interesting mathematical activities for her children to do. She especially enjoyed whole class activities, practical and creative work in shape and measure, and games. She was slightly anxious that her colleagues (or the children's parents) might disapprove or feel she was wasting the children's time, so she was careful to make sure the children knew which aspects of maths they were tackling in each activity they tried, and she added explanatory notes to their classroom and corridor displays to make the mathematical content more explicit.

Anne realised very quickly that children and staff from other classes were interested in what she was doing. Some staff asked for copies of worksheets, or for notes about how best to introduce an activity, or for help with collecting resources for a piece of practical work. Anne tentatively suggested that she would not mind setting a maths 'puzzle of the week' for the remainder of that term, and staff agreed. She began to feel that some of the very negative and obstructive views she had heard from some staff previously were based on feelings of anxiety about their own lack of confidence in mathematics, compounded by a lack of experience in teaching without a maths scheme.

Anne decided that the least threatening way forward was to concentrate on practical resources. She initiated a review of what was available to each class, and persuaded the head that an investment in calculators, measuring and construction equipment, and storage boxes for each room was worthwhile. She asked individual members of staff to try out equipment borrowed from other schools, or bought enough for one class for staff to review before purchasing more, and she arranged short 'reporting back' sessions at their weekly whole staff meetings to talk about what children had been doing and why it was mathematical.

Working with a colleague's class

Many co-ordinators must have had colleagues say something like 'Yes, very nice, but it won't work with my class'. Tony works in a special school for children with moderate learning difficulties, aged 5 to 19.

Tony was concerned to reassure staff of the value of the mathematical work already going on throughout the school, to acknowledge the importance of number work but to encourage further work on shape and space. He also wanted to increase and improve the use of maths resources which were available in the school, and decided that the best focus for his allotted in-service time with the whole staff was using the 'Roamer' programmable floor robots, since many staff confessed they had never used the two which the school owned. He used the session to show what he had done with his own class (following some work he had done on a 20-day course) concentrating on describing the progression which was possible for each child, and he gave teachers the chance to try the activities for themselves. He volunteered to visit any class on request, to take a short introductory session along with the class teacher.

Tony's visits to other classes enabled their class teachers to spend time observing children they knew well taking part in a new activity, and they were able to talk to individual children about what they were doing without having to feel responsible for the rest of the class at the same time. Tony also took an extended 'story time' with all the children he had worked with, so that their teachers could get together to discuss what they and he had done, and to plan what they might do next.

SUMMARY

The characteristics of effective co-ordination for mathematics throughout a school are, of course, similar to those in other curriculum areas.

- The co-ordinator needs time to reflect upon his or her own work with children, and to think about what is important about mathematics both in society as a whole and in school. He or she will want to encourage colleagues to do the same.
- Maths *is* a subject where people who have been badly taught themselves (resulting in anxiety or confusion) may tend to feel that it was their own innate inability with the subject which caused their problems, and they perpetuate their own difficulties with children in their class by using the same teaching methods which failed them. The co-ordinator needs to acknowledge this.
- Co-ordinating change is never easy, so it is important to share ideas, plans and responsibility for carrying them out. Sometimes it may be most appropriate to look at overall policies first; alternatively, as we have shown, it may be more sensible to focus on a smaller-scale issue as an agreed priority.

If they are to be successful in using mathematics and to enjoy doing so, children and adults alike need to feel involved and interested in the outcome of changes in their ways of working.

Chapter 9

Science

Tina Jarvis

INTRODUCTION

Before the introduction of the National Curriculum what little science was done in the primary school tended to be natural or biological rather than physical science. Now, as one of the three core subjects, science has taken on far greater importance. As this is a very recent development, many teachers do not have academic science backgrounds and have limited experience of teaching science to young children. Consequently they lack self-confidence, perceiving themselves to have low levels of competence to teach the subject (Barnes and Shinn-Taylor 1988, Bentley and Watts 1994, Wragg *et al.* 1989). Therefore the science co-ordinator is involved in ensuring not only that the *children* have an appropriate and progressive science curriculum using suitable materials and equipment, but that their *colleagues'* competence, enthusiasm and confidence to teach science is also developed.

THE SPECIAL NATURE OF SCIENCE

In order to teach effectively, it is important to be clear what science is and how it differs from other subjects. Otherwise there is a risk that teachers will provide activities which have a scientific *content* but do not, in practice, develop science *skills* and *concepts*. Unless the latter are clearly identified in the lesson plans, the language and/or technological elements of the task may become the prime focus of the learning instead.

Science aims to explain the existing physical world by creating ideas or generalisations that fit all situations, whether in India, England, Australia or on Mars. Therefore the hypothesis or explanation is central to scientific activity. These are frequently arrived at through practical investigations which involve setting up fair tests that identify and control variables. The value of using skills for the specific purpose of forming *hypotheses* or *explanations* has not always been recognised in the primary school. In the past, primary teachers have focused on a limited range of science skills such as *observation* and *classification*. In addition, they have avoided setting up activities that encourage children to raise their own *questions* that will help them *identify* and ultimately *understand* fundamental science concepts (Cavendish *et al.* 1990).

As phenomena and their relationships continue to be examined, scientific ideas have to be reviewed and, if appropriate, revised. Even the most established explanations of scientific evidence can only be regarded as tentative. After all, there was a time when many distinguished scientists believed the Earth was flat! Therefore, the style of providing practical investigations in the primary school, where children question and explain what they see, simulates the scientific process far more than an activity that demonstrates an apparently fixed truth. This practical approach gives children a taste of the excitement of scientific discovery and may help them to recognise that they can have a role in the future in revising and improving current ideas, and exploring aspects such as magnetism which still baffle scientists today.

DISTINGUISHING BETWEEN CONTENT, CONCEPTS AND SKILLS IN PLANNING AND PRACTICE

The science co-ordinator should aim to help teachers to focus on *significant* science ideas in practical classroom activities, which also develop the whole range of science skills. In order to do this it is essential to distinguish between the activity or lesson content, concepts and skills.

Although a science concept or skill should be the main focus of a lesson, it has to be presented within an activity or context that is of interest to the children in order to demonstrate the relevance of science and hence to assist the children's understanding. In the past, many teachers have provided a series of potentially suitable activities, but because they have not been clear about the underlying concepts and skills, effective scientific learning has not been achieved. It is important to explain to children, and colleagues, *how* the activities will be used, as each activity can have the potential to teach different concepts or even different curriculum subjects.

> For example, making and testing a parachute could be used to teach that things fall because of a force of attraction towards the centre of the Earth; air exists and has properties; air resistance is a force that slows falling objects; or that different materials have different properties. The same activity could be used to develop children's abilities to devise fair tests.

It is likely that a combination of only a few of these will be appropriate depending on the age and experience of the children concerned. However, if the teacher has not planned to develop such concepts and skills, the making and doing process might easily dominate and become the focus of the activity. The co-ordinator may need to help colleagues to clarify their objectives before teaching, so that discussion and questioning enable the children to recognise significant observations and relationships.

In order to establish understanding each concept or skill needs to be encountered several times. Fortunately, the same concept or skill can be incorporated in many different activities.

> For example, the concept that water resistance is a force that slows down moving objects might be introduced by testing and making model boats, examining the movement and shape of fish, and/or by talking about how to maximise speed in different swimming strokes.

There is a danger that by focusing only on developing concepts that science lessons become a disjointed series of one-off activities. This can be avoided by developing a whole school plan which shows a *progression* of concepts and skills linked to suitable activities. The co-ordinator first needs to identify a possible progression of science skills and concepts that will satisfy both the National Curriculum and the specific needs of the children of the school. Then he or she should collaborate with the whole staff to identify a series of topics or activities that will enable these skills and concepts to be delivered in the school, taking into account the needs of other curricular subjects as well as colleagues' personal interests and abilities.

Such whole school planning in science will be enhanced if it is accompanied by in-service training to improve the teachers' understanding of the science concepts and skills. Moore (1992a) found that teachers most appreciated science support from their co-ordinator in the form of whole day INSET workshops, resource packs on science topics and team/joint teaching with the co-ordinator in the teacher's own class. Classroom teachers did not favour being taken out of their own class to have demonstration lessons in the co-ordinator's classroom nor did they like exchanges with other teachers' classes.

THE RELATIONSHIP BETWEEN SCIENCE AND TECHNOLOGY

When developing a whole school plan, co-ordinators may wish to optimise time and enhance children's learning by linking science and technology. Technological activities provide contexts for introducing science concepts and demonstrating that science is *relevant* and *socially important*. In addition, as long as the teacher is explicit about the science skills and concepts to be developed, design and make projects can enable children to *apply* their science knowledge, help to establish understanding and provide assessment opportunities for the teacher. However, unless teachers are clear about differences between science and technology, both subjects are likely to suffer.

> *Science* is explaining the real world by making generalisations, whereas *technology* is concerned with changing it to create unique solutions to solve human problems and needs.

Some of these new technological developments can prompt scientists to wonder how they work, so encouraging questions to be posed that lead to new scientific ideas or force existing ones to be reconsidered.

Although both disciplines use similar skills for testing, the purpose of the investigations is different. In *science* these skills are used to make a generalisation, whereas in *technology* they are intended for testing how successful a product is or to decide what making technique and material to use.

Technologists use scientific ideas to ensure that their products work effectively, but they also use skills from all other subjects – art, economics, mathematics, history, geography and English.

> For example, when designing and building a bridge the technologist considers the special geological situation of that particular location, the skills of the labour force, the proposed type and volume of traffic, the aesthetic requirements of the culture concerned, and the available budget. It is essential to take into account scientific concepts of forces in balanced structures and the properties of the available materials, but economic, aesthetic and geographical factors also have to be applied.

Therefore, if technology is only perceived to be the appliance of science the children will have too narrow an experience and the potential of technology to enhance all subjects in the curriculum will be impaired. Consequently, the science and technology co-ordinators need to work together to raise colleagues' awareness of how each subject can support the other and when they should be taught separately.

PROMOTING APPROPRIATE TEACHING METHODS IN THE CLASSROOM

Although teachers' knowledge of science concepts and skills is important, appropriate pedagogical skills are also essential. Inexperienced teachers with high academic qualifications in science can have a detrimental effect on the children's learning as they tend to use excessively complicated language and attempt to present abstract ideas that young children cannot appreciate (Jarvis and Cavendish, 1994). This complexity can have the effect of increasing the children's confusion and possibly discouraging interest in science. Therefore, the co-ordinator needs to act as a role model and explore methods of effective classroom presentation with colleagues.

First-hand practical activities are essential for developing a wide range of skills. Additionally, when the children carry out simple experiments for themselves the experience is more lasting and the concepts involved clearer than when secondary sources are used. It is also easier for the teacher to recognise when a concept is misunderstood or if language is used inappropriately.

> Whenever possible, science activities should include an *open ended* element. If the children are given a 'recipe' for an activity or investigation, their ingenuity and imagination will not be developed.

Children are more likely to learn how to set up a 'fair' experiment, raise their own questions, suggest hypotheses and interpret data if they are involved in the decision-making process. If the work is both practically based and has an open ended problem-solving element, *all* children can participate effectively at their own particular intellectual level. The less able children understand what is happening because it is tangible and immediate. They will often arrive at a solution (although one probably not as sophisticated as their peers), and they are less restricted by the requirement to read before being able to join in effectively. The very able child, on the other hand, is able to investigate and solve problems in a more advanced way. As the activities should not only be practical but the content should appeal to girls and boys from all cultures, it is important to develop and monitor the whole school plan to ensure that a variety of suitable activities are covered.

Initially some teachers can feel apprehensive about providing open ended practical activities. Some are concerned that discipline might be difficult to maintain or that they will be unable to answer the children's questions. The co-ordinator may need to provide support by working alongside colleagues, ideally in the classroom but where this is not feasible through some joint planning of a few lessons and exploring some practical activities in science focused staff meetings.

ORGANISATION AND USE OF SCIENCE EQUIPMENT

A practical approach has both *equipment* and *organisational* implications. Although a lot of very expensive material is not necessary to enable the children to pursue a broad, balanced and practical science programme, a variety of suitable resources does take some time to accumulate. Access to only a limited amount of equipment means that teachers have to organise small-group work with a few children carrying out an experiment while others are involved in other subject work. As this is organisationally difficult for every science lesson, hopefully the school will, over a period of time, be able to buy sufficient equipment for the teacher to choose to carry out whole class practical activities on at least some occasions.

Some items specifically used for science will need to be *bought*, such as:

- magnets;
- mirrors;
- batteries;
- bulbs;
- bells;
- microscopes;
- biological collecting equipment.

Some of the more expensive, infrequently used items, e.g. light boxes, might be acquired by a cluster of schools or loaned from a nearby secondary school. Those items which are found in the home such as recyclable materials, fabrics, working toys and simple household machines could be collected with the help of parents. Whether bought or not, items should be chosen bearing in mind the general physical and manipulative skills of young children.

> For example, monocular microscopes which only cater for slides and require careful positioning of a mirror to ensure sufficient light will have far less value in the primary school than simple, robust binocular microscopes with one simple control for adjustment.

Once equipment has been acquired the co-ordinator, in consultation with the staff, needs to consider how to store it. If it is stored in a central location, it is easy to *monitor* use and breakages as well as enabling teachers to have sufficient equipment for a whole class to carry out an experiment at one time. In this case, the labelling of the storage containers is essential so that busy teachers are able to collect and return materials quickly. A *recording* arrangement indicating which class is using the equipment is helpful for other colleagues who might need similar items. Frequent overlap of special items such as rock and fossil specimens can be minimised by taking this into account when devising the whole school plan.

Some schools may prefer to house equipment in individual classrooms, encouraging children and teachers to respond to scientific questions as they arise. Additionally, if everyday materials and basic measuring equipment required to make models and carry out tests are easily visible and available to the children, this helps to stimulate their imagination in designing investigations. This classroom based approach, however, usually requires a more generous provision of equipment.

Staff may need suggestions for adapting their teaching strategies to enable young children and those with special educational need to use science equipment which appears to require relatively demanding mathematical skills. For example, some thermometers have scales which range from negative numbers to numbers over 100, and force meters can require the comparison of decimals. If the children have not used the device before, some introductory activity may be necessary.

> For example, many young children do not realise that the fluid in the thermometer rises as it gets hotter and falls when cooled. Without this basic understanding measuring temperature will be meaningless. In this case the children can be asked to place a large, clearly marked class thermometer in different locations to watch the change of the fluid level.

Subsequently if the children are unable to read the scale or handle comparative calculations their activities can often be simplified by using a matching technique.

> For example, in an investigation to find out which mug keeps soup hot the longest, the children could draw around their thermometer and colour in the height of the liquid at each reading. A comparison of the series of drawings will show which mug was the best insulator.

The activity may then enable the teacher to introduce the mathematical skills such as reading scales and showing the children how to carry out the calculations involved.

The principle of *matching results* can simplify many of the mathematical demands of science activities, including recording results to identify *patterns*.

> In a test to find the effect of increasing the slope on the distance a toy car travels, the final stopping point of the car for each slope-height could be marked on the floor, so removing the need for linear measurement and difficult graph design.

Obviously when children have the appropriate mathematical skills these should be used, as this enables the children to apply mathematics in a relevant context.

CHILDREN'S IDEAS OF SCIENTIFIC PHENOMENA

Even if plenty of practical hands-on experiences are provided, effective learning may be inhibited unless teachers take children's existing deeply held *beliefs* into account. Young children have already developed a set of explanations to rationalise everyday events before they arrive at school. Many young children, for example, consider the world is flat and the Sun goes round the Earth (Baxter 1989, Nussbaum 1985). The problem is compounded in that many teachers, including those with science qualifications, have also built up alternative science concepts (Kruger *et al.*. 1992, Mant and Summers 1993). Therefore, science co-ordinators and their colleagues may need to update and develop their own knowledge by taking opportunities to attend in-service courses or by using distance learning packages and information for primary teachers in professional science journals. By identifying children's common alternative beliefs, primary teachers should be better able to avoid language and tasks that might compound or prompt the children to develop *inappropriate concepts*. They should also be enabled to improve the quality of science activities so that their children will question and change their cherished notions to develop scientifically more acceptable ones.

Children's beliefs are often related to the way words are interpreted in common use. The terms 'light', 'energy' and 'force', for example, are used in everyday conversations in a different way than when used by a physicist. Therefore, teachers need to be careful with the way that they use such words in the classroom. For example, it is important not to equate energy with force, as the first involves the capacity to do work and the second is a push or pull. In addition, if teachers encourage the children to share their understandings at the very beginning of new science topics, many misunderstandings can be clarified. Such action, for example, would have avoided one teacher's puzzlement when her class could not find any signs of 'animals' on a nature walk. This was because they thought only furry four-legged creatures were animals, a common misconception in children identified by Bell and Freyberg (1985).

Other alternative ideas arise because children do not recognise the existence of all the factors that are involved in a situation. For example, many young children do not *perceive* that air exists. After all, it cannot be seen or felt. This means that children do not appreciate the effect of air resistance, making the understanding of forces difficult. Newton discovered that once a force has been applied to an object it will continue in the same direction and speed indefinitely, unless another force acts on it. Children find this difficult to believe, as their real life experiences appear to refute this notion. When they kick or throw a ball it inevitably slows down. If the primary teacher helps children to appreciate the existence of air and its effects, as well as pointing out the influence of friction and water resistance, secondary pupils' problems understanding Newton's laws may be avoided later.

The foundation of many abstract and complex scientific ideas can be effectively laid in the primary school, by providing practical activities that teach the language and simple basic ideas involved.

> For example, the kinetic theory of matter describes how the changes between a gas, liquid and solid can be explained by the movement of different sized infinitesimal particles that vary in their rate of movement according to the amount of heat applied. This abstract idea is beyond most primary children. However, if the primary teacher is able to introduce practical experiences that enable the children to use the words gas, liquid and solid correctly; help children recognise that the same material can be in gas, liquid and solid form; and that change between these states occurs when there is a change of heat; the teacher will have provided an excellent basis to enable pupils to understand the complex theory in secondary school.

When new experiences are provided the children will not necessarily modify their views immediately. It is quite normal for them to appear to hold conflicting ideas simultaneously, as it takes time to change views. The co-ordinator may need to give colleagues reassurance that in the long term it is quicker to spend time establishing an important idea *well*, than to succumb to pressures felt by some teachers to introduce many concepts *briefly* in order to cover the requirements of the National Curriculum.

ASSESSMENT

In order to find out about children's existing ideas it is helpful to assess them at the *beginning* of each science topic. Even if the topic has been taught before, some ideas will have been forgotten or confused, but others will have been extended by experiences outside the school and by watching television and reading. By identifying the class's ideas, activities can build on *existing* knowledge and deliberately set out to *challenge* any misconceptions. In addition, sensitively sharing and discussing the range of ideas in a class can help children to question their beliefs, helping them to develop more sophisticated science concepts.

Once the children's initial ideas have been identified, *on-going assessment* of science skills, which is a part of all topics, as well as monitoring concept development will be required. It is relatively easy to assess factual knowledge and most formal written tests concentrate on this, but it is much more difficult to assess skills and understanding of concepts.

Questions (oral or written) which enable the child to offer a range of answers, annotated drawings, concept maps and observations during practical work all provide opportunities to assess children's concepts.

Level of skill development can only really be assessed by observation during practical activity (Cavendish *et al.* 1990, Russell and Harlen 1990, Schilling *et al.* 1990).

Self-assessment by the pupils might also be included in the school's assessment strategies, as this is particularly useful in helping to identify the level of individual performance in practical group situations.

Teachers need to build up knowledge of how scientific skills and concepts develop and how children demonstrate their competence in these. This will take time. If possible the science co-ordinator should devise an action plan to assist *colleagues* to develop their *assessment* skills. This might be achieved by providing time for individuals to observe small groups; helping teachers to plan for *focused* assessment in the normal teaching situations; and providing opportunities for small groups of teachers to share and *discuss* the responses of different aged children to similar activities.

Assessment throughout the whole school will be assisted by producing a whole school plan for science indicating when different skills and concepts will be introduced and what assessment methods are appropriate. The Science National Curriculum provides the basic framework as it indicates what skills and concepts are appropriate at different key stages but this will need to be expanded to show individual year teachers what to focus on in their teaching and assessment. If this whole school plan is produced in collaboration with all the teachers, they should come to a clearer, shared understanding of what children can do and how this might be recognised. This collaborative process should also enhance individual teachers' personal understanding of science skills and concepts and their assessment.

LIAISON WITH SECONDARY SCHOOLS

Primary science cannot be a simplified version of secondary science as young children are unable to understand complex *abstract* concepts. However, guided practical experiences in the primary school relating to the children's personal experiences will enable them to make sense of these generalised concepts later in secondary school. It is also an opportunity to introduce scientific language and basic ideas before too many alternative beliefs have developed and become entrenched. As both girls and boys come to enjoy the practical nature of primary science and hence grasp basic science ideas, hopefully more children will want to persist with science throughout secondary and higher education. The *unique* value and style of primary science needs to be shared with secondary schools so that effective progression can be ensured. This will involve primary science co-ordinators liaising with their secondary schools so that staff from feeder primary schools and secondary schools can visit and collaborate to share and co-ordinate the work of both phases, treating both with equal value.

SUMMARY

Many teachers are reluctant to teach practical science because of a lack of confidence in their *own* knowledge. This reluctance is compounded by the time and organisation necessary to prepare and clear up such activities. The science co-ordinator can assist in ameliorating both problems by helping to develop colleagues' science knowledge and pedagogical skills, alongside organising efficient access to appropriate materials and equipment throughout the whole school. In addition, by producing a whole school plan for assessing and developing children's science concepts and skills, the effort put into each lesson can be used effectively.

Chapter 10

Design and technology

Aileen Dunkley

INTRODUCTION

Technology as a subject in the modern curriculum may be new but technology itself is not new. Even in the earliest times the aim of technology was not unlike its modern counterpart, being concerned with generating products, for example clothing, tools, weapons, buildings, all to satisfy human needs (Newton 1991). In education, early nineteenth-century schools, for example, introduced children to practical skills such as needlework for girls and woodwork for boys. Important influences came from thinkers such as Froebel (1782–1852):

> Froebel expected that children should play with Gifts which made up the resources for the key Occupations for learning in a carefully prescribed manner. It is fascinating to note that when the Occupations were done by rote in the tiered galleries of the monitorial schools, the purpose was defined as 'to train hand and eye', an appropriate technical skill for future artisans.
>
> (Anning 1991)

More recently, in the context of the National Curriculum, Jarvis has observed that:

> Children need to develop creativity and skills of analysis and problem solving in all areas of the curriculum but the opportunity for their development is more obvious in Design and Technology, particularly as primary teachers are under considerable pressure to focus the children's attention on specific areas of knowledge and concepts in other subject areas in order to respond to all the requirements of the National Curriculum.
>
> (Jarvis 1993)

In this chapter we begin by examining the nature of design and technology.

THE NATURE OF DESIGN AND TECHNOLOGY

Design and technology in education is essentially a practical process which involves having ideas and then purposefully and thoughtfully engaging in designing and making activities leading to the creation of a product. The 1995 National Curriculum orders do not even seek to define D&T, rather they choose to identify a 'capability' which children are to be taught to develop:

> Pupils should be taught to develop their D&T capabilities through combining design and making skills with knowledge and understanding in order to design and make products.

(DfE 1995a)

D&T is a very diverse area of the curriculum. It draws on and links with most other subjects and the range of activities which can constitute D&T is huge. One of the main contributions to diversity is the wide range of materials which may be used in primary D&T. This includes wood, textiles, clays, doughs, paper, card, wood, plastic, found materials, electrical and mechanical components and construction kits. 'Capability' with these materials calls for a wide range of knowledge and skills and can lead to the creation of many widely differing products.

The process through which the children pass is very important in terms of:

* the teaching which it demands;
* the various forms of learning which can take place; and
* the thorough assessments which need to be carried out.

The end product will in no way tell all of the tale and will, by itself, be of very limited use for assessment purposes. The product will, nevertheless, be significant for the child in terms of perception of the subject and of capability. A great deal of valuable learning takes place during a process which leads to a seemingly disappointing final product. However, usually it is easier for the teacher to understand the value of this disappointment than the child! Whilst an occasional failure will probably not do the child too much harm, teachers will naturally feel that they need to ensure that the same child does not experience repeated failures. It is very important that children build positive attitudes towards their own capabilities and this will largely come from success. In the best scenario children find the process purposeful and pleasurable and are proud and satisfied with their end product.

The co-ordinator may take steps to help teachers to devise activities where there is a degree of built-in 'guaranteed success'.

DISPLAY

One way to encourage the school to emphasise and value the whole process is for the co-ordinator to ensure that it is not just the final products of children's D&T activities which go on display. Displays can include, for instance, description of the context, drafts of preliminary discussions, early designs, detailed designs, mock-ups, children's accounts of the process, evaluations, etc. This way the display can still be attractive, whilst at the same time being far more informative and interesting for the observers be they pupil, member of staff, parent or visitor.

KNOWLEDGE AND UNDERSTANDING

D&T does not have an empirical body of knowledge, but rather draws on knowledge from other curriculum areas, notably science, but also maths and art. However, when knowledge gained in these areas is applied in D&T it is far more likely that, through its use in relevant, purposeful and practical activities, knowledge will be converted into true understanding. Frequently applied areas of knowledge in primary D&T would include knowledge about:

- structures and strength;
- structures and stability;
- forces and energy;
- movement and simple mechanisms (e.g. wheels and axles, levers, linkages, pulleys and gears);
- electricity (e.g. circuits, batteries, bulbs, switches, motors and buzzers).

In addition D&T is intended to increase children's knowledge and awareness of materials with regard to:

1 their properties such as strength, rigidity, weight, insulation properties, texture, flavour, etc;
2 their properties such as response to heating, combining, etc;
3 working with them, such as cutting, joining, etc.

Equally children develop a knowledge and understanding of tools, with regard to correct choice and safe use (i.e. aspects of health and safety).

SKILLS

We can identify some generic headings within designing and making under which appropriate skills can be grouped.

1 Designing skills include:

- Visualising (i.e. picturing in the mind)
- Describing (e.g. talking, gesturing)
- Drawing (e.g. use of pencil, ruler, plan views, enlarged details, 3-D drawing)
- Perspective
- Annotating (i.e. labelling)
- Measuring (e.g. use of ruler, checking availability)
- Selecting materials (e.g. making patterns and mock-ups).

2 Making skills involve:
- Measuring (e.g. using ruler, weighing scale)
- Marking (e.g. using pencil, chalk)
- Cutting (e.g. with scissors, knife, hacksaw)
- Joining (e.g. using different adhesives, stitching, nailing)
- Finishing (e.g. painting, icing, embroidering).

Some aspects of work with certain materials do not fit easily into these categories and some additional headings may be necessary. For example, when working with food, 'combining' is a useful category. One of the most important skills, however, and that which sets D&T apart from straightforward craft work, is the skill of being able to *apply* knowledge and understanding to good advantage.

PROGRESSION

Progression in knowledge and understanding is relatively easy to chart and much will come from work children cover in other areas of the curriculum. Children will gradually build on their existing knowledge and understanding to cope with wider areas and more complex concepts. There are certain materials which come later in progression simply because younger children are not yet ready to handle them. With materials, the physical strength of the child will often influence the order in which materials become appropriate. Balsa wood precedes thin wood which, in turn, precedes thick wood. The use of paper will precede card which in turn precedes thick card which precedes board. Occasionally the teacher may have to prepare some materials before an activity can proceed. For example, a paper and card model may need a strong base or a sturdy upright support made from card which is too thick for the children to cope with. In this case, the teacher may cut some beforehand to ensure that the task focuses on the learning objectives to be met and that the activity stands a good chance of being a success.

One fairly tangible aspect of progression can be developed by gradually introducing children to new materials, or to new applications of familiar materials. For example, children may build up knowledge and understanding about simple mechanisms by using construction kits and by modelling with paper and card. It will only be later that they can be given similar tasks using wood, since wood is a more difficult and time-consuming material with which to make *mechanisms*. In the mean time, they may be developing their work in *wood* through more simple tasks which enable them to concentrate on skills and quality of workmanship. In other words, children shouldn't be given a difficult task in a challenging material before they have had plenty of opportunity to develop both the knowledge and understanding for the content of the task, and the skills for the material. A rule of thumb might be

challenging material–simple task   challenging task–simple material

It is difficult when working across a diverse range of materials to define a progression of skills. For instance, who is to say whether peeling and separating a tangerine is more difficult than hitting a nail with a hammer? Even within one materials area it is not always easy to determine whether one skill should precede another – for example, some teachers might feel that young children can stitch fabric before they are capable of cutting it. What we can say, though, is that once an initial skill has been introduced much of the progression becomes a matter of 'doing it better'. This will come through practice, children needing not to be continually moving on to new skills, but to have time to consolidate and improve existing ones. Aspects of skill development such as accuracy, precision and neatness will then gradually improve as children have the opportunity to 'get a feel' for the material and for the tools with which they are working. Hence we would see a progression in quality.

Another aspect of progression lies within the process of D&T. As children progress they become capable of handling more difficult tasks involving a longer and more complex designing and making process. Attributes such as planning ahead and the ability to solve incidental problems become very important.

The most important and most elusive aspect of progression in D&T concerns the issue of 'capability'. Capability involves something far more difficult to define than knowledge and skills. It is an application of these, combined with higher-order skills and attitudes, which constitutes real capability in D&T. This may involve decision making, independence, motivation, perseverance, patience, management of time, handling of choice, improvisation, etc., so that gradually the child learns to manage himself or herself all the way through the designing and making process.

TEACHING STYLE

The preceding paragraph needs to be borne very much in mind when considering appropriate teaching styles for D&T activities. The kinds of skills and attitudes just described in terms of capability are too intangible to be able to *teach* them – rather they have to be allowed for, fostered and encouraged. What the co-ordinator needs to remember when helping colleagues to plan, is that it would be very easy, by adopting certain teaching styles, to *exclude* children from having the opportunity to develop real capability.

During the introduction of the National Curriculum it was often said that the orders would lay down what had to be taught, but not how to teach it. In some ways, the 1995 orders for D&T do come close to prescribing teaching styles when, in section 1 of the programmes of study for all key stages, they refer to giving pupils experience of three distinctly different learning modes:

1 assignments in which they design and make products;
2 focused practical tasks in which they develop and practise particular skills and knowledge;
3 activities in which they investigate, disassemble and evaluate simple products.

However, the investigational activities described in mode 3 above do give the teachers and the pupils a good, concrete starting point. Pupils can be taught to build up a bank of knowledge by investigating the products of other designers and makers. They can learn how to look for good and bad points in design, consider the appropriateness of different materials for different jobs, see how form can conflict with or enhance function, check for environmental friendliness and consider fitness for purpose.

The focused practical tasks described in mode 2 give teachers another opportunity to 'input' knowledge and/or skills. Teachers will use their assessments of children's past work to help decide what the children need to learn next, and then devise activities to meet these specific learning objectives. Such activities can be very effective for teaching conventions of design, defined areas of knowledge, or skills specific to certain tools and materials. Such tasks may be short or long, simple or complex, but they are teacher led, and planned with specific learning objectives in mind.

Primary teachers usually feel they have a better grasp of teaching English than D&T and co-ordinators may find the following analogy useful when explaining ways of teaching D&T. The investigative activities of mode 3 can be compared with looking at books and reading stories by other authors, listening to stories read aloud, etc. The focused tasks of mode 2 are similar to English exercises in handwriting, spelling, punctuation, joining sentences or using adjectives. The assignments described in mode 1 are like asking the child to make up his or her own story and write it out.

We all know that standards of handwriting and punctuation produced by a child can be high in isolated English exercises. However, when the same child is in the mode of creative thinking and writing these skills sometimes appear lost. The same may well happen in D&T. Skills which the children appear to have mastered during focused tasks may be poorly applied during an assignment. This may be because the child is preoccupied with creative thought, or is rushing for fear of not finishing on time, or because someone else is using the tools required, or because the child has tackled tasks in the wrong order. The teacher may feel disappointed, disillusioned or frustrated at this apparent lack of carry-over of skill, but the fact is that the child will need plenty of opportunities in 'assignment' style activities before he or she can handle the whole process well. For most children it takes years before they have good handwriting, spelling and punctuation in their creative writing. The same will be true for creative making.

A further issue concerns the teaching styles and learning approaches set up by the teacher. As primary classroom practitioners we would never expect that we could prepare the children for creative writing solely through English exercises. No – we use all sorts of strategies to give children the best possible chance of success in their creative writing. We might give them an opening sentence or two to help get them started; or we suggest a beginning, middle and end to help with story structure; or we work on descriptions of scenes and characters which can later be incorporated into a story. We can use similar strategies to help with D&T assignments.

The notion of built-in or 'guaranteed success' was alluded to early on in this chapter as a means of ensuring that children have positive learning experiences. But we can also see the importance of giving children enough freedom to develop the 'capability' aspect of D&T. The co-ordinator can help the classroom teacher to plan for both, through developing teaching styles and learning approaches to satisfy the two apparently conflicting sets of requirements. Activities can be organised whereby children are taught specific skills whilst making a basic product. This can then be developed in a more open ended way with individuals or groups employing attitudes and skills not usually required in a focused task. For example, when working with textiles children may make a bag. During the initial focused task they would be taught the specific skills of following a simple pattern, cutting fabric, and joining using a sewing machine, running stitch or adhesive according to ability. This would give every child a basic bag, i.e. 'guaranteed success' has been built in to the activity. From here children would be given the opportunity to select and use a variety of materials and techniques to realise their individual designs for the decoration of the bag. This would enable the children to exercise their D&T 'capability' in applying the knowledge, understanding and skills they have acquired through previous experiences. Open ended activities are challenging to teach and do not suit everyone's teaching styles, but the co-ordinator must encourage opportunities for the use of attributes such as independence, perseverance and decision making since these are the essence of true capability and are generic to all materials areas.

LEARNING APPROACHES

We have stressed that a variety of teaching styles need to be employed, because different styles suit different aspects of D&T. Further, some styles will suit the child as learner better than others. By varying the style the teacher favours different children. It is the same with children's learning. Some children thrive on teacher led, instructional situations, whilst others do not come into their own until they are given more inventive, creative opportunities. One important variable which affects the child as learner is the amount of time given to a particular activity. Some D&T tasks should be short; for example a construction kit assignment may take less than half an hour. Others may be very long and extend over several weeks. From the outset the teacher should share with the class information about how long an activity is expected to take so that children can pace themselves accordingly. Teachers should try out tasks so as to set realistic time goals. When children are rushing it may be that they mistakenly think they have very little time in which to complete a task, or it may be that the teacher has allowed insufficient time.

Children sometimes perceive that they are good at working with one particular material used in D&T, but not good at working with another. The teacher can help the child to see how much of the knowledge and skill is transferable from one materials area to another, and that the stages in the design process are much the same regardless of the material used. It also helps the learner to see that attitudes and high-order skills such as motivation, co-operation, perseverance, precision and attention to detail are very useful attributes in any D&T situation.

SPECIAL ISSUES FOR THE D&T CO-ORDINATOR

The role of the co-ordinator of D&T can be a particularly challenging one since D&T is perceived as a relatively new subject and many primary phase teachers lack the confidence to deal with the orders. Many feel, often wrongly, that they have little in their background to equip them to deal with the subject, and the original National Curriculum orders, with their use of specialist technical terminology, did much to undermine what confidence there was.

Essential to the role of the co-ordinator is the ability to enthuse and encourage other members of staff. Usually colleagues have greater expertise than they are prepared to admit. The co-ordinator should help them to increase their knowledge and skills and build on their existing practice. To ensure that help given is at an appropriate level the co-ordinator should carry out an audit of existing practice and this really needs to be done by observation in the classroom, since many capable teachers are overmodest about their current work. Equally, some teachers, although doing plenty of practical work, may be keeping practice so tightly controlled that children have little chance to think for themselves. At the other extreme, some may leave tasks too open, with no teaching of specific skills. It is difficult to identify such situations through conversation alone, and looking at the outcomes of children's D&T activity will not reveal enough about the nature of the teaching and learning styles in operation during the process. Once the co-ordinator is familiar with the classroom practice of colleagues, then he or she is in a good position to give appropriate help in planning by making suggestions for practical activities which meet identified learning objectives, often within the context of a particular topic or theme. Eventually the whole staff, led by the co-ordinator, will need to be involved in charting the children's main D&T experiences onto the school's curriculum map. A cross-check can then be made, looking for breadth, balance and progression in materials, type of task, context and products.

The core subjects always command a great deal of attention, whilst D&T is traditionally a low-status subject. The co-ordinator may well have to fight to ensure that D&T is given a fair amount of staff meeting time, curriculum time and funding, and that it is catered for in the School Development Plan. Such action should help to improve the status and quality of D&T within the school.

Where a number of staff require support then it may be that the most efficient way to deal with this would be for the co-ordinator to arrange or run a whole day INSET workshop.

Many of the tools, materials and processes for D&T are potentially dangerous and the co-ordinator needs to ensure that all staff are aware of relevant health and safety procedures, including risk assessment.

RESOURCES

All curriculum areas have some resources to manage, but for the D&T co-ordinator the task can be quite a mammoth one. Because of the overlap between their two subjects the science and D&T co-ordinators may share some resources and they may wish to work together to set up a combined storage area. In some schools, for example, each classroom is equipped with tools and materials for practical work whilst in others it is stored centrally for use by a year group, a key stage or the whole school. Much depends on finance, the historical tradition, and the physical size and layout of the school buildings, so it is difficult to make general recommendations. What can be made clear, though, is that it is *not* the job of the co-ordinator to keep resources tidy. The co-ordinator's role can reasonably be expected to cover the control of the budget for D&T resources, selection and ordering, the setting up of a system for storage, retrieval and monitoring, and advice regarding resources. It needs to be understood by all concerned that it is the responsibility of all users to see that the storage area is kept tidy, that unused items are returned to their place, that resources are used appropriately and that waste is kept to a minimum. Any teacher who knows that they are going to use a large quantity of a particular item, or who uses the last of any item, should notify the co-ordinator. Children need to be given access to resources so that they can exercise choice. Such choice can often be arranged by taking a selection of resources to the classroom but, as children mature, part of their progress may include access to and selection from a main storage area. If this is the case, the class teacher must ensure that children are aware of any rules and that they conduct themselves sensibly. Similarly, the co-ordinator must ensure that dangerous items are not left accessible in an unsupervised situation. It is often advisable to keep small and tempting resources in a 'Teachers Only' storage place.

SUMMARY

In this chapter we have examined design and technology as a medium through which children may develop and apply their knowledge and skills. A key role for the co-ordinator is to encourage colleagues to develop this nebulous quality of 'capability' amongst children. In order to do that, an awareness of progression – in skills development, in the experience of using a range of materials, in gradually and increasingly complex technological applications, and in the ability to work independently – is essential.

Chapter 11

History

David Walker

INTRODUCTION

History is a subject with a content full of rich and vivid stories of the past; it has a limited amount of specialist subject jargon; and its themes and issues are well represented in the popular media. Above all, history has the power to engage with pupils' curiosity in finding out about their past.

The changed world of the late twentieth century created a debate within the teaching of history (Aldrich and Dean 1991). In a multi-cultural and diverse society, whose history should we teach about? Should it be the history of great political events or should it be concerned with the past lives of ordinary people? Should we be encouraging our pupils to develop the skills of historical analysis? And what should the relationship be between these skills and the historical content of history courses? The National Curriculum has created a new focus for history teaching within the primary school and the opportunity to review what we are trying to achieve when we teach history.

THE ROLE OF THE HISTORY CO-ORDINATOR

The role of the co-ordinator involves the provision of support in developing teachers' understanding of and expertise in the subject. This has two aspects.

First, there is the teacher's understanding of the process of learning history – the concepts and skills that need to be developed, how children develop an historical understanding, and the kinds of activities that are most appropriate to that development.

Second, teachers need support in understanding the key features of historical periods and in identifying significant events.

The National Curriculum, in prescribing areas and periods of study, has introduced new and often unfamiliar content for teachers, who may need to develop their own confidence in understanding what is of significance and of interest within this content. Both these areas of need should be addressed in the organisation of support through the provision of in-service training, advice and guidance, the selection and packaging of resources, and the use of exemplar activities and demonstration activities. Together these should provide an on-going programme of support based on an early identification of teachers' needs and concerns.

GETTING STARTED – WHAT IS HISTORY?

History is a vast and ever expanding subject area, potentially encompassing the evidence of everything that has happened in the past. Within the primary school pupils can be found building models of pyramids, creating Aztec designs, producing illustrations of historical scenes and reading works of fiction set in Tudor times. For many of us this adds to the attraction of the subject and to the enjoyment of the children. While the links that can be made between historical themes and studies are to be encouraged and developed, we do need to consider what exactly historical learning is, and how we can know if children are developing historical knowledge and understanding. A starting point for the co ordinator could be to consider the following characteristics of history and to use them as a basis for an audit of the school's provision for history, to discover if and where genuinely historical learning is taking place:

- History is about the ways of life, events and attitudes of human beings in the past. Study of, for example, what dinosaurs might have looked like is not history.
- Historical understanding involves developing historical skills and concepts. These include an understanding of chronology, causation, change, using historical sources as evidence, and discussing interpretations of the past. This means that historical learning is not about producing models or pictures about the past without first identifying the purpose of the task and how it will develop children's historical understanding. Children could, for example, produce models of structures from the past after first studying the available evidence as to what they may have looked like.
- Learning lists of facts and dates from the past does not in itself constitute historical learning. To remember the date of an event, for example, only becomes part of an historical understanding when we talk about its significance, what it led to, how we know about it, etc.
- Historical understanding needs to be developed within an historical context. This means that, for example, sequencing pictures of the stages of growth of an animal, while it may provide an interesting way of introducing change and chronology, does not in itself constitute historical learning.

- History is about asking questions about the past and providing opportunities for children to interact with historical sources. Copying from a book, for example, does not allow children to question how we know about the past, or to construct and take part in their own enquiries.
- History is about imagining what the past was like. This imagination needs to be rooted in an understanding of the past, or proceed from and allow for an interaction with the evidence of the past, if it is to contribute to an historical understanding.

CAN CHILDREN REALLY UNDERSTAND HISTORY?

Research into how children develop an understanding of historical concepts is limited, particularly with regard to young children. Theories of cognitive development do not always easily lend themselves to a description of the development of historical thinking, and many historical concepts are difficult to isolate and define. What research is available would suggest that young children are able to make historical inferences, develop a sense of historical imagination and an understanding of key historical concepts. Although broad patterns in the development have been identified these are only loosely related to age, and a variety of developmental stages are likely to be present amongst a group of children of a similar age. The key factor in the development of historical thinking would appear to be in the ability of the teacher to provide interesting learning experiences, ask appropriate open ended questions, build up children's historical vocabulary, and allow for pupils to discuss and explore their own ideas of the past (Cooper 1992).

A central concern of many teachers is in regard to children's understanding of the concept of time itself. If young children are unable to develop a sense of chronology and understand the place in historical time in which periods studied are located, then studies of distant periods of history, or the significance of historical events, will have little meaning. Smith and Tomlinson's (1977) studies of children between 8 and 15 demonstrate that children are capable of a range of understandings of historical duration. West (1989) has pointed out that concern over children's understanding of time is usually associated with a concern over an understanding of number associated with time. Although young children are unable to estimate age or the distance of periods and events in history, they are more successful in sequencing stereotypical historical images and artefacts, and are able to deploy appropriately terms such as 'long ago', 'long, long ago', etc.

The development of a sense of time is supported by the constant use of classroom time lines, which should be a feature of all classrooms where historical learning takes place. Timelines should be flexible to accommodate different periods of time, dealing at first with broad categories of time and becoming more detailed as children's understanding and ability to make use of an increased historical vocabulary become more refined. Timelines can act as reference points in the growth of children's historical understanding and a strong visual reinforcement of their own maps of the past.

Children's knowledge of the past comes from many different sources, of which perhaps those located in the classroom are in the minority. TV films, book and comic illustrations provide a rich stock of images of historical events and periods which children can bring with them to the classroom. This aspect of children's historical learning and its effect on conceptual development needs to be taken seriously by teachers. Images from films can, for example, enable children to identify correctly artefacts from the past and relate them to other features of an historical period, and to develop a sense of what living in that period was like. These sources of knowledge can be utilised as useful reference points for the development of an historical understanding and as a means of widening the scope of historical studies. Many of these images will take the form of stereotypical interpretations of the past and will be presented within the conventions of contemporary popular forms of entertainment. Teachers need to discuss carefully the nature of images which the mass media present, and stereotypes need to be progressively challenged with reference to other interpretations and with the evidence of the past.

PLANNING THE HISTORY CURRICULUM

It is useful for the co-ordinator to view the planning of the school's provision for history in two overlapping phases:

• the planning of the history curriculum across and between key stages; and
• the planning of individual units.

Planning is needed to ensure that the provision for history is coherent and balanced and enables children to progress in their historical understanding. This should involve the co-ordinator in an audit of the curriculum to ensure that the overall amount of time devoted to history is sufficient (an average of an hour per week would be reasonable) and, where teaching is organised around topic work, there is a sufficient number of topics with a specific history focus and bias.

The units of work chosen should reflect available resources and, across a key stage, enable a variety of perspectives to be covered. *Coherence* can be built into the curriculum by ensuring a balance of approaches, skills and concepts, and opportunities to use and explore a range of historical sources. *Progression* should be evident in differences in the breadth and depth of historical knowledge being accumulated. As children develop a knowledge and understanding of a greater range of historical periods, they should be encouraged to make comparisons between them, both to build up an understanding of change and to deepen their understanding of historical terms and concepts.

An overview of the history curriculum also involves the co-ordinator in liaison with the secondary school. The National Curriculum programmes of study for Key Stage 3 include revisiting periods of history studied at Key Stage 2. Liaison is important to establish that children's experience of history is continuous and progressive and that the secondary school recognises the child's achievements within the primary phase and is able to build upon them.

Teachers are likely to need most support in the planning of individual programmes of study. Periods for study in history can present daunting masses of content. How can teachers begin to select and organise content for young children to cover, for example, 'The way of life, beliefs, achievements of the ancient Greeks, and the legacy of ancient Greek civilisation to the modern world' (DfE 1995b)? Successful planning involves making a selection from all the possible content and lines of enquiry through the provision of a clear focus for work. What is there about a period of history which could provide an interesting area of enquiry, and can these lines of enquiry be supported by available resources or opportunities for local studies?

A study of life in Tudor times might, for example, lead to enquiries into 'How did religion change during the period?', 'How big a threat to Elizabeth was the Spanish Armada?', 'What was life like in Elizabeth's court?', 'What did the Tudors know about the world?', and 'What was life like in a Tudor mansion?'

Creating enquiries or key questions for the coverage of a period both makes content manageable and encourages children to find out about the past. Within these enquiries co-ordinators can provide advice about the learning objectives that could be identified.

An enquiry into the Spanish Armada could, for example, lead to children being able to trace the course of the Armada, understand the way different groups of people thought about a Spanish invasion, and suggest reasons for the Armada's defeat.

Encouraging teachers to identify learning objectives for units of work helps create a clear focus for learning activities, and enables them to ensure that both historical content and concepts are being covered and to check that children are making progress.

DEVELOPING APPROPRIATE TEACHING APPROACHES

A variety of methods and styles should be encouraged and there is room in the history classroom for narrative description and the well told story as well as individual or group enquiries. The coordinator should encourage a balance of approaches with opportunities for the teacher to provide information about the past and for children to engage actively with ideas, information and evidence. The history curriculum for younger children needs to be grounded in the familiar and the present day which should provide a way into comparisons with the past and stories about past events. Older children should be able to cope to a greater extent with activities which enable them to explore different features of life and events in past societies.

Teachers may react to the unfamiliarity of a period of history under study with an overreliance on textbook exercises and schemes of work or an overemphasis on project work. The first of these can produce a narrow approach to the subject and often inappropriate activities and the second runs the risk of producing unstructured work with a heavy element of copied material.

Support will be required to ensure that teachers are aware of the full range of possibilities for developing work from textbook material. Pictures and portraits from the past, for example, can be 'read' to discover evidence about people and personalities as well as information about clothing and places. Documentary evidence introduced within the appropriate context and through appropriate teaching strategies can produce more than comprehension style questions.

- A seventeenth-century inventory can provide the basis for children producing their own *Through the Keyhole* style TV programme.
- The Monteagle letter, from the Guy Fawkes story, can be the start of a mystery 'Whodunit'.
- A document from one of Cortes' men describing the city of Tenochtitlan can be the start of a class produced guidebook to the Aztec world.

Producing good history activities often has less to do with the quantity of resources provided as with the quality of resources, the way they are presented and the strategies provided for their use.

Project work has often been a significant element in primary school history teaching. It offers opportunities for children to follow their own interests, work independently or in groups and to develop reference skills. Project work carries with it, however, the danger of ending up with little which extends historical understanding. The co-ordinator should give clear advice as to what constitutes good project work.

- Are children given a clear structure to work with?
- Do they have a clear idea of what they are finding out about and why?
- Is there an understanding of how the children's work will contribute to their development of historical skills and understanding?
- Has thought been given to the audience the children are producing

work for (other children in the class, children in other years, adults etc.)?
- Does work give children the opportunity to produce a variety of written forms (newspaper reports, wall displays, etc.)?
- Do children have opportunities to discuss and share their work?

The past only becomes meaningful when we are able to think ourselves into it. Numerous strategies can be explored to develop children's historical imagination. These include producing diaries of people in the past, discussing different viewpoints of people in past situations, using literature, describing the 'feel' of a place in the past and, above all, through the use of drama. Using drama for history teaching requires careful thought if it is to be more than dressing up in historical costume or asking children to imagine they are people from a past which they know little about. Children 'enter' the past with a range of assumptions and contemporary anachronistic understandings and 'recipes'. Imaginative work in history needs to ensure that these are methodically challenged. Drama work, for example, needs to provide opportunities to work from real historical evidence, to provide space for children to discuss their actions in the drama and to compare their actions and decisions within the drama with those of real historical characters.

The co-ordinator's role involves not only clarifying classroom approaches and strategies but also in finding opportunities to encourage teachers to develop them. How this is achieved will depend on the context of the school:

- Are there opportunities to provide school based in-service training within school meetings?
- Are there opportunities to share planning or for joint teaching?
- Can displays of children's work be used to demonstrate approaches and methods?

ASSESSING CHILDREN'S WORK?

Assessing progress in historical understanding is a far from straightforward process. Not only has it been difficult to define with precision what exactly should be assessed in historical learning but also chidren's progression in historical understanding is far from unilinear and is often dependent on the content of the unit of work being studied. The co-ordinator has a responsibility to take a lead in developing a policy for and approaches to assessment.

Whatever policy for assessment is developed the co-ordinator could consider the following:

- Do teachers have a clear understanding of the key elements of historical skills and concepts which should be assessed and are they aware of progression within these?

- Is some attempt made to use assessment to baseline children's understanding of periods of history so that teaching can take account of what children already know about the past?
- Are there opportunities for teachers to share their assessments of children's work with each other?
- Does assessment enable children's progress within a variety of forms and types of work to be measured?
- What use is made of assessment to inform children of their progress and to enable teachers to plan effectively?

RESOURCING THE HISTORY CURRICULUM

History is a subject characterised by the immense volume of potential teaching resources. Historical periods provide the context for much of the output of film and television productions and fictional publishing, while historic buildings and reconstructions of the past are part of a substantial and growing heritage industry. The past is present in both specialist documents and artefacts in record offices and museums and within our own communities and homes in documents, photographs, personal possessions and in memories. The role of the co-ordinator involves the identification and selection of relevant teaching resources, making contact with external resource providers, and drawing attention to techniques and methods for the use of resources to develop children's historical understanding.

A starting point for the co-ordinator is an audit of the school's current provision of resources:

- Is an adequate level of resources provided for all periods of history studied?
- Is access provided to a range of historical sources, pictures as well as texts, IT software as well as artefacts?

An essential part of any audit is the consideration of the sort of history available resources give access to. History is about the experiences of men and women, rich and poor, and the history of Britain is the history of a multicultural society with a variety of distinct cultures and cultural heritages. Images in books should reflect these different histories, and attempts should be made to avoid a reliance on stereotypical images, for example depicting women only in domestic roles and not as producers, as passive, not active, members of society.

Historical learning should include provision for pupils to interact directly with the evidence of the past. Many museums and archaeological units will provide handling sessions or loan collections of artefacts. All schools should be able to create their own classroom museum of artefacts from the more recent past either by appealing to colleagues and parents, or through some low-cost purchasing in antique shops. Children need to be provided with clear structures to enable them to make use of artefacts for historical learning and to ensure that they become more than background displays. Artefacts need to be studied carefully, and children encouraged to record their findings about their shape, what they feel like, their weight, what they may be made of, and how they were made, before being encouraged to speculate about what they tell us about the time they come from and the people who once owned or used them.

Visits to museums, historic sites and the world outside the classroom are an essential ingredient in any strategy which aims to make history come alive to children and demonstrate its relevance to their own lives. The historic environment comprises all the elements of the past which exist around us. Anderson and Moore (1994) usefully divide the historic environment into three elements: *the built environment*, whether 1960s council houses, Tudor mansions or medieval castles; *the landscape*, which contains the evidence of thousands of years of human activity; and *the portable historic environment* of collections of artefacts from the past in museums and galleries. Any use of the world outside the classroom requires careful preparation to ensure the suitability of the site and the practicalities of a visit. Co-ordinators need to take a lead in providing advice for the preparation of children for a visit, and in considering how it will connect with their work in the classroom and how it will be built on.

Preparing pupils for visits may involve devising strategies to help children develop a sense of place – what sort of place is it? – and for historical enquiries – how has this place changed? how was it built? what was it used for?, etc. The key to successful visits is to ensure that children have a clear focus for their enquiries which will involve them in searching for evidence and clues to answer particular questions. Organising children to work in groups focusing on particular enquiries and reporting back will enable them to build up a picture of the site through a study of the evidence it provides. No historic site remains exactly as it was in the past, and most will involve an element of reconstruction and interpretation. Children should be increasingly encouraged to challenge the way in which the past is presented and to ask questions such as why some parts of an historic house are visible or accessible but not others, which parts of structures have been reconstructed and which are original, which museum objects are displayed and what is missing, how artefacts are grouped in collections and what impression about the past is being presented.

The resources selected should also enable the study of history to connect with the lives of children themselves, the histories of their school, their communities and their families. Oral histories collected from relatives can be a means of involving children in gathering historical evidence and of helping them to realise that history includes their own past and the pasts of their families. The school itself may provide a useful starting point for oral histories. Whatever the age of the building, there should be opportunities to collect information about the past from previous pupils, children and adults, and to use these to enquire into change or to look for additional evidence from records, change in the use of rooms, or additional building.

SUMMARY

The history co-ordinator has a responsibility to ensure that the curriculum of the school provides for the delivery of the requirements of the history orders, and that teachers are supported in this with adequate resources and advice on planning and the development of valid and appropriate historical activities. However the curriculum is organised, history should be provided as a coherent experience which enables children to make comparisons and connections between the events, personalities and periods studied, and to build on their understanding of historical skills and concepts.

Differentiating between fact and opinion, understanding how to handle and analyse evidence, explaining why things happen, the effects of discussions and events and discussing the moral dilemmas of the past, are important accomplishments for young children. History therefore has an important contribution to make in explaining the present, its environment and concerns, and so aid the development of informed, active and aware citizenship.

Chapter 12

Geography

John Stout

INTRODUCTION

Geography is not a new subject but, until recently, its existence in the primary school curriculum has been spasmodic and very often coincidental. The inclusion of geography as one of the foundation subjects in the National Curriculum, and therefore a subject which should form a compulsory part of every child's school experience, has changed that. The geography that did exist pre National Curriculum was usually something incidental to a wider 'topic', or something to do with maps or a part of 'local studies'. It may well have been little more than the occasional book based study of a place, often distant and usually exotic, the end product being an attractively presented 'project'. Or alternatively, geography was about maps. Consequently, the main skills that children learned were simple map skills without any practical application.

Against this background the role of the new geography co-ordinator could seem like an impossible task. That person may not be a subject specialist, may not have colleagues with any formal qualification in the subject nor, for that matter, any real knowledge of, or experience in, teaching geography. That co-ordinator's understanding of the subject may well be coloured by distant memories of the geography which he or she did at school. The confusion created by an initial National Curriculum order for geography, which was both structurally flawed and over-laden with content, can have done little to contribute towards any feeling of confidence.

Geography co-ordinators have a number of clear goals if they are to see the successful implementation of the subject, and are to ensure that the children have a worthwhile geographical experience as part of a broad and balanced entitlement.

- First, there is an immediate need for co-ordinators to come to terms with the nature of the subject itself and what it has to offer to their children.

- Second, there is the need to initiate a sequence of curriculum planning which will build the subject naturally into the whole school curriculum.
- Third, there is the need to plan a programme of activities which will enable children to make progress in all aspects of the subject.
- Fourth, those activities need to be resourced.
- Fifth, a reliable and valid system of assessment, recording and reporting needs to be developed.
- Finally, but no means least of the tasks, will be the need to support the professional development of colleagues, to give them a better understanding of the subject and to create the confidence and enthusiasm which they will surely need if they are to enthuse the children in their classes with the sense of excitement that geography can bring.

THE NATURE OF GEOGRAPHY

It is worth beginning this section by exploding a few myths and misconceptions about what geography is. The most common substitute for the subject is 'mapwork'. This is an aspect of geography with which many people feel entirely comfortable and therefore very confident. But mapwork on its own is the province of the cartographer and is not the exclusive right of the geographer. It is, in fact, quite easy to see where maps can be used in many different areas of the curriculum.

Neither is a knowledge of the location of places all that constitutes this subject. A detailed knowledge of places is more properly the province of the travel agent or the compiler of a world gazeteer or encyclopaedia. Equally, the pure aspects of the physical world belong to the geologist, the geomorphologist, the meteorologist, the climatologist and the earth scientist, whilst human geography belongs to the sociologist, the economist and the agriculturalist.

It is essential therefore that co-ordinators help their colleagues to develop a more sophisticated understanding of what geography really is, if they are to teach the subject successfully to their children. Without that, there is always the danger that they will give their children activities which outwardly may appear to bear some resemblance to geography, or to one of its component parts, yet does not help the children to make any real progress in the subject, nor enhance their understanding.

What makes geography unique, then, is the blend of knowledge, understanding, skills and experience that together give a child a sense of place, and which gradually enlarge that child's mental map – a mental map together with the related knowledge and understanding of the world which is unique to every child. To teach geography is not always 'to teach about' but to provide the opportunity to 'have experience of' an ever changing world of which the child is a part. Children will learn geography without the teacher, will gain a knowledge of the world, a sense of place and a set of values and attitudes as a part of growing up. This geography will be learned from a very wide range of influences which bear upon the child. Part of the critically important role for the teacher is to ensure that the children's geographical growth is supported and guided so that they may gain the knowledge, understanding, skills and values which will enable them to develop a sense of morality more human than animal.

Geography co-ordinators, then, have to lead their colleagues away from the stereotypical geography substitutes to a real understanding of the subject. This is not always an easy task. The child audience is captive and often captivated – mapwork is fun. Learning interesting facts about exotic locations is fascinating and confronting worthwhile environmental issues is relevant. It is important, therefore, to recognise the importance of seeing how the components of geography need to come together, if the school experience of the subject is to have some point.

The diagram in Figure 12.1 indicates that geography consists of three components and demonstrates how they should overlap. It shows that geography consists of:

• knowledge and understanding of places and themes – this is the content of the subject; it has for long been at the heart of the subject, and is regarded by some as being undervalued;
• geographical skills – as well as the instantly recognisable skills of mapwork, this also includes the skill of pursuing enquiry supported by work outside the classroom;
• values and attitudes – it is this which builds on the experience of children and allows them to understand and make judgements about the global environment, and which gives a practical purpose to all work in the subject.

It is easy to see how a teacher could be mistakenly led into concentrating on just one of these components at the expense of the others, or indeed to spend a disproportionate amount of time and effort on a combination of just two at the expense of the third. Children are really only pursuing true geography when they are at the centre of the diagram, when they are developing their knowledge and understanding of geographical themes and issues in real places, through the use of a wide range of skills.

To do this, then, children must be pursuing an enquiry or an investigation which enables them to journey on a voyage of discovery with other children and with their teachers, a voyage in which their own personal knowledge and understanding will grow and their experience will broaden and deepen.

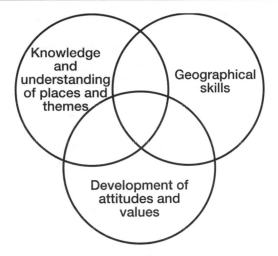

Figure 12.1 The overlapping components of geography

PLANNING FOR GEOGRAPHICAL ENQUIRY

A significant role for the geography co-ordinator is to initiate a planning process. This will put in place in the curriculum a number of opportunities within which children can pursue meaningful geographical enquiry. The focus of this enquiry is the issues which are at the heart of understanding about the interrelationships between people and their environment, wherever they are and whatever that environment may be. This means that all geography must start with questions: those the teacher asks and those the children ask. The children must be encouraged to ask questions and must in fact be taught to ask questions. They must learn what questions to ask and how to ask them. To begin with, these may be simple questions of the 'What is it?' or 'Where is it?' variety, or perhaps more difficult questions which require description and explanation of the 'Why is it like that?' variety. But eventually the children need to be asking questions with some significance, questions which raise important issues and which question values and attitudes, questions of the 'Is it important?' or 'Should it be protected?' variety.

The geography co-ordinator will need to give a lead in this planning cycle, in shaping the key enquiry questions. These questions are going to form the basis and give the structure to all the work which the teachers and their children will subsequently do. Identifying the curriculum package in geography is not so much about creating a series of content led topics or units, but more about setting up a range of enquiries into issues of some importance. These enquiries will then dictate the content areas that need to be explored, the places that will need to be visited, both literally and metaphorically, and the geographical skills that will need to be utilised.

The creation of key questions for enquiry will lead naturally to the identification of a set of learning objectives. If the key questions are the first critical stage for the co-ordinator as a part of the planning process, the determination of these learning objectives is the second. These will reflect the aims that the school has in the subject and can be guided in content by the relevant parts of the programmes of study for Key Stages 1 and 2 in the National Curriculum order for geography. These learning objectives will become, in fact, the core of what is taught and learned and will of course contain specified knowledge and understanding and specific references to place content. It has occasionally become unfashionable to suggest that children should learn geographical facts. Indeed, one of the major criticisms of the subject in recent years has been that children do not apparently have any geographical knowledge of the locational variety. Frequent horror stories, highlighted in the press, tell us what percentage of the population cannot identify where they live on a map or cannot name the capital city of a range of countries. To teach factual knowledge did at one time become unfashionable, but not because it was considered unnecessary. Rather it was because that factual component grew disproportionately at the expense of others, with the result that it was all that children ever did in geography.

A clear set of learning objectives which have grown as a natural part of an enquiry gives some purpose to learning factual knowledge and will hopefully lead children to acquire the factual knowledge which is necessary to them. It will also give a purpose to the development of their understanding of ideas and concepts. Most importantly, it will give a purpose for the development of those skills, including mapwork skills, which are now being learned and practised in many schools demonstrating good practice, and not just for their own sake.

With an enquiry led structure and a range of learning objectives in place, the third part of the planning process for the co-ordinator is the development of activities for their colleagues to use with their children both inside and outside the classroom.

An invaluable way of planning through the three stages of key enquiry questions, learning objectives and learning activities is to use an outline planning sheet something like that illustrated in Figure 12.2.

The main left-hand column provides space for the key enquiry questions, the second column for learning objectives and the right-hand column for identifying learning activities. Space at the bottom can allow for a range of comments. The example shown here includes space to demonstrate how the work relates to the National Curriculum programme of study, to list essential resources, to comment on opportunities for using information technology and to identify some particular

⊕	OUTPUT PLANNING SHEET FOR KEY STAGE	
Year:	Unit:	
Enquiry questions	Learning objectives Children can:	Suggested activities
	•	
	•	
	•	
	•	
Programmes of study references	Information technology	Resources
Assessment		Place focus

Figure 12.2 An outline planning sheet for geographical enquiry

aspects of assessment which only apply to this unit of work. A small 'notepad' can be used for any additional notes of guidance for the teacher.

The most effective use of outline planning sheets like this would be in medium-term planning in order to provide a structure within which the co-ordinator can then provide support to individual teachers or year teams in managing their short-term planning. The activities are simply identified on the outline planning sheet – short-term planning would entail more detailed description of the activities and of exactly what it is the children would do and the resources they would use. It is at this short-term planning stage that individual assignments would be written.

PLANNING FOR PROGRESSION

A key part of the work of the geography co-ordinator will be to ensure that the work being planned for the children, both long term and short term, does in fact provide opportunities for the children to make real progress in their geographical knowledge, understanding and skills. This will involve developing amongst colleagues an understanding of the meaning of progression in a geographical sense. It is not enough that children simply collect additional snippets of factual knowledge as they go through the key stages and the school. Regrettably, the geographical curriculum in recent years has encouraged and allowed children to make only limited progress because it concerned itself with content at the expense of other aspects of the subject. The co-ordinator will need to build into any schemes of work opportunities for progression in all of the following:

1   Progression of enquiry – this will involve providing a structure within which the children move gradually from answering questions set by the teacher to formulating their own questions, to identifying for themselves the issues and eventually determining their own line of enquiry. The children should become more independent learners and more able to pursue independent enquiry.
2   Progression of scale – that is to say that children at first will work on a very small scale and will subsequently work at larger scales and at a range of scales. For example, a small-scale enquiry into a distant locality in Key Stage 1 may focus upon just one small aspect of the life of a person or a family in a village community in a developing country – an aspect such as going to school, which is a familiar experience to a child. Later, in Key Stage 2, such an enquiry would be on a larger scale, and would include a study of the village community itself and of more than one aspect. So the scale of the work has broadened both spatially and thematically.
3   Progression of experience – this is the increasing ability and confi-

dence with which a child can comprehend less familiar aspects of the subject. This does not imply a concentric approach to the study of places. Even very young children can comprehend the notion of distant places if they are learning about it via a familiar experience. The progression is from the familiar to the unfamiliar.

4 Progression of place – the scheme of work should allow children gradually to enquire into a greater range of places.
5 Progression of skills – here we mean progression not just in terms of learning more skills but also in terms of learning further applications for existing skills and learning to be selective in the choice and use of skills as part of the enquiry process.
6 Progression of knowledge and understanding – this means in the children's grasp of human and physical themes. It refers also to their ability at first to describe, then to explain, then to evaluate and so on. This is not to imply that young children can do no more than describe and that making evaluative judgements should be left to older children. It is again a question of the range of circumstances in which children can apply these skills and the number of variables which they can articulate. At first, for example, children might make comparisons between one aspect of two places and then, later, more than one aspect of a greater range of places. Progression here includes increasing one's knowledge about places and about the processes which shape those places and which give them their character. It also implies an understanding of the patterns which result.

PLANNING ACTIVITIES FOR GEOGRAPHY

The importance of promoting good-quality activities for teachers to use with their children should not be underestimated. Colleagues will turn naturally to the co-ordinator for guidance and a role model to help them to engage their children in good-quality learning situations. It is essential, therefore, that the co-ordinator develop a range of sample activities, using high-quality resources to exemplify to colleagues how to set about doing good geography. There is, it should be emphasised, no one way of teaching geography that is better than any other. A wide range of activities should be used within the enquiry. The co-ordinator may wish to discuss with colleagues the range of activities which could be used to teach geography.

One thing which is certain in geography, though, is that active is better than passive. This is not to say that there is no place in geography for whole class teaching nor even for the occasional use of didactic methods, but in general these will be rare. If part of the process of progression in geography is the fostering of independent enquiry and learning, then most work will be individual and small-group work.

Additionally, all activities must cater for the individual needs of children, which means a range of differentiation techniques will need to be applied in the setting of assignments, in the resources provided and, most importantly, in the support offered to the individual by the teacher. The role of the co-ordinator is critical here in terms of offering suggestions for ways of working and, if possible, working alongside colleagues to support their professional development.

RESOURCES FOR GEOGRAPHY

Fortunately for the co-ordinator, and for the class teacher, a good quality geographical experience is possible for all children with a small and limited range of resources. This is contrary to what many believe. The job of acquiring, cataloguing, storing and maintaining those resources is a further, essential, part of the co-ordinator's role. It may be worth considering the resources as being of three types. The first, and without doubt the most valuable, is the most freely available. It is also the one which can provide the most problems in using. It is, of course, the world outside the classroom. If geography is to be experiential then work outside the classroom is essential. Sometimes, unfortunately, such activities are traditionally known as fieldwork and come complete with images of inclement weather and boots. Similarly they can become lost in an activity known rather loosely as the 'class visit'. Good, first-hand observation and information collection has no substitute, and the co-ordinator must build into all schemes of work as many opportunities as possible for all children to observe and record some detail of their environment at a scale appropriate to their age and ability.

The second type of resource is that which the co-ordinator will want to provide for every teacher in their own classroom: items such as a globe, a small set of good up-to-date atlases and a small range of resource or reference books for the use of both teachers and children.

Then, third, there are the resources which will be stored and managed centrally, again for the use of both teachers and children. Traditionally, the core of such a resource collection would be various large-scale maps and plans, including those of the local area. But good quality, coloured photographs are now regarded as being of increasing importance for the teaching of children of all ages. The co-ordinator may want to consider working with other co-ordinators within the local cluster or family of schools to acquire high-value items that are infrequently used but nevertheless important.

ASSESSING AND RECORDING GEOGRAPHY

This will perhaps be the main area in which colleagues will turn to the geography co-ordinator for advice and support. Certainly, the co-ordinator will want to develop a policy which is both consistent with the school assessment and record-keeping policy yet which respects the individuality of the subject and the statutory requirements of the National Curriculum. The advantages of a geography curriculum, with systematic and careful planning of geographical enquiry at the centre, can now be seen. The identification of a precise set of learning objectives, as part of the structuring of the enquiry, provides at the same time its own set of assessment objectives. A system of assessment and recording developed on the basis of those learning and assessment objectives can readily be devised.

As with all subjects, on-going formative assessment, whether formally or informally, will inform the teaching and learning process and ensure the continued progression of the individual child. This is a natural and normal part of the process of teaching and learning in geography. It is shared between teacher and child, and provides valuable, and valued, feedback to both. This assessment may well be recorded by the individual teacher in whatever way the year team or the school may wish to develop, but will certainly not take the form of exhaustive tick lists.

Periodically, and on preplanned occasions, individual teachers will want to review the progress of every child and to make a summative judgement about the standard of achievement of that child. This, again, can be done against the original learning objectives. The co-ordinator's role in devising a simple but effective method of allowing individual teachers to record their judgements about individual pupils is clearly an important one. The original set of aims which describe the nature of geography, and the aspects of the subject in which progression should be expected, could form the basis of such a recording system. This system may reflect the levels' descriptions in the Attainment Target for geography in the National Curriculum Order, as it may be against those levels that final summative observations will be made.

LIAISON

If geography co-ordinators are to support fully both the curriculum development and the professional development that will be necessary to allow geography to grow in their school, they will want to encourage that development within the wider context of the school and its whole curriculum and, indeed, the wider context of the learning of individuals throughout their school career and beyond. The geographical development of the child cannot be seen in isolation from the other areas of the curriculum. Much is made of the closeness between geography and history, and between geography and science, but clearly there are complementary overlaps which go far beyond these particular subject boundaries. Geography has a part to play in promoting the core skills of numeracy and literacy in children. This has been recognised in the new National Curriculum order for geography which includes reference to the use of language and information technology in particular. The geography co-ordinator will, therefore, want to liaise with other subject co-ordinators to exploit any and all opportunities which are of mutual benefit. Links will be essential with the co-ordinators of Key Stage 3. Initially, perhaps, this will be only to exchange information but later it will be to ensure that there is a shared approach to the teaching of geography.

SUMMARY

In this chapter we have examined the nature and purpose of geography as an essential part of the primary school curriculum. Geography can no longer be seen in terms of exotic places and the names of cities and rivers, nor as the acquisition of a discrete set of mapwork skills. The role of the co-ordinator of geography is to foster a spirit of enquiry amongst colleagues and children, one which allows children to use and enhance their geographical skills and knowledge as they attempt to make sense of and question the world around them.

Chapter 13

Co-ordinating the physical education curriculum

Angela Wortley

INTRODUCTION

The primary aim of the physical education (PE) co-ordinator is to raise both the status and profile of physical activity in the school by improving the quality of all physical activity experiences. This task has never been easy and has been made more difficult in recent years as a result of PE's late appearance in the National Curriculum (NC) implementation programme. The perceived status of PE has been further confused both by the stated intention of central government (Major – Conservative Party speech 1994) to 'restore competitive games in schools and increase the time allocated to them for all pupils under 16' and by the re-emergence at national level of health and fitness concerns as a result of recent studies such as the Allied Dunbar National Fitness Survey (1992). These studies predict a bleak picture of physical and cardio-vascular health in the future as the current young and middle-aged progress into old age. The findings are reinforced by the work of Armstrong and Sparks (1991) whose research reveals the very low physical activity levels in many of the children they have studied.

The competitive games and health and fitness issues that contribute to these concerns are, of course, of genuine interest to all PE teachers and will influence their teaching through the curricular activities selected and the ways in which these are taught. However, they are not central concerns, and should not unduly influence the PE programme that each school develops in response to its staffing and expertise, resources (including facilities) and time available. Nevertheless, such developments have succeeded in undermining the confidence of primary teachers in their ability to teach the activity content of their PE programmes and to decide their priorities as they are developing their policy statements.

Such a confusing and complex scenario goes some way to describing the minefield that is likely to face a co-ordinator in this area. This is exacerbated by the limited training in PE that has been given to primary teachers over the years and indications are that this specialist training is likely to diminish further. Some of the basic equipment and resources required to teach the PE curriculum are expensive and unless the schools have invested in PE over a long period they will find it impossible to resource adequately in the short term.

In contrast, the co-ordinator can take heart from the positive attitude of two groups, the children and their teachers. The highest percentage of primary age pupils named PE as their favourite subject (ILEA Research and Statistics 1987). Similarly, prior to the implementation of the NC, research by Williams (1983) revealed that primary teachers named PE third in *importance* behind maths and English. To the co-ordinator this indicates that children value their PE time and that their teachers also recognise its value – even though, when questioned, their reasons may not have been deemed educational (Williams 1983). We can assume from this that improving the quality of the programme and its frequency will be welcomed by the pupils and that any benefits from this will be to the advantage of the class teacher.

This chapter identifies some of the ways in which the co-ordinator can support and help develop colleagues so that their teaching of PE can be structured, challenging, planned, purposeful and stimulating in order that children experience a sense of enjoyment and achievement. We begin by looking at some general issues of co-ordination and then we consider specific PE activity areas.

THE WORK OF THE PE CO-ORDINATOR

The starting point for co-ordinators is to empower themselves with knowledge – knowledge about their subject and about what is going on in their school in relation to their subject. *Subject* knowledge will enable co-ordinators to feel confident about their rationale for PE: its unique contribution to each child's education and its potential for supporting other areas of the curriculum. Subject knowledge enables them to be up-to-date with thinking about successful practice and familiar with resources to support, develop and extend the teaching of their subject. Subject knowledge requires co-ordinators to have considered the pressures on their programme from outside bodies (particularly for health and competitive games) and to have a clear idea of how to take advantage of these initiatives whilst maintaining the needs of all children at the heart of the programme.

In order to acquire the *local* knowledge about what is going on in school the co-ordinator needs to carry out an 'audit'. This needs to be kept as low key and as non-threatening and non-intrusive as possible. Much data can be gathered about *resources* through a simple inventory – how much, the variety, quality and where they are located. The headteacher will provide information about the available *budget* for resources and hire or access to specialist facilities. Individual staff will need to be asked what *activities* they intend to teach during the year and to share any *schemes of work* and *assessment documentation* they are using. The information about *frequency* can be collected through observation more easily than for other subjects because of the need for access to large, open and easily monitored spaces. Analysis of these data will enable the co-ordinator to build up a picture of how the subject is viewed by the school.

The availability and quality of documentation, the extent of co-operation between staff and the range, frequency of use and state of equipment will all indicate PE's relative importance to staff. The documentation will reveal the extent to which individuals have been encouraged to work to a whole school plan and whether continuity, progression and assessment are planned for in a systematic way. The pervading philosophy may be inferred from the documents and the extent to which the subject is used to contribute to the curriculum in a wider context. The audit will also reveal areas of good practice, subject expertise, and the potential for future development. Equally, the audit will identify areas and activities where there is a need for the development of staff skills and knowledge.

Irrespective of the school it can generally be assumed that a number of issues concerning the teaching of PE will need to be considered by the co-ordinator. These will be tackled through discussion of the contributory activities that make up the primary curriculum:

- gymnastics;
- games;
- dance;
- athletics activities;
- swimming and water safety;
- outdoor and adventurous activities.

The agreed curriculum will indicate how the school has decided it can best fulfil the minimum statutory requirements for all activity areas for all children. It will reflect the relative strengths of the school in terms of expertise and resources. It will have drawn upon the expert advice of the co-ordinator in matching the developmental stages of the children to the content base of the schemes of work and it will contain agreed expectations of what children will be able to achieve at various stages in each activity area.

The co-ordinator will need to lead the staff through consideration of a series of questions in order to develop a whole school curriculum that will fulfil the aims of the policy statement and statutory requirements. These questions will enable staff to understand the necessity to plan block or serial timetabling for different activities – questions such as how often? how much? in what stage in the child's development will particular activities and concepts be appropriate?

Much of this discussion will be new territory for many teachers and will help them to understand what they are trying to teach their pupils and why, and what the children should be able to do at the end of each unit of work. The discussion will develop their understanding of the importance of planning for progression and continuity; achieving a balance in the type and frequency of activities throughout each planning phase; and in discussing the scope for developing activities neglected in the past.

GYMNASTICS

Many teachers have genuine and deep rooted anxieties about either their ability to teach using apparatus without putting children at risk of physical injury because of their own lack of expertise, or being unable to maintain control of pupils so that the likelihood of accidents is increased. The co-ordinator can raise the quality of teaching in this area through a planned programme of staff development to increase individual confidence and by establishing agreed safety procedures that are adopted by all staff. These will include:

• lesson plans that give adequate time for warming up and preparing the body for exercise and cooling down afterwards;
• agreed routines for carrying and erecting apparatus;
• organising planned and safe storage areas for apparatus when not in use; and
• agreed rules for pupil behaviour when working in the gymnasium or hall.

In providing photographs, plans and diagrams which are displayed prominently next to the apparatus the co-ordinator can provide a permanent reminder to staff and pupils of safe practice. Clearing the storage and teaching space of other bulky items often 'lodged' in the room allocated for gymnastics will increase the safeness of the area and improve access to equipment. Ensuring easy access is more likely to increase the use of large apparatus.

The major aim of gymnastics is to develop skilful control of body movement. The co-ordinator needs to help staff to understand what this means at each phase of child development and how to identify and develop skilful movement in their lessons. For example, at the infants stage a forward roll may be judged successful if the child can roll over his or her head along a mat in a tucked position but remain in a supine or seated position on the floor; in the early junior phase the roll would be judged successful if it had a clear beginning and end and finished in a crouched or standing position; in later juniors it would have a clear beginning and end, show control throughout, with a change of pace to enable the pupil to return to a standing position without using his or her hands.

The next stage is to get staff to consider how they can help children develop their skills. Essentially, staff need to develop their observational and analytical skills and, where they lack expertise, they can be pointed towards resources or work alongside the co-ordinator for a short period. However, it may be necessary for the co-ordinator to develop schemes of work for staff lacking confidence to enable them to experience working in a systematic way where each *lesson* in a unit builds on the previous one and each subsequent *unit* advances either the physical skill level or requires children, for example, to work in a more complex way with others or to use more taxing combinations of apparatus or to link several themes together in longer sequences.

Through these approaches the staff will develop more confidence because they have a clearer understanding of what they are trying to achieve and a structure in which to become successful. Agreed approaches to lesson structures and codes of behaviour will elicit safe responses from pupils who generally enjoy and look forward to participating. Over time, increased confidence will enable teachers to develop their teaching strategies. Safe practice is often equated to un-challenging and narrow experiences which discourage inventive and more advanced gymnastic movements. Confidence developed through increased understanding and expertise will enable the co-ordinator to try out less teacher directed approaches. These allow more scope for inventiveness from pupils and, importantly, provide opportunities for pupils to plan their own work and to evaluate their own and others' work in relation to how successfully it meets the demands of the task set.

Teachers can be encouraged to develop task cards, to provide apparatus plans for groups of children to follow, to have skill cards for individuals or groups to refer to when practising a new skill, to vary the limiting lesson structure often followed and to use apparatus arrangements that enable children to exploit the theme.

The co-ordinator could effectively spend time with early years teachers to establish good practice, particularly in relation to establishing a routine for

- dressing/undressing;
- awareness of and consideration for others when moving about the room;
- safe handling of apparatus;
- establishing responses to teacher commands;

- developing quiet working in the room to encourage concentration and reduce the opportunities of distraction and the risk of accidents.

Gymnastic type activities may provide the only opportunity for many children to experience a range of movements such as balancing, taking weight on hands, hanging and swinging, jumping from a height and climbing. These movements provide the kind of exercise necessary to promote the full development of healthy bone and muscle tissue. Modern lifestyles often limit the opportunities for this type of activity. Health surveys paint a bleak picture of brittle bones and poor muscular health in a growing percentage of the ageing population. There is much evidence to support the inclusion of vigorous physical activity through-out life in order to maintain physical and cardio-vascular health. This must depend also on ensuring a healthy, early, physical maturational progression. Vigorous exercise is vital to this process. For some children gymnastic type lessons will provide their only opportunity for this type of exercise.

DANCE

Together with gymnastics and games, dance has a major role to play in the PE programme in the primary years. It is probably this area which exhibits maximum variability in its delivery. Some schools will have well developed curricula linked into classroom and whole school issues, led by a knowledgeable teacher and be well resourced; other schools will have little or no dance or may simply link into television programmes; yet others may rely on a limited exposure to a narrow dance form, such as country dance. This variety will exist within as well as between schools.

Established good practice will need little support from the co-ordinator other than through the sharing of good practice, the provision of a wide range of music resources, and introducing staff to dance forms that would enrich their curriculum.

Variable or limited provision will necessitate a long-term plan drawn up with the staff to establish a dance policy with which they all feel comfortable. Considerable INSET and support teaching, probably bring-ing in local advisers, will be necessary to establish a sufficient level of confidence amongst staff for them to teach dance well. Co-ordinators can provide a role model for staff through their own enthusiastic teaching and their willingness to be observed, through being prepared to work alongside anxious staff and to discuss and share ideas for dance lessons. Developing whole school themes at certain times could help to raise staff confidence levels and raise the profile of dance in the school. Introducing dance festivals which last from one day to a whole week, in which local teachers work with invited experts to develop a varied programme ending with some dance production, could provide a way of raising the profile of dance for staff and pupils. Dance does provide a unique context to explore issues and themes and can enrich children's language, creative and expressive powers.

GAMES

Games teaching forms the basis of the PE programme throughout schooling. It is the area which most teachers feel confident to teach. Yet it also provides most examples of poor practice particularly in relation to matching tasks set to pupil ability and engaging all children in activities where they are likely to get maximum participation and practice throughout each lesson.

Limited initial training and personal experience combine to produce lessons that frequently provide enjoyable experiences but with little opportunity for developing and improving skills and strategies in a systematic way. Subject experts have stated that the games education in primary schools should concentrate on the development of a wide range of games skills, understanding the principles of attack and defence, the nature and importance of rules and making up and playing small sided games adapted from adult versions. Practice often contradicts this approach both in lesson time and in the persistence of interschool leagues based on full sized teams – these often focus on accomplished performers only and favour boys at the expense of girls.

The educational role of games has to be openly debated in order for the co-ordinator to produce a whole school programme that carries the support of staff. Agreement to plan lessons to develop individual skills alongside small sided games throughout the primary years will go a long way to raise the standard of children's participation. Facilitating an understanding of the stages from skill development to successful execution of skills in a game situation is vital. Too often the skill teaching takes up too much of lesson time and allows little scope for individual interpretation. The games parts of a lesson frequently do not emphasise the skills taught earlier and involve too many children for effective practice and learning to take place.

However, good games education cannot take place unless there is sufficient equipment, both in terms of variety and quantity, to implement recommended teaching strategies. Equipment will need to be suitable for successful practice throughout the school. The co-ordinator can facilitate good practice through providing a wide range of resources. Dividing resources into made-up baskets that contain specified numbers of a variety of equipment, colour coded for easy identification, will encourage small-group work building up a wide variety of games skills. Further support to all staff can be provided through the development of the spaces to be used by, for example, identifying rebound walls, providing a variety of permanent markings on walls and in playgrounds/playing fields to ease lesson management, and providing several high rings and other target areas for shooting practice. The co-ordinator can provide staff with ideas of how to adapt simple equipment to make nets, goals and court dividers. These practical ideas will enhance the variety of types of game that can be played and help to ensure that all participants in any game situation are fully involved for most of the time. No child can hope to improve any games skills if that child spends most of his or her lesson time being denied access to practice by more successful peers.

If games making does not exist in the curriculum the co-ordinator can use this as a new area for staff development. The debate stimulated about the nature of games and the purpose of rules is likely to have benefits in the general teaching of games. It will introduce a new teaching approach based on problem solving and valuing pupils' ideas. Games-making cards are available commercially that will help staff make a success of this approach.

ATHLETICS

Athletics activities involve children in developing all aspects of their *running*, *jumping* and *throwing* abilities. During the nursery years these activities will be developed in a general way in games and gymnastics lessons.

Athletics lessons are often dismal and disappointing. They mirror athletics competitions, involving children in fiercely competitive situations that motivate some but are humiliating and dispiriting for many others. The co-ordinator can provide ideas for stimulating and challenging *all* children to improve their athletics skills through using a wide variety of activities that develop sound techniques and encourage maximum effort. Challenges that encourage every child to improve against their previous best result, or against a progressive standard, are more likely to engage their full co-operation. An extensive list of interesting events with management suggestions and simple testing ideas is likely to be welcomed by colleagues who are fully aware of the misery some children suffer during these lessons but are unsure how to remedy the situation.

SWIMMING AND WATER SAFETY

Safety regulations ensure that all school practice adheres to LEA guidelines using appropriately qualified instructors and pool supervisors. In their initial audit, co-ordinators will need to be certain that all guidelines are followed and the qualifications of all teaching and supervisory staff appropriate and up to date. Where there are problems fulfilling the swimming programme because of problems getting into a local pool on regular basis or the lack of funds to support this activity, the co-ordinator will have to liaise with the headteacher and governors to try to fulfil their obligations in the future. The co-ordinator could provide a fresh look at the timetabling of swimming. Teachers often resent the time taken out of school for swimming. If this could be concentrated into shorter half-termly periods with more frequent visits during this time it might prove more attractive and achieve their support. In the early learning stages, learners are more likely to achieve their objectives if they have more frequent practice. Unfortunately, this flexibility of planning is often missing as access to pools is dictated by availability.

Regardless of access to water the co-ordinator can provide a well structured water safety programme that can be taught independently or as part of a topic on personal safety. This element of the curriculum is often neglected but could provide children with information and strategies to save their own and others' lives near water, in particular where the practical input is very limited. The ASA has developed an excellent school resource pack suitable for primary age children.

OUTDOOR AND ADVENTUROUS ACTIVITIES (O&AA)

The inclusion of this area of activity has caused a great deal of anxiety in schools. Much of this has been due to a misunderstanding of the terminology. The co-ordinator's role in this area will be to interpret what is meant by O&AA and to assure colleagues that they already fulfil much of the orientation/navigation and environmental awareness components through their *geography* and *science* curricula. Depending on the expertise available in the school, units on pitching tents, packing and carrying rucksacks and lighting and cooking with camping stoves could be developed to contribute to a cross-curricular topic on environmental education or to precede a residential visit. Problem solving in this area provides stimulating challenges for children by encouraging genuine co-operation. A staff development session could provide for both trial and evaluation of lesson materials while engaging staff in worthwhile team-building exercises. It is important to assure the staff that this activity need form only a minor part of the total PE programme.

SUMMARY

The development plan for PE will probably need to have an extended implementation period for most schools. The role of the co-ordinator will be to prioritise the target areas and devise the strategies for implementation. It is important that all developments can be easily monitored and

... the effectiveness of the changes to the quality of the

...ge to practice will be facilitated if co-ordinators lead by
... their own enthusiastic teaching, accessibility to other
...ss to support others in the classroom and through the
... curriculum support material and the development of a
...rces. In the early stages the co-ordinator will have to be
prepa... lead a good deal of school based INSET and to organise
festivals and sporting events in order to raise the awareness of the staff
to the value of PE and to improve its image throughout the school.

The following examples provide ideas for whole school initiatives that
could easily be implemented and would, hopefully, gain support from
colleagues.

- *Organise extra-curricular activities and competitions with access for all children*. These could be offered over short periods to give opportunities for all age groups at some stage in the school year.
- *Organise a sports festival or traditional sports day*. Provide new ideas on organisation that involve all children throughout the event, balancing competition and co-operation. Suggest that a senior class, with teacher support, be given the responsibility for organising such an event each year.
- *Enlist the help of other staff, parents and governors*. Encourage them to contribute to the extra-curricular programme and provide them with appropriate training (the National Coaching Foundation provides much support material).
- *Develop an active playground*. This could be a difficult project but very worth while. Once designed and installed, equipment could be provided from school funds. Ancillary staff need to be convinced of the value of the scheme and be willing to help to monitor equipment and play. This type of scheme would raise the profile of physical activity in the school very quickly and provide an important aspect of the PE curriculum often neglected – the opportunity for children to practise their skills and to engage in regular vigorous activity when they choose to – in an effort to develop an active lifestyle.

Chapter 14

Art

David Williams

INTRODUCTION

The changes and developments implicit in the National Curriculum document for art have redefined the role of the art co-ordinator. Important among these changes is the necessity to develop a set of guidelines which articulate clearly the responsibilities of the individual class teacher together with the implications for changes in the teaching and learning of art in the whole school. A major focus of this change will be that of support for developments for a broad and balanced art curriculum which highlights the emphasis of continuity and progression within the school and beyond.

The first part of this chapter will address the aims and objectives of art in the primary school and will draw on recent research in this area. The second part of the chapter deals with the more specific issues relating to planning for art teaching, whole school policies and innovation.

Almost all recent surveys and reports of the practice of art, craft and design in our primary schools have observed that the quality of children's experiences and the work that they produce varies widely. The practice and experiences made available vary not only from school to school, as may perhaps be expected, but also from teacher to teacher within a school. Some observers have suggested that part of the explanation for these differences lies in the range of views held by teachers regarding the value and purpose of art for children. Within any one school quite different views can exist. One widely held view is that of an inflexible belief in the natural creativity of children, which means that little or no teacher intervention takes place and children's work in art is accepted almost without question. Another commonly observed teacher approach is that which is heavily structured, with particular skills being emphasised and taught, perhaps in isolation from the process as a whole.

In the introduction to *Art in Practice*, Gillian Figg (1993) suggests that the eternal dilemma for the teacher is when and how to intervene. Indeed, she suggests, the National Curriculum was established in part as a reaction to the non-interventionist philosophies practised by some teachers in the past. Moreover, this non-interventionist philosophy could be said to be a response to earlier prescriptive practices which did not allow children's creativity and expression to develop fully.

It is against this background that art in the National Curriculum was introduced in an attempt to afford a structure and framework within which all teachers can operate. The inclusion of art as an integral component among the foundation subjects provides a challenge, the intention of which is to build upon existing energy and good practice.

Many schools will recognise their own and their children's existing practice in the art orders. Others will be encouraged to develop new strategies and practices. The role of the curriculum co-ordinator is crucial to these developments and the co-ordinator's skills are essential in encouraging and supporting these changes. Developing a climate in which structured and coherent change can take place needs the support and co-operation of all those involved, including the headteacher, staff and parents. An essential prerequisite to the development of a spirit of change and enquiry in other professionals is confidence in the ideas and beliefs which give the practice some personal meaning and direction for the co-ordinator.

The art co-ordinator has a range of possible approaches to developing and implementing the subject and ensuring that the children have a soundly structured developmental programme. In *Art for Ages 5 to 14*, published by the Department of Education and Science in 1991, the Art Working Group identified a range of factors which they believe are common to those primary schools where there is evidence of consistently good practice in the teaching of art and design:

- The head and teachers share aims and objectives, often expressed in a clearly stated policy document.
- The continuity provided by individual teachers' planning within that agreed policy is important.
- The staff give clear guidance having analysed the steps that pupils need to take to gain a skill or understand a concept.
- There is balance between the activity of making art, craft and design with opportunities for pupils to reflect upon and discuss their own work and the work of others.
- Children's drawing abilities are developed to the point where they are at ease using drawing as a tool, for example to aid thinking.
- Children develop confidence, value and pleasure in making art, craft and design.

The quality of art work within the primary school is determined by the way in which teachers respond to the above factors guided by a confident and skilful co-ordinator.

THE NATURE OF ART

In order to provide colleagues with well articulated support it is important that the co-ordinator has a clear and clearly expressed view of the role of art which in turn is developed and shared by the staff. Many writers and researchers have attempted to identify the specific role of art and its unique contribution to the curriculum in the primary school. *Most agree that it should be an essentially practical experience making use of a clear and logical, visual and tactile language.*

This practice is supported by responses to, and an understanding of, man made forms both past and present. The *Warwickshire Primary Schools Art and Design* booklet (1988) contains a preface by the then County Education Officer who makes some important observations about the place of art in the primary school curriculum.

> The first is that all schools endeavour to promote among children self confidence and a sense of personal identity, resourcefulness, judgment, powers of observation and a respect for the world around them. Schools seek to encourage children to come to terms with their emotions, to explore their imaginations and to give expression to these in ways that they can handle. In some degree every aspect of the curriculum should contribute to the realisation of these aims, but I believe that art and music do so more readily and perhaps for more children than any other.

The unique contribution of the arts to the education of children is again succinctly stated in the following quotation:

> The prime value of the arts in education lies in the unique contributions it makes to the individual's experience with and understanding of the world. The visual arts deal with an aspect of human consciousness that no other field touches on: the aesthetic contemplation of visual form.
>
> (Eisner 1972)

The dual roles of the *practical* nature of art and its parallel *critical* aspects are identified in each of the above extracts. It is possible to see that these two areas are emphasised in the National Curriculum orders for art:

> 'Investigating and Making', with its emphasis on the practical, investigative and exploratory nature of art; and
> 'Knowledge and Understanding', which reflects the critical, contemplative and language aspects.

It is important that the co-ordinator helps colleagues to understand and develop the relationship between these two aspects of the work in such a way that they emphasise that they are two parts of the same whole.

Without this unity there is the danger that the child will fail to understand the contribution of each, and that the child will imply a priority order between the two which is clearly unintended. In particular, the introduction of the critical studies aspect of art will be a new challenge to most primary teachers and will therefore require support from the co-ordinator or others outside the school who are familiar with this area.

It is easy for the child to assume that art is wholly a practical area and that the newer areas are additional and intrusive rather than integral. The interdependent qualities of the two attainment targets will need great emphasis especially at the beginning of the developmental planning period.

In practice, many teachers of younger children in our schools have found that they already have many of the skills required to develop their critical understanding. All teachers use pictures and book illustrations to extend or introduce an idea or develop a narrative. Initially it may be a short step to extend the looking and discussion to include objects and illustrations which are art forms. In addition many teachers have used stories and poems as a stimulus for work in art, skilfully using language to link the medium of art, whether it be in paint or clay, to the medium of language. All of these activities require the teacher to involve the child in discussion of his or her own work within any practical work. Any extension of these strategies will require particular support from the co-ordinator at the planning stage. The role of language in art and the relationship between the use of appropriate language and art activities could become the basis for staff discussion or perhaps in-service support.

Experience has shown that many teachers use words to steer the path of practical activity in art lessons. They use instructional language more than they use aesthetic language. The latter can considerably extend the vision and imaginative potential of art for children. The quality of language contributes considerably to the successful teaching of art. It will need to be positive and encouraging in addition to being appropriate and illuminating. Careful use of expressive and descriptive language with children helps them both to plan for and reflect upon the qualities of the topic being explored and their own responses to it. Considered discussion will also reflect the value given to art by the teacher and the child. Acquiring and developing practical skills is therefore only part of the role of art.

Experiencing and developing an understanding of things seen provide a basis for developing the imagination and expressing ideas.

This visual understanding deepens their aesthetic responsiveness as no other mode of learning can by enhancing the imagination and intensifying feelings, ideas and sensitivities. Pupils come to recognise order within the complexity of the changing environment. The ability to see clearly and to draw, paint, model and handle the associated technical problems is essential in a world that relies increasingly on direct visual communication.

(DES 1991)

It is clear that to develop a rich and meaningful art curriculum for children all of the staff must come to see it as an essential vehicle for exploring the world of art, the children's environment and other areas of the curriculum. One of the strengths of art is that it is easily organised to support a school's thematic approach. This helps to reinforce the perception of the wholeness of the curriculum for children.

PLANNING FOR ART

An important role for the art co-ordinator is to guide and support the planning process. Whatever the strategy developed for the school in respect of curriculum planning, part of the role of the co-ordinator is to help the teacher make 'connections'. These connections may be in different forms and at different levels according to the stage of development and level of understanding of the teacher. One connection might be made by investigating the opportunities for learning between religious and cultural artefacts and art. Another might be achieved by seeking connections between the subject of children's own paintings and paint ings by other artists.

> It is relatively easy to program children to make well observed drawings or attractive objects to take home to their parents. The challenge is to find ways to enable children to use art and design purposefully and to be educated through the making of art.

Many schools have suggested that they find that a structure and sequence to the work in art is needed now more than ever if the learning framework produced is to be meaningful. The necessary framework is one which links and supports the school's major themes or topics and at the same time introduces experiences and promotes the development of skills and concepts in art. It is clearly not enough for children to acquire discrete little packages of information and skills related to art as they progress through the school. Using the National Curriculum as a guide it will be possible to devise an aid to planning which considers the following questions:

- Where do the ideas and developments come from? What resources, experiences, visits, etc., will be needed?
- What are the key art concepts to be considered? Are they colour, pattern, texture, line, form or shape?

- How will the activities be extended? Will it be through printmaking, textiles, modelling, collage or clay work?
- How will memory and imagination be used?
- An additional question to ask could be: will the work be individual, group or whole class?

If, for example, the key art concept to be used is *colour* then there are implications for the whole school policy. Strategies about the role of drawing and the use of media may need to be considered. If paint is to be used many questions can be raised about the type of paint, use and storage of brushes, etc. Many schools have a very clear statement in this regard and have analysed the educational reasons for the inclusion of a particular range of colours to be made available to the children. Indeed, some schools insist that the quality and range of materials and the way in which they are stored and presented need not vary greatly from classroom to classroom.

ATTAINMENT TARGET 2

The demands of Attainment Target 2 have raised some areas for concern for teachers. Teachers are aware that they should be using works of art with their children but often feel inadequate about their ability to select and comment appropriately. In using the work of art as a point of discussion it is necessary to

1 identify areas for development; and
2 decide which aspect of the work to focus upon for further development.

Rod Taylor (1986) suggests that children can actually be taught to engage with all manner of works of art so that they can spend time with them, discover their secrets and learn to value and trust their own responses, observations and judgements. To this end he has, with the support of practising teachers, devised a strategy for investigating and exploring art works. The model is based on the following four areas:

- Content;
- Form;
- Process;
- Mood.

This model allows children to come to a fuller awareness of a work and helps them to make connections between their own work and that of others. Although the model was first set out to aid the classroom teacher it can, with some adaptation, form the basis for work with all children. In essence the four areas pose the following questions:

- What is the work about?
- How has it been organised and arranged?
- How has it been made?
- What effect does it have upon me?

This may provide an adequate model for teachers who feel less secure and could also be the basis for staff discussion and further development led by the co-ordinator or other specialists.

Resourcing for work in Attainment Target 2 needs careful consideration if appropriate and economical resources are to be made available to the staff. Over a period of time a wide range of visual and other source material should be made available to children to support their work in art. It may be useful to investigate the range available before deciding which are most appropriate to your situation.

As with many aspects of primary school development the balance between the use of *human* and *physical* resources is an important consideration. Much of the impetus for the inclusion of 'Knowledge and Understanding' in the art curriculum is a consequence of seminal work by art educators and teachers in British schools. Thus much of the research and curriculum development is both easily available and directly applicable.

Pupils need to be introduced to the work of artists and crafts people in a variety of ways, for example through direct contact with an artist in a workshop situation, demonstration or talk. This may be organised by the primary school, a linked upper or comprehensive school or as part of LEA, INSET or cluster group arrangements. The artist may be local, a member of staff of a linked school or part of an artist in schools scheme organised by an LEA or regional arts association. Access to artists can also be made by creating links with a nearby college of art or college of education. Direct contact with a practising artist can be a powerful influence upon children's perceptions and work. Choice of an artist needs to be carefully considered. Part of the role of the post holder will be to co-ordinate the range and type of artists your school may need and how best to use them. Some excellent examples of good practice in art have been introduced and developed in the important and influential *Educating for Art* (Taylor 1986).

Some of the work related to Attainment Target 2 will be introduced to the children through the use of secondary source material. The range of reproductions of paintings, drawings and prints available can be overwhelming and again care must be taken to utilise these resources. As these resources will build up gradually, and supplement those already in existence, it is important to consider which items may be used across the curriculum. Artefacts used as resources in religious education and multi-cultural education, for example, could also be useful as art resources.

Postcards bought on a gallery visit may also be useful for drama or English. Catalogues of exhibitions held locally or further afield are excellent sources of illustrations, commentaries and biographical notes. Although some high-quality packs of illustrations and postcards are now available, it is important to remember that these have been selected by someone else, perhaps with commercial rather than educational interests in mind. With the exception of a very limited few which have been written and compiled through practical teacher involvement, prepared packs of illustrative materials are likely to prove difficult to fit into the programme of topics you may wish to explore.

CREATING AN ENVIRONMENT FOR ART

Much has been said and written about the effect of the school environment on children's learning. The way in which a school uses its space and visual resource materials is a reflection of the attitude the teachers in the school have to children's learning and motivation. Indeed the quality of presentation and care with the details of display can communicate to the children the pride that teachers have in sharing their work or presenting ideas to them. Some writers suggest that there are three main purposes for displays. Simply stated these are:

- Those which stimulate ideas and responses.
- Those which summarise a particular project.
- Those which show work in progress.

Although these three types are separated for convenience, in practice they are often seen in combination. Over a period of time all teachers should consider using each of the display types as part of the day-to-day teaching in the classroom and in the school in general. Many teachers are of the opinion that the ability to produce a display requires skills which only a few practitioners seem to have acquired. Some basic skills do need to be explored and this will be an easier task for some if they are exposed to the model of a confident teacher. This not only supports the development of the requisite skills but also leads by example. Teachers will need to be aware of simple ways of mounting and displaying artefacts, children's work and the work of others. The co-ordinator may have the responsibility of supporting and promoting the visual environment of the school. Art, particularly, has the ability to enhance and enrich the whole school environment. The opportunity to share the children's work with a wider audience or to bring into school the work of others should not be overlooked. Activities may include exhibiting the work of the school in a local venue or showing the work of the feeder secondary school to, in particular, the older children in the primary school.

Art for Ages 5 to 14 (DES 1991) suggests that the introduction of the National Curriculum will ensure common aims and consistency of practice. Progress between the phases of education is discussed, as are the important issues of *communication* and *liaison* to promote continuity of experience for the children. A direct consequence of encouraging contacts with and between related schools is the development of a well structured programme of art in each of the schools with clear documentation to support this. The staff of each school will devise their own plans to clarify their understanding of continuity and progression. Discussions with colleagues within the school and across the phases will do much to help to clarify and interpret the role of each school within the three key stages. The reality for some schools is that they can only develop by sharing valuable physical and human resources and by using the potential and expertise of a wider range of professionals.

SUMMARY

Many primary school teachers may in the past have been reluctant to teach art because they claim that they lack the skills to do so. The training of primary teachers in the arts in general and the visual arts in particular has historically lacked structure and purpose. This leaves teachers themselves to find a route through the perceived difficulties and basic concepts of art whilst in post. Recent changes in the primary curriculum, including art, have raised new concerns for the less confident teacher. Art co-ordinators can assist greatly in building the confidence of other staff and to this end must themselves be assured in their role. They should lead by example, have high expectations, value the work of children and help teachers to understand the merit of using the highest-quality materials with children. Confidence is also gained by the use and development of a well structured whole school plan for art which builds upon the skills of experienced primary teachers, whilst introducing and developing the less familiar concepts in art. The co-ordinator for art is presented with a number of opportunities for the support and development of colleagues which can be aided by other professional support and promoted through a sensitive and realistic approach to change over a period of time. The range of issues and challenges which face the co-ordinator are varied and dependent upon stage of development of individual teachers and the staff as a whole. The issues outlined in this chapter include the following:

- Developing and extending pupil skills, attitudes and experiences.
- Maintaining the high profile of art in the school.
- Keeping well informed about art and informing others.
- Developing liaison and continuity.

- Developing an ethos for art in the school through the use of appropriate aspects of the school environment.
- Using a range of opportunities to involve outside support.

Only if the support and enthusiasm of the whole school, the headteacher, staff, the children and parents are utilised can the co-ordinator support the subject and professional development of the staff which will help to provide the full range of opportunities and experiences in art to which children are entitled.

Chapter 15

Music

David Wheway

INTRODUCTION

Recent developments in primary curriculum music (DES 1992, SCAA 1994) have encouraged reflection on current practice and highlighted the need to develop a music scheme which promotes accessibility for all children. This has considerable implications for the teacher responsible for music.

The teacher with responsibility for music has often operated as a specialist in the past. Many schools now recognise that this role needs redefining to that of a music co-ordinator. The music co-ordinator is seen as someone who can offer support to other teaching staff and enable them to provide a broad and balanced curriculum for all children, as well as the person who continues to provide many of the opportunities for music making previously associated with the role of a specialist.

However, there are significant issues for a co-ordinator of music which may differ from other curriculum areas. There are a considerable number of primary teachers who have little or no experience of teaching curriculum music, and may have some misconceptions about the skills and knowledge required to deliver curriculum music.

The first part of this chapter addresses some of the issues for co-ordinators related to curriculum music and, in particular, the areas of performing, composing, listening and appraising. The second part of the chapter addresses some of the management issues for the music co-ordinator.

CURRICULUM MUSIC

The National Curriculum for music outlines four main areas for study:

- performing;
- composing;

- listening;
- appraising.

Performing

Children should have opportunities to:

- perform their own work;
- perform the work of other children; and
- perform the work of other composers.

There are similarities between the value of performance in music and, for instance, that of performance in dance and drama, creative story readings, and display of art work. Performance and display give value to the piece. In addition, awareness that a product will be made 'public' hones skills, and encourages children to remain 'on task'. It aids assessment and planning. It the development of individual skills in elements such as pitch, pulse and rhythm keeping and listening skills. Performance also encourages participation in planning and performing. Not least performance gives children in the 'audience' the opportunity to note the ways in which another child or group has interpreted the task within the given parameters. This often sparks off new ideas, e.g. 'We could do that', or better still, 'We could adapt that'. It also highlights for the performing child or group, in a way that no amount of preparation can, the strengths and weaknesses of their performing and composing skills and, through this heightened awareness, promotes the development of these skills.

Creating time for performance is an issue for many teachers and it may be worth considering the following points:

- Children should be encouraged to assess when their piece is ready for performing, e.g. can they keep together, is it free from errors, could the sounds be improved, etc.?
- It is often preferable to listen to and discuss a performance in detail rather than listen to a series of performances. Children can amend their performances after considering the performance of another group in detail.

What other times of the day might performance occur:

- at the start of the day;
- when the children have 'cleared away' before a break;
- at the end of the day;
- by creating a break in other activities to listen to children who have been working as a group?

It is important to remember that concerts for audiences other than the rest of the class, e.g. other classes, assemblies, concerts for the local community, and interschool, offer valuable opportunities for children to develop further their performance and composition skills, and to have these skills recognised and valued by the wider community. Non-specialist teachers may require much support and reassurance regarding the quality and readiness of children's work when preparing for a performance to an audience beyond the classroom.

Composing

The processes involved in the production of a composition are similar to creative processes involved in other curriculum areas. They include exploring, problem solving, developing ideas, presenting and evaluating.

Children should have opportunities to:

- Explore the potential for, and build a repertoire of sounds from, a variety of sources, e.g. percussion, vocal and body sounds, sounds from the environment, from keyboards, etc.
- Investigate ways of combining and organising sounds. This might be achieved:
  1 in response to a stimulus such as a poem, story, picture trail, painting, etc.;
  2 through selection of sounds to create a desired effect;
  3 within musical structures.
- Refine and develop ideas through practice, recording, performance and evaluation.

To develop composing skills children need the opportunity to explore sounds from a variety of sources. Through these exploratory skills children are more able to consider, for instance:

- Which instrument(s) to choose to achieve a desired effect, for instance the sound of a clock or a sad mood.
- Storing ideas for future use, for instance the sound of paper scrunching to represent rainfall, or wind, or walking across pebbles.
- Classifying sounds: high or low, hard or soft, etc.

Non-specialists may require considerable support when organising their classrooms for music sessions in order to accommodate such exploratory activities. Co-ordinators and teachers might consider whether there are areas where children can continue such activities in small groups, for instance within the classroom, or around the school. Such areas are important for many different aspects of composing and the trialing of ideas as well as for exploratory work. Indeed, they are as valuable as their counterparts in other curriculum areas, for instance: 'Home Corners', 'Reading Corners', IT terminals, 'Wet Areas', Writing Tables, etc. Introducing the above music activities into the school day raises a number of issues which may require careful discussion. Staff need to consider, for example:

- How to cope with an activity which is potentially 'noisy'.
- How to introduce such activities into an already busy day.
- How to oversee and evaluate such activities.

Class teachers may require support in considering different approaches to composition. They may wish, for example, to experiment with producing whole class compositions by adding sound effects to a story, poem or picture trail, or developing patterns or sequences with sounds, rhythms and/or melodies.

Furthermore, co-ordinators can support their colleagues in considering ways of extending and refining their children's compositions, for instance through the use of the following:

- repetition;
- different sound sources;
- different elements (dynamics, timbre, etc.);
- adding more layers of sound;
- exploring different accompaniments;
- considering different forms (such as Binary, Ternary, Rondo).

Many non-specialists are concerned that their personal lack of knowledge of traditional notation will prove a handicap when encouraging recording and performing skills with the children. It is important that colleagues are reassured that traditional notation is not the only method of recording, that it is not necessarily required at Key Stages 1 and 2, and that it is only one way of recording music. Other methods of recording such as the use of pictures, symbols, audio-tape recorders, or the memory facility on keyboards are all suitable and desirable methods of recording children's compositions.

Listening

Children should be encouraged to:

- Develop an awareness of different sounds.
- Develop an ability to distinguish between sounds.
- Develop a vocabulary to describe sounds.

Children need to be encouraged to listen to, and talk about, sounds from percussion and everyday materials as well as sounds in the environment (for instance, in the playground or on a nature walk). Children should be given opportunities to distinguish between sounds, e.g. a drum and a triangle, between different musical elements, e.g. pitch, timbre, dynamics, and between the characteristics of pieces of music, e.g. a mood or an action. Mastering such skills assists in the acquisition of a vocabulary to describe what has been heard and also to describe what is required for composing and performing purposes. It also supports the language development of the child.

Children should have opportunities to listen to music from a variety of sources including:

- music they have composed, e.g. on cassette;
- music by other children;
- music of other times and places.

Providing opportunities to listen to their own music gives value to the piece, and offers opportunities for appraisal. Music stored on computer disk, audio or video cassette, as well as offering the opportunity for listening to and refining pieces, can be a useful way of keeping records of children's work.

Children should also have the opportunity to listen to music of other times and places. Young children are generally receptive to many types of music, and therefore should be offered every opportunity for a broad range of listening. Music can be introduced through a variety of contexts. For example:

- through topics related to different times and places;
- through accompaniments to drama, movement, creative writing, art, etc.;
- as a stimulus for children's own compositions;
- in its own right for analysis or pleasure.

When choosing music for playing to children, teachers might prefer to start with their own preferences in order to gain confidence. It is relatively easy to talk about music we know and like, e.g. what instruments are being used, what images was the composer trying to convey, how often is a theme repeated?

However, children should also have the opportunity to listen to music of different styles and cultures, and teachers should be prepared to broaden their own personal knowledge of different types of music. This can have resource implications for the music co-ordinator, in terms of providing a wide range of back-up CDs, audio-tapes, etc.

Below are some practical issues which staff will need to consider when playing music to young children:

- Keep the extract short (e.g. 30 seconds to two minutes).
- Don't expect the children to identify what the composer's intentions were. There are no 'wrong' answers when children are talking about what a piece of music makes them feel or think about. For example,

Fingal's Cave might make a child think of an elephant because there are loud bits.

- Encourage the children to talk about the music, or to be actively involved in responding to the music after or whilst listening.
- Provide opportunities to listen to a broad range of music.

Appraising

Appraising occurs in two major areas.

- Appraising their own, and other children's, compositions.
- Appraising music by others, e.g. on tape, disc or live.

Encouraging dialogue is not always second nature to the generalist teacher of music, but dialogue is vital in raising awareness regarding different aspects of a performance, and in relation to composition. Expectation that dialogue will ensue helps to focus the listening of the audience, which in turn helps to develop their own performance and composing skills. The questions listed below offer useful starting points for children's discussion of their own compositions:

> Can you tell us about your music?
> - How did the piece start/finish?
> - What did you like about it?
> - What contrasts or changes did the piece contain?
> - Does the piece fulfil the task set?
> - Was it performed fluently and appropriately?
> - Could it have been improved, and if so, how?
> - Could the piece be extended, and if so, how? (e.g. repetition, contrasts, new material, different instruments, etc.)
> - Did the audience listen well?
>
> (Wheway and Thomson 1993, p. 4)

In the same way, teachers should develop questions to encourage appraisal of recorded music.

MANAGEMENT ISSUES

This section of the chapter considers issues related to the management of curriculum music in primary schools. These include:

- developing a whole school policy for music;
- INSET (other staff, personal and that provided by local services);
- developing resources.

Developing a whole school policy for music

A whole school policy for curriculum music should encourage continuity and progression and support teachers in their planning. It should raise awareness for the music co-ordinator about the nature of current practice within the school. It should also identify areas for development, possible INSET needs and resource implications. Music co-ordinators should be reassured by having their attention drawn to a recent report in which Ofsted (1993c) found that curriculum music was satisfactory or better in four-fifths of Years 1 and 3 classes in a sample of 174 primary schools. However, the report identified a number of issues for development of the music curriculum in primary schools. These included:

- breadth relating to all programmes of study;
- progression across Key Stages 1 and 2;
- types and styles of music addressed;
- schemes of work in line with National Curriculum requirements;
- assessment, recording and reporting;
- the role of the co-ordinator;
- resources of musical instruments;
- information technology to create and record music.

Co-ordinators need to balance development of music within the school against a realistic view of what is possible, taking into account issues such as staffing, INSET requirements and financial constraints. Developing a scheme of work to which colleagues can work with a degree of comfort and confidence is vital.

A useful process might be to involve staff working in small groups. These groups could compile an audit of current practice and pool the results. In most primary schools there will be a variety of musical activities already occurring, for instance: 'greetings' or birthday songs; songs about 'ourselves'; communal songs; nursery or other rhymes; rhythmic playground chants and 'dips'; use of radio and television; movement to music; school productions; various occasions when recorded music is utilised; etc.

Staff should consider and prioritise areas for development, including tasks for the co-ordinator such as:

- developing resources;
- liaising with secondary colleagues;
- support for individual members of staff, e.g. support for teachers wishing to develop composition and recording;
- support for the whole staff, e.g. developing records.

These priorities need to be dove-tailed into the School Development Plan. Financial implications should be considered as well as the need to avoid overburdening the school's INSET programme and to identify possible conflict with other curriculum areas. The co-ordinator will need to consider a programme for successfully addressing a prioritised area for development:

- What is the main focus?
- Who will be involved?
- What is the time-scale?
- What resources are required?
- Are there any financial implications?
- How will this fit in with priorities for other curriculum areas?
- What will be the success criteria?

The following example may help to clarify the process: a member of staff wishing to develop children's composition and methods of recording through notation may require an initial meeting of an hour to discuss this aspect of curriculum music. The co-ordinator might organise sample lessons over a period of several weeks. Cover for the co-ordinator, and other possible costs, will require careful consideration. A series of short meetings with the member of staff in order to plan and evaluate a series of lessons might follow, and the success criteria might be a performance of children's compositions and a display of their scores.

In-service training (INSET)

There are various ways in which a co-ordinator may support colleagues. The development of certain skills (e.g. composing, rhythm) might be introduced through 'teacher days' or workshops. It may be helpful to introduce one activity and consider how it could be developed at different stages. Staff could trial the activity at an appropriate level with their children, and feed back evaluations of their sessions in a future staff meeting.

Additional support for resources, workshops, classroom based INSET, etc., is often available through the Local Education Authority Advisory Services (see the section on local services, below).

Providing sample lessons and follow-up support in the classroom is often a valuable way of supporting colleagues. Non-specialist teachers appreciate the educational value of curriculum music when they have the opportunity to observe someone working with the children. Over a series of sessions, control of the lesson can gradually transfer to the class teacher, with the co-ordinator always close at hand to support and offer advice regarding planning, organisation, on-going classroom music, etc.

Support in the classroom offers the opportunity to develop a scheme of work which is relevant to the class teacher, utilising any particular subject strengths that the class teacher possesses. Planning for this collaborative approach might consider the possibilities of linking:

- poetry and composition;
- art and pattern;
- maths and groups of sounds;
- history and listening.

In addition, the co-ordinator might consider utilising the ways in which a particular teacher manages the class. For example, exploration activities in music can provide valuable starting points for a teacher who values exploratory work in other curriculum areas. Class teachers may appreciate further specific advice and support on:

- music objectives and assessment;
- classroom organisation;
- progression and continuity.

Personal INSET

It is important that the co-ordinator keeps up to date with developments in music education, including new initiatives and resources. Local Education Authority courses can support by raising awareness of current developments and by responding to issues raised by teachers. It is important for a co-ordinator to remain in close contact with these services, therefore, and keep colleagues back in school informed of issues (see the section on local services).

Liaison with colleagues from other schools in the locality, both primary and secondary, is valuable for meeting other teachers, planning joint projects, sharing ideas and possible concerns, and also for moderation purposes. Such meetings can raise awareness of the developments in primary schools, and ways in which primary colleagues can support children in readiness for transfer. Such communications with other colleagues also help to ensure continuity and progression.

Local services

With the transfer of funding to schools, many LEA services are being reorganised or in some cases disbanded. Schools now have the option of choosing support from the LEA services or from other agencies which may be offering their services to schools. Co-ordinators purchasing support will need to consider carefully value for money and quality of service. Schools should take care to verify that appropriate staff checks are made on suppliers of teaching services (such as peripatetic specialists), especially where they will operate *in loco parentis* (LEAs already check records of support staff).

Developing resources

For many schools music resources are a major issue. This is partly a result of the relatively recent introduction of classroom music onto the curriculum. Whereas in other curriculum areas there has been a process of restocking and culling over the years, it is not unusual to find a poor stock of music resources such as percussion, recorded music, recording/ playback equipment and activity and text books. This situation may be even more acute where the staff of a school have in the past failed to prioritise the resourcing of curriculum music.

Under these circumstances a 'chicken and egg' situation may arise with staff failing to appreciate the potential for good quality music making and therefore not appreciate the need to channel funds into music resources.

However, it is important for the co-ordinator to ensure an annual budget for music resources, and the following areas might be considered:

- A wide range of percussion instruments, including good quality, well maintained tuned-percussion.
- A broad range of recorded music and good quality equipment for playback.
- A 'set-aside' amount for repairs (tuned-percussion) and wear and tear (it's not just your school where tambourines and tulip blocks get broken!).
- A supply of activity books and resources which can be utilised both by teachers who have previous musical experiences, and those just beginning to introduce music into their classrooms.
- Song materials with consideration for teachers who cannot read traditional notation and/or cannot play an accompanying instrument. Some song materials have accompanying tapes. Alternatively a music co-ordinator might provide a tape recording of sung or played melodies.
- IT resources for reference, recording and performance.

SUMMARY

The music co-ordinator in primary schools faces many challenges which will include some or all of the following:

- Support for colleagues with little or no previous experience of classroom music.
- The introduction of a music curriculum which may differ substantially from previous models within the school.
- Developing resources which may initially be minimal or non-existent.

- Developing a programme of INSET with colleagues who may feel anxious or threatened.
- Offering enhanced musical experiences, such as choirs, ensemble groups, peripatetic support, etc.

The music co-ordinator, possibly to a greater extent than his/her counterparts in other curriculum areas, needs to proceed sensitively when supporting colleagues, and adopt a realistic approach to what is achievable in both the short and long term.

Chapter 16

Religious education

Mark Lofthouse

INTRODUCTION

Charles Handy (1994) has recently written a book entitled *The Empty Raincoat*. As a symbol and metaphor for the end of the twentieth century, *The Empty Raincoat* is immensely powerful. For Handy it signifies the paradox of increased economic progress leading those in work to feel anonymous cogs in a great machine. For the increasing numbers of those out of work, *The Empty Raincoat* only too vividly symbolises the emptiness and void in which their lives are lived. Handy is currently one of a number of philosophers re-examining foundational values (Barrow 1993, p. 1). These appear to be most elusive and problematical just at a time when they are most needed because materialism and technology are not automatically delivering happiness. As Handy suggests, many are now seeking values and meanings to underpin 'candyfloss capitalism'.

This context helps to explain why RE is back on the map. For long periods during the 1960s and 1970s, RE lay becalmed in a sea of indifference because the possibilities and achievements of secular materialism seemed limitless. During the 1990s we have painfully discovered these limits and politicians and opinion formers are worried. A search has begun to recreate the kind of social glue needed to hold together increasingly disparate, atomistic societies.

RELIGIOUS EDUCATION: THE LEGAL AND LEGISLATIVE FRAMEWORK

For England and Wales the 1992 Education (Schools) Act places a responsibility upon schools and staff working in them to promote the 'spiritual, moral, social and cultural development of pupils' (NCC 1993). To counter suggestions that using such high-sounding words was an exercise in empty rhetoric, the Office for Standards in Education (Ofsted) was instructed by the then Secretary of State to report on the spiritual, moral, social and cultural developments of pupils during inspections of all schools (DES 1989). As the inspection framework has been developed Ofsted inspectors have been required to comment on 'the ethos and values of an institution' and have additionally been tasked with producing inspection evidence concerning the planning and teaching of RE, and the arrangements made for worship, in all schools (Ofsted 1993a). The 1988 Education Reform Act stated that collective worship in schools should be 'wholly or mainly of a broadly Christian character' (ERA 1988, 7:1, 7:2). The Act made it mandatory for a Standing Advisory Council for Religious Education (SACRE) to be set up in each Local Education Authority. The key function for each SACRE was to 'Advise the authority upon matters connected with Religious Worship in county schools and Religious Education to be given in accordance with an agreed syllabus' (ERA 1988, 11,1, (a)).

RE curriculum co-ordinators have every reason to be grateful for the combined legislation of 1988, 1992 and 1993. Collectively it provides a charter for bringing RE out of the shadows and giving it a place in the sun because the legal and statutory powers presently available to co-ordinators have been identified. What is not so readily apparent from the legalistic framework is an enabling and empowering dimension within the legislation which many at first feared was not present. The phrase 'wholly or mainly of a broadly Christian character' attached to collective worship led many teachers and media analysts to fear that the clock was being turned back ignoring multicultural, multifaith Britain. As both Brown and Bastide point out, these initial fears are proving premature (Brown 1992, p. 21, Bastide 1992, pp. 11–13). 'Broadly Christian', has been defined by the DfE as encompassing material from other religious traditions, providing this material is in sympathy with the main streams of Christian belief (DES 1989). Not all acts of collective worship in schools need be broadly Christian – provided that a majority are and a majority can be defined as 51 per cent! In the same spirit the Act softens the law on collective acts of worship, enabling assemblies to be held during any part of the school day and in groupings and locations which take advantage of year groups, forms and classes. In short, what at first appeared draconian is infused with a good deal of pragmatism.

THE AIMS OF RELIGIOUS EDUCATION

The aims of RE have shifted over time, but in Britain since the Second World War three broad approaches to the subject can be identified:

1 the Confessional Approach;
2 the Giving them the Facts Approach;

3 the Understanding Religion Approach.

(Bastide 1992, p. 5)

The central aim of a *confessional* approach is to commit children to belief in a defined faith. The values, attitudes and creeds of a faith will be explored with a view to children acquiring and believing them. Such a process is characteristic of *denominational* schools. However, Brown (1992, p. 4) cogently makes the point that 'The RE programme of any school (including denominational schools) would not be complete without the study, in appropriate depth, of some non-Christian religions'. The same point, in reverse, would apply for all other faith schools. Contemporary society has an overriding need for there to be tolerance and respect for differing beliefs. Attitudes of tolerance and respect are not well served by an exclusive focus on one faith to the exclusion of all others.

The 'giving them the facts approach' has been the dominant method in English primary schools since 1944. Rejecting notions of encouraging children to believe in any particular faith, the *factual* approach adopts a neutral stance to whether any religion is true or false, right or wrong. The factual approach notes that religions exist, treats them as being equal, and accepts the right of children to *know* about them all, rather than *believe* in any one. Given the secular tendencies of many western societies (including Britain) it is not surprising that approach has gained in popularity. However, it has its problems. A dispassionate approach risks draining out all life and interest in the subject, reducing it to a meaningless exercise in information transmission (Lofthouse 1994a, p. 102). This deficiency has been highlighted in a sharply critical report by Ofsted on the teaching of RE in primary and secondary schools during 1993 (Ofsted 1994d, pp. 3–5).

The third strand, *understanding religion*, rejects both the confessional and instructional methodologies. Adherents to, and advocates of, this approach insist that the essence of religion lies in getting inside it, *feeling* it, *experiencing* it, *valuing* it through understanding and empathy. In achieving these 'dispositions' children are encouraged to examine religions sensitively and to explore them, in part, in terms of a *personal search*. This term can best be understood from work undertaken by the Schools Council. In 'Discovering an Approach', the team of researchers argued:

> Religious Education can build upon the desire to make sense of life. It tries to help pupils to enter imaginatively into the experience of a believer so that they can appreciate the importance to him/her of what he/she believes and does.
>
> (Schools Council, *Discovering an Approach*, in Bastide op. cit., p. 10)

Clearly this is ambitious, with high expectations of teaching and learning outcomes. In approaching this style of RE teachers need to appreciate that their primary role is that of *facilitator*. As a 'personal quest' is potentially a lifelong activity, the main task of the primary teacher is to lay down foundations and equip children with tools of understanding. Such a style of work reaches back to the kinds of primary practice championed in the Plowden Report: experience is valued and cherished, 'learning by doing' is encouraged. All of this is exciting but exceptionally demanding, placing upon teachers very high expectations in terms of their levels of commitment and enthusiasm.

WHAT CONSTITUTES GOOD PRACTICE?

The philosophy and rationale underpinning 'Understanding Religion' explicitly, or implicitly, underpins the majority of books and schemes of work devised for RE work in schools (Hyde 1990, pp. 10–35). This is useful knowledge in terms of knowing the drift of informed opinions. However, while 'Understanding Religion' is an excellent approach, I am reluctant glibly to recommend it. First, it is absurdly arrogant to pontificate as to what actually constitutes good practice because this shifts in terms of differing environments and institutions. Second, what can and should be invoked by any co-ordinator endeavouring to put in place 'good practice' is the notion of *fitness for purpose*. With this conceptual tool in place, good practice involves offering high-quality learning experiences, created and offered in the right places, at the right times and in the right ways. Curriculum consultants can be very helpful in enabling a school to carry out a *strategic review*. Initially this task requires accessing relevant information:

- the national framework: current legislation;
- the local framework: advice from SACRE.

This process can be extremely time consuming and while the co-ordinator needs to be both involved and informed, he or she does not necessarily need to undertake all the work. The head, parents, governors, teaching staff and children all have a role in determining and agreeing aims. It is often easier for someone outside the school to act as a facilitator, working between and with the above groups, so as to achieve agreed aims. While the co-ordinator has the right to play an important part in identifying aims, the critically important role is in translating aims into policies and practice.

GETTING STARTED

Expectations of what can and should be achieved by co-ordinators have risen sharply during the last five years. A review of such responsibilities and duties (focused on the RE co-ordinator) provides a current list which can be divided into 'traditional' and 'acquired' responsibilities. Traditionally RE co-ordinators have been expected to initiate and advise on:

• policies;
• schemes of work;
• resources.

With the development of inspection frameworks there is now an expectation that co-ordinators will have 'acquired' additional responsibilities for:

• monitoring work;
• moderating work;
• reporting on work.

The processes of monitoring and moderation will necessarily involve the co-ordinator in:

• guiding;
• training;
• advising.

Collectively this is a formidable list, which needs 'reflection before action'. The critical point is that the co-ordinator is the real expert in knowing what is achievable and judging 'the art of the possible'. What is possible, in getting started, depends on the co-ordinator accurately assessing colleagues' personalities and professional potential. The importance of getting this right in the field of RE cannot be overstated. The Conscience Clause, embodied in the 1988 Act, means that no teacher can be *required* to undertake RE; they can only be invited to do so. Refusal and non-co-operation by staff have recently led Ofsted to report that the teaching of RE in 20 per cent of primary schools was 'invisible' and in another 20 per cent 'negligible'. Overall, half of the primary schools in a survey conducted during 1992–1993, were either not teaching RE at all or teaching it badly (Ofsted 1994d, pp. 4–5). Clearly if this situation is to be avoided in a school, it argues that the RE co-ordinator needs to get policies and schemes of work clear, visible, understood and *owned*. Without consensus and whole school support, the RE co-ordinator may find that he or she is single handedly shouldering the burden of teaching the subject throughout the school.

Determining how much scope there will be for the RE co-ordinator to *guide, train*, and *advise* is an early litmus test of how seriously an institution is taking the co-ordinator's role. If action, under all three headings, is declared to happen only on training days and outside the normal teaching day, it suggests that the RE co-ordinator is going to have to be properly assertive in ensuring that other role activities are supported during school time. *Monitoring* and *moderating* work undertaken by colleagues and students demands an allocation of *time* within a school day.

If such an allocation is not made it suggests that responsibility is de-volved to the co-ordinator, but without the power to ensure action and implementation.

Despite the slimming down of the NC achieved by the Dearing Review, the total demands of the revised curriculum leave most primary teachers fighting for every minute of time and space that can be conjured up during a school day. This is bad news for high-quality RE teaching, especially the style and type of RE that demands 'Understanding Reli-gion'. Without time, personal and curricular, the RE co-ordinator cannot function. Therefore a *time audit* will be a critical information tool in informing the RE co-ordinator whether:

1 the job can be done;
2 what kind of job can be done.

When the size and scale of the enterprise is agreed, time auditing quickly leads into *curriculum mapping*. The challenge for the RE co-ordinator is to achieve a whole school RE curriculum which makes the best use of all available time, interest, talent and commitment. Ideally, classroom time will be linked to assemblies and both identified in the School Development Plan. While schemes of work will reflect the unique circumstances of differing schools, in constructing a whole school RE curriculum a co-ordinator needs to bear in mind four factors:

> *Balance*: Does the scheme of work reflect different aspects of the many sided nature of religion?
> *Cross curricular involvement*: Does the work take into account teaching and learning in other areas of the curriculum? Is there really an R.E. element? If so, what is it? How can it be identified?
> *Progression* and *Continuity*: Does the scheme of work keep pace with, and extend, the developing capacity and experience of the children?
> *Differentiation*: Does the scheme of work provide for the needs of all abilities, including the least able and most able children?
> (*Eggshells and Thunderbolts* 1993, p. 7)

This is a challenging task, but the RE co-ordinator can take heart from the fact that a wide range of excellent schemes and materials are now available. (A recommended list of such materials is reviewed at the end of this chapter.) The RE co-ordinator can take further comfort from know-ing that good resources play a critical part in empowering and encourag-ing teachers (Lofthouse 1994b, pp. 87–92). However, some commercial schemes do not always identify teaching and learning opportunities and outcomes. When they do, the advice offered may not be appropriate for a particular school. Thus, the RE co-ordinator has the important responsibil-ity of linking content and resources to learning methods and experiences.

In short, 'It's not what you do, but the way that you do it' which is of 'primary' concern.

The RE co-ordinator as human relations expert

Many adults carry around within them 'secret gardens' of values and beliefs acquired during childhood. Because these gardens are very special places we may not visit them very often. Whether we do or not, we certainly do not want strangers trampling around them. RE co-ordinators, by the nature of their job, may be perceived as the unwelcome visitor. Any consideration of contemporary RE teaching is liable to challenge values and raise emotions. Teachers happy to consider changes in a variety of curriculum areas suddenly become defensive and angry when RE is reviewed. The outright hostility of the non-believer can be mingled with the rage of those who feel their personal beliefs challenged by 'multifaith' teaching and worship.

As the RE co-ordinator is entirely dependent on the goodwill of colleagues in planning and teaching RE, negative, emotionally charged meetings should be strenuously avoided. RE co-ordinators need, above all other co-ordinators, to appreciate that while they possess *influence*, they are short on *power* (Warnham 1993, pp. 62–75). Recognising this is salutary in reminding the RE co-ordinator to adopt a 'softly, softly approach' in terms of human relationships.

THE RE CO-ORDINATOR AND STRESS

While acknowledging that all teachers and co-ordinators are exposed to stress, I want to argue that the RE co-ordinator is often placed in a uniquely stressful position. This arises because potential sources of stress are built into the role in the following ways:

• The RE co-ordinator is the recipient of feelings and emotions, from colleagues and pupils, which find expression through the *subject*.
• The *values* held by RE co-ordinators may drive them to work too hard and generate feelings of *guilt* if imperfections are perceived.

This list can be greatly extended (Nash 1988, p. 43), a process which is counter productive because it only serves to increase feelings of personal and professional depression. The important point to seize upon is that recognising stress factors, endemic within the RE co-ordinator role, is the first step to acquiring *stress skills* which enable you to do the job better (Nash 1988, pp. 33–43). Negatives need to be turned into positives and RE co-ordinators, often skilled at doing this for others, are not always very good at doing it for themselves. Peculiarly unhelpful to them are unacknowledged feelings of guilt and resentment. A syndrome of responses along the following lines may be identified:

- Nothing is too good for RE, my *faith* demands *perfection*.
- If *perfection* cannot be achieved I have *failed*.
- Failure cannot be explained in normal terms, e.g. I cannot *blame others*, therefore I *blame myself* and *feel guilty*.
- *Guilt*, *anger* and *resentment* are internalised and *stress* accumulates.
- Stress and *anxiety* cause insecurity.
- Feelings of *insecurity* provoke questions of *faith*; if my faith is strong enough, why am I feeling like this?

Now it may be observed that this is a circular process, one which can become a downward spiral. Fortunately, most teachers *recognise* the pressures, especially if these are brought into the open. Having worked with many groups of RE teachers on in-service courses, I never cease to be happily surprised at the *relief* felt by course participants when symptoms from the above cycle are shared. Suffering in silence is a negative not a positive response. With in-service opportunities now harder to find, RE co-ordinators have an urgent need to set up 'self-help' groups where professional *sharing* and mutual *encouragement* are absolute priorities.

SUMMARY

In some ways this summary may be premature. A recommended list of books, materials and organisations follows. The list is not intended to be exhaustive but it is intended to be helpful and 'time saving'. In a tangible way it expresses the approach adopted in this chapter. In response to the paradox of *The Empty Raincoat*, everyone needs to begin somewhere. Robert Pirsig in *Zen and the Art of Motorcycle Maintenance* offers a timely and positive philosophy:

> The place to improve the world is first one's own heart and head and hands, and then work outward from there. Other people can talk about how to expand the destiny of mankind. I just want to talk about how to fix a motorcycle.

For the RE co-ordinator 'fixing the curriculum' may be the vital first step in expanding the destiny of the next generation. A list of helpful 'spare parts' is now provided.

RE in Britain

Brown, A. (1992) *Religious Education*, London: The National Society.
A 32-page booklet which brings a mass of information together and makes it accessible to busy teachers. Nine sections dealing with 'why teach RE' to Spiritual and Moral, Assessment and Management issues. Although written from an Anglican perspective, provides the kind of information necessary and relevant for co-ordinators working in non-denominational schools.

Bastide, D. (1993) *Good Practice in Primary Religious Education 4–11*, Lewes: The Falmer Press, ISBN 1–85000–639–3.
Extends the themes dealt with more concisely by Brown, who contributes a chapter on 'worship' in primary schools. Chapters on planning RE across infant/primary schools are especially relevant for co-ordinators.

McCreery, E. (1993) *Worship in the Primary School*, London: David Fulton, ISBN 185346–233–0.
A detailed review of all aspects of 'worship' in a primary school following the Education Reform Act.

Books for practical application and planning

Owen-Cole, W. and Evans-Lowndes, J. (1991) *Religious Education in the Primary Curriculum: Teaching Strategies and Practical Activities*, Norwich: Religious and Moral Education Press, ISBN 0–9002/1–32–8.

Provides professionally focused information and will be of particular use to teachers seeking both teaching styles, strategies and lesson outlines.

Two books which supplement and extend the same kind of approach are:

Hughes, E. (1994) *Religious Education in the Primary School: Managing Diversity*, London: Cassell, ISBN 0–304–32656–9.
Jackson, R. and Starkings, D. (1990) *The Junior R.E. Handbook*, Cheltenham: Stanley Thorne, ISBN 1–871402–31–X.

Books and materials for use in schools

Eggshells and Thunderbolts Multimedia Resources for Primary R.E. (1993) BBC Education and Culham College Institute.
Quite simply a 'best buy', especially for those primary schools where Christianity is given substantial treatment. Pack contains audio- and video-tapes, interactive disk and teachers' manual. The last not only provides excellent practical advice and activities, but additionally has exercises for RE co-ordinators to engage colleagues in formulating aims and planning curriculum outcomes.

Grimmitt, M., Grove, J., Hull, J. and Spencer, L. (1991) *A Gift to the Child. Religious Education in the Primary School, Teacher's Source Book*, Hemel Hempstead: Simon & Schuster, ISBN 0–7501–0128–8. Particularly strong on multifaith approach to RE. Provides clear theme and lesson planning with a rationale for multifaith worship and approaches described in the introduction as 'A New Realism in Primary R.E.'.

Two books which have good layout and especially easy formats and printing for children to use are:

Rankin, J., Brown, A. and Hayward, M. (1989) *Religious Education Topics for the Primary School*, Harlow: Longman, ISBN 0–582–00334–2.
Co-ordinators will find it helpful that topics are divided/planned by age range, 5–7, 7–9, 9–11 years. This book is supplemented by

Rankin, J., Brown, A. and Hayward, M. (1991) *Religious Education Across the Curriculum*, Harlow: Longman, ISBN 0–582–06052–4.
This book provides a series of themes and symbols, 'Water', 'Fire', 'Time', and links these ways of teaching and learning. The whole approach enlivens traditional ways of teaching R.E.

Books for RE co-ordinators

In addition to the teachers' manual in *Eggshells and Thunderbolts* the RE co-ordinator will find the following 'activity book' most useful:

Ainscow, M., Hopkins, D., Southworth, G. and West, M. (1994) *Creating the Conditions for School Improvement: A Handbook of Staff Development Activities*, London: David Fulton, ISBN 1–85346–310–8.
Provides an excellent range of 'hands-on' activities, including on pp. 85–89 practical activities, skills for co-ordinators. Book can be photocopied and exercises used on training days.

Following up themes raised in the chapter:

Warnham, S.M. (1993) *Primary Teaching and the Negotiation of Power*, London: Paul Chapman, ISBN 1–85396–228–7.
Nash, W. (1991) *At Ease with Stress: The Approach of Wholeness*, Longman, ISBN 0 252 51777.

Both books are recommended because, as well as identifying a problem, both offer ways in which teachers can confront and overcome difficulties.

Useful organisations

Co-ordinators may wish to establish contact with a member, or adviser, on their SACRE Committee. Registered charities are often pleased to be involved in school projects. Lists of such organisations, and other helpful information, are available in Brown's booklet *Religious Education*, pp. 29–32, reviewed earlier.

Part III

The extended curriculum

Chapter 17

Getting started

The process of implementation

Neil Kitson

INTRODUCTION

Since the imposition of the National Curriculum, the role of the subject co-ordinator within the primary school has become more significant, more specific and more involved. Post holders have increased levels of responsibility and accountability to colleagues, governors and outside bodies. Also, as Whiteside suggests in Chapter 3, the role of the co-ordinator is very diverse. It varies across schools from that of resource gatekeeper to planning and resource facilitator, to subject consultant and critical friend who works alongside other teachers in the classroom. Irrespective of how the role is perceived in your particular school, or in your area of responsibility within the school, it can be seen from the chapters in Part II that there are a number of common strategies which need to be considered when developing the role of the co-ordinator in order to make your work more effective. In this chapter we look at the most significant of these strategies: acting as a role model; auditing practice; action planning; and staff development. Finally, some specific suggestions are offered as to how you might begin the process of encouraging experimentation and change.

ACTING AS A ROLE MODEL

Without exception, all the contributors in Part II have referred to the need for the subject co-ordinator to be a good classroom practitioner; the most effective strategy for promoting any subject area within a school is to demonstrate by example. In your own classroom, putting into practice those key aspects of sound teaching that you would like to see in place across the school, and letting others see what is occurring, will have a significant effect. The effect will be not only on the way that others take on board the ideas that you are developing but also on their willingness to receive these ideas and develop their own teaching strategies. Look for opportunities to enhance the profile of your curriculum area by being ready to offer ideas for colleagues to try out. The profile of your subject area will be raised by your willingness to develop ideas and make suggestions in staff and general curriculum meetings. In this sense you are creating a positive atmosphere for the development of your curriculum area.

SETTING UP AN AUDIT

With regard to the formal development of your curriculum area, one of the first activities that co-ordinators need to undertake is to increase their knowledge: to find out what is currently being taught as part of their area of responsibility; and, more generally, what relationship their subject has with other things that are being taught within the school. Such an audit can begin by looking at the extent and location of existing resources, in effect 'seeing what's there and where' in the school. This analysis helps begin to create an overall picture of how the subject is viewed by both the classroom teachers and the school in general. The level of access to shared resources, and the degree of flexibility shown in teaching aspects of the curriculum, will indicate how your subject is perceived and understood. The audit will show you existing areas of strength and identify where help might be needed in the development of skills and subject knowledge in staff. Looking at the work that children produce will also be important in order to establish the range and extent of differentiation of development across classes and across the school as a whole. Whatever it is that you feel you are looking for in your audit it is important not to alienate colleagues. As a teacher there is nothing worse than feeling threatened by a co-ordinator asking for yet more evidence or information in a subject where you have little confidence. Match your enquiries to the prevailing ethos of the school and be sensitive to the needs of staff. Whilst it may be appropriate at times to send round a questionnaire, an informal chat over coffee may have a greater effect.

Having a look at a sample of work from a year group will often yield as much useful insight into your curriculum area than will a detailed study of lesson plans for the year. That is not to say that the questionnaire and the lesson plans are not important but it might be more appropriate to save such approaches until you have gained the trust of staff. I recently witnessed one approach to a whole school audit that the school concerned found very useful. The approach builds on the issues and strategies which have already been discussed in this chapter. On a whole staff INSET day, trays of work from a particular curriculum area, chosen by teachers as a representative sample group of children, i.e. one child of above average attainment, one of average and one of below average attainment in each of the classes in the school, were set out in sequence in the hall. The staff then spent some time looking at the evidence in terms of: curriculum coverage, differentiation, progression, and continuity. From this they were able to discuss where it was felt that gaps occurred, where further progression was needed and where additional support would be beneficial. It also gave staff the opportunity to see the extent and range of work across the years rather than the more usual fleeting insight into the classes just above and just below the ones they teach.

PAPER DOCUMENTATION

Paper documentation also plays a significant role in the understanding of existing thinking and philosophies within the school. This documentation can take a number of forms ranging from formal policy statements through to the individual teacher plans mentioned earlier. At a very basic level the sorts of questions to ask are: Do documents exist and, if so, which? How co-operatively were they devised? Do staff use them and, if so, how? Recently I encountered a curriculum document in a school which had received awards for both its staff and curriculum development work. By studying the documentation in none too detailed a fashion it was clear that there was a significant rhetoric gap between the philosophies expressed, which were very sound, and the schemes of work which were, one felt, just a reinterpretation of the same type of work that had always been done. One can look at the work of individual class teachers. A lot may be inferred from whether they have identified individual lesson plans for specific learning areas in your subject or whether your curriculum area is seen as 'a part of everything that children do'. One can also consider wider whole school applications which, again, indicate the level of curriculum development undertaken by the staff.

Such applications might include:

PE – How are aspects of games skills reflected in the children's playground experience?
Geography – Do school visits encourage reflection upon aspects of geographical enquiry or are they just things to do in the summer term?
English – Is there consistency of policy for marking across all areas of the curriculum or do people have one set of marking criteria for English and another for other curriculum areas?
Art – Does the display policy reflect the ethos of the school across all classes or is display used to fill blank spaces on the wall?

TOWARDS AN ACTION PLAN

Having undertaken an audit the co-ordinator, with colleagues, is in a position to draw up a statement of areas of strength and weakness based on evidence drawn from actual practice. From this it is possible to draw up an action plan of priorities, taking into account the culture and structure of the school. It is important not to attempt too much too soon. Rather, co-ordinators should prioritise the actions to be taken. For resources, this is crucial as one must consider curriculum development needs in the light of available finances. For the development of skills, ideas and practices amongst teachers, the co-ordinator needs to be aware of the discomfort that change will bring and the need to progress at a suitable pace. Change will take time to implement and your curriculum area will have to take its 'turn' in the curriculum development cycle of the school as a whole. The action plan must provide a series of attainable goals and targets acceptable to all and which can be monitored and evaluated as targets are reached.

STAFF DEVELOPMENT

A lot can be achieved within the school on an individual basis simply by identifying with the school the help that teachers require in your curriculum area and supplying ideas and advice where appropriate. Beyond this it may be necessary to look outside the school in order that your work as a co-ordinator can be supported by other agencies. Through the audit or assessment of staff development needs it is possible to identify areas where specific support can be given from within the school, within the family of schools, or by external consultants. Support can often be in the form of workshop sessions or seminars. They can be run by the co-ordinator either formally or informally. Alternatively staff can be encouraged to attend suitable courses offered in the area by the LEA or by other providers in higher education institutions. The benefits of attendance on such courses can be maximised back in school if those attending share what they have learned with colleagues. Alternatively, a visit from an enthusiastic and energetic advisory teacher or inspector, either for a twilight session or on a training day, can boost the interest levels of colleagues and help introduce new ideas into the school.

Whilst these consultants may well repeat what you have been saying for some time, and the ideas that they offer replicate those you have been implementing with your own class, the fact that they have been suggested by someone from outside the school will not only reinforce and vindicate your actions, but also provide you with some ammunition for the future! Once the needs of staff have been identified it is important to make colleagues aware of the wide range of support and resources that are available, both in school and beyond, to help them in their teaching, and to encourage them to take full advantage of this help.

GETTING STARTED

The most important responsibility of the co-ordinator is to raise the quality of teaching and learning within the school. There is the danger that you attempt too much, too soon in this role. To help avoid unnecessary conflict and stress it is worth drawing together and reiterating some key points made by the authors in Part II.

Give yourself time to establish a good standard of teaching in your own classroom before moving onto wider whole school issues.
Look to see what is going on in the school both in terms of curriculum documentation and classroom practice.
Explore with colleagues how consistency of approach and a planned progression can be achieved across your curriculum area.
Develop a strategy for change which enables those affected to feel ownership of the change process.

All staff will be involved in some way in the teaching of your curriculum area so they must all be part of and have responsibility for the developments.

Once changes have begun to occur the role of the co-ordinator alters. In addition to maintaining interest in and enthusiasm for the developments, and to acting as a gatekeeper of resources, you will have to help colleagues make sense of and evaluate developments in your curriculum area. You will need, for example, to review documentation coming into school, interpret and disseminate it for others as well as create opportunities for discussion. Above all, however, it is worth repeating that the co-ordinator's key role is to be an enthusiast who makes the curriculum exciting; to demonstrate this through good classroom practice; and to enable colleagues to develop their own knowledge and skills.

Chapter 18

A curriculum for all

Sylvia McNamara

INTRODUCTION

The role of special needs co-ordinator may at first appear rather daunting to many teachers as it contains within its brief some specific legislative and statutory obligations. The 1993 Education Act and the accompanying Code of Practice (DfE 1994) require schools to have a Special Educational Needs Co-ordinator (hereafter referred to as SENCO). SENCOs are responsible for:

- maintaining a register of children with special educational needs and overseeing the records of all these children;
- liaising with and advising fellow teachers;
- contributing to the in-service training of staff;
- the day-to-day operation of the school's special education needs policy (this will include the identification and assessment of children with special educational needs, and the planning and reviewing of programmes and monitoring of progress for such children);
- co-ordinating provision for children with special educational needs;
- liaison and consultation with parents of children with special educational needs as well as with agencies who can offer additional support and/or advice about the most effective way of helping such children to reach their potential.

(See paragraph 2.10 for details on the policy and paragraph 2.14 for the role of the SENCO, Code of Practice, 1994.)

It will be argued in this chapter, however, that there are a number of ways in which the various functions of this role can be carried out: different schools will address the requirements with different systems.

CONTINUUM OF SPECIAL EDUCATIONAL NEEDS

When addressing the issue of special educational needs there has always been a tension between *identification* and *labelling*. This tension continues, despite successive education acts of the 1980s and 1990s, and can be described as a continuum of public opinion, which manifests itself in staffrooms, school offices, playgrounds, governor meetings and PTAs. The tensions are summarised below.

On the one hand, the argument goes, if children who experience difficulties in learning do not have their special educational needs identified early on, then the interventions from teachers and other professionals which may create significant improvements for the child are lost. Examples of such interventions are the provision of spectacles, radio microphones or food at appropriate times, for children who have visual impairment, hearing loss or diabetes.

Thus, some teachers and parents of children with special needs and parents of 'ordinary' children think that it is important to have early testing, screening, observation and identification. Some teachers and parents also think that, once identified, such children should have their needs met in the special school because that is where the best resources are housed. These resources may include both specialist equipment and people with expertise.

The role of the SENCO according to this attitude and viewpoint is one of the 'expert', who will be familiar with a range of assessment techniques in order to identify and diagnose children's difficulties, and who will be the one to deliver an appropriate curriculum, either in the classroom as a support teacher or in another corner of the school in a withdrawal situation.

On the other hand, there is the view that the very act of identification creates a label which may become a *stigma*, whether the label is special needs, hearing impairment, or some of the less empathetic playground labels such as 'thickie'. The arguments against labelling are outlined below.

The problem with labelling children is that it can mean that ordinary classroom teachers fail to look at the particular needs of the *individual* child. In turn, this may lead to low expectations of children who have been labelled as having learning difficulties. An example of this is shown in the research carried out by the London Institute at Key Stage 1 SAT pilot testing. The results of the research showed that teacher assessment was much lower than SAT assessment. Labelling may also mean that the teachers feel de-skilled or disempowered to meet the child's needs. This is a common response to labels such as Down's Syndrome and cerebral palsy. An example of this is a child who had the label 'Down's Syndrome'. He had received ten years of his schooling in mainstream settings, including a repeat year in primary school, but found it very difficult to get a transfer place to his next school. The school that all his classmates were going to refused him an interview on the grounds that they could not meet the needs of a child with Down's Syndrome in their institution. The response in that school was to the label not the child.

The problems caused by labelling give rise to a number of different attitudes towards and expectations of the SENCO. The teachers who feel de-skilled as a result of the label may see that the role of the SENCO is to take the child away or 'off my hands'. Another reaction to a label is to suggest that the child needs the protection of a separate school. Some parents of children who have been given a label feel very strongly that they want their child removed from the negative comments they feel sure will come from the other children in the class. These views may be shared by mainstream primary teachers who tolerate the SENCO in their classrooms but all the time believe the child would be better provided for in a special school setting. Other teachers and parents of children who do not have special needs may resent the child with the label being in their child's class. They may assume that children who behave differently or who work differently will create a bad influence, or hold the others back, or take up too much of the teacher's valuable time. These feelings are often behind demands for 'extra resources', by which teachers usually mean another teacher to support the child. In these cases the SENCO is seen as responsible for providing other adult help in the classroom or removing the child to another space to have 'extra help' so that the education of the 'rest' is not interfered with. Thus, the tensions between identifying children and labelling children get played out in terms of provision for special needs.

THE SENCO ROLE IN SUMMARY

In their research into current practice Dyson and co-workers (1990, 1991, 1993, 1995) identified three different approaches to special needs provision.

The 'withdrawn' approach

Pupils are withdrawn for basic skills and they are seen by most of the staff as the responsibility of the SENCO. Most functions of the role, including the statutory duties at Code of Practice stages 1 to 3 are carried out solely by the SENCO.

The 'support' teacher approach

SENCOs and their team either support in the classroom all the time or do a combination of withdrawal and in-class support, some of which is support for the child and some support for the teacher. SENCOs are seen as the ones with expertise, and are highly sought after by the staff because they do a fair amount of differentiation by task and text access preparation. The formal functions are likely to be shared between the SENCO and the headteacher.

The 'consultant' for teaching and learning styles approach

In this scenario, all staff see the learning of all children as their responsibility and are experimenting with differentiation by group work and outcome (Lewis 1991).

In this situation the SENCO will become adept at co-ordinating teams of people such as volunteers, parents, older children, YTS, ancillaries and welfare assistants to help with the support part of the special needs provision. The functions of the SENCO role may well be shared out evenly between the staff as a whole.

As SENCOs start to move towards the model of consultant they will be involved in:

* thoughts, discussions and training that will influence staff development;
* discussions and training about children's learning;
* training on the effects on children's learning of particular styles; and
* approaches of teaching.

From this list it can be seen that the bulk of the work of the SENCO as consultant is not with children at all but with *teachers*.

There are, however, some basic functions that the SENCO needs to ensure get done (this is not the same as doing it yourself). We examine these below.

FUNCTIONS

The functions are to do with creating a systematic approach to the business of identification, assessment, diagnosis, individual target setting (Individual Education Plans (IEPs) in the Code of Practice), record keeping and evaluation.

If the policy on special needs is to be meaningful then there should be systems in place to fulfil these functions and to meet the legislative requirements as set out in the 1993 Act and the Code of Practice stages 1 to 3 (see above).

Identification

One important way for children who experience difficulties to be identified is for the class teacher to be encouraged to look out for difficulties and to identify children who give cause for concern.

However, in order to break the cycle of

- label,
- stigma,
- low performance because of feelings of low self-worth brought about by the stigma attached to the label, and
- low teacher expectations of child's academic work and/or behaviour because of the label,

then problems which are either noticed by colleagues or reported to the the SENCO for them to act on should be followed up by detailed and systematic observation.

For example, one child came to reception class with a poor 'behaviour' record from nursery school and was drawn to the attention of the SENCO as having special behavioural needs and behaving in a disruptive way. The SENCO carried out a series of *observations* and noted other contributory factors such as other children blaming him: when a pot of crayons was knocked over, the children on his table told the teacher that he had done it. The SENCO observation sheet showed quite clearly that this was not the case. Equally, the class teacher was observed explaining things to him in an impatient manner with no encouragement, either verbally or non-verbally. This also seemed to be affecting his behaviour. The SENCO was then able to work out a programme with the class teacher which included public and private praising. Not only did the child's behaviour change but so did the attitude and behaviour of his peers towards him. (Further details of the way to approach observation, moving from open field notes to systematic schedules, are laid out in Ann Lewis' book, *Primary Special Needs and the National Curriculum*, 1991.)

In terms of staff development, training in observation skills is helpful for:

1 *Intervention research work* – for example, observing how well children acknowledge the contributions of all group members when working in groups. Then teaching the children the skills to do this acknowledging work. Then observing again to see if they are any better at it.
2 *Evaluation of classroom teaching and learning effectiveness* – that is to say, gathering *evidence* about the *actual* effectiveness of particular styles of teaching in terms of pupils' learning before introducing a change in teaching style. Observation combined with group interview with children is, for example, what Ofsted inspectors do.
3 *Establishing baseline data* – to ascertain how often, with what frequency and what level of intensity inappropriate behaviours occur amongst children with emotional and behavioural difficulties, in order to introduce a behavioural change programme.

It is therefore well worth spending time on whole staff training in the area of observation skills. Once this has been done, the role of SENCOs can be either to do the observation of children causing concern themselves, or to cover the class of the teacher concerned in order for the class teacher to do the job.

Assessment and diagnosis

Once children have been identified, either through observation or through screening, the next stage is to make a judgement about the exact nature and extent of their needs. Again, attitudes to 'within child' and 'environmental' models tend to guide the way the assessment is made.

If, for example, the assumption is made that a child aged 8 years with a sight vocabulary of 20 words has a reading problem (the within child model), it is quite likely that the decision will be to withdraw that child every day for a specified time to do work on reading until he or she 'catches up'. Failure to progress under this regime may well be seen as either the wrong approach to the reading, or the need to introduce more phonics/flashcards/word shapes/matching games or a mental processing problem.

If, however, the class teacher is encouraged by the SENCO to draw up a list of the child's total strengths and weaknesses and any social or behavioural strengths are added then a different picture may emerge (the environmental model). The same child, with a 20 word sight vocabulary, may also be a large boy who is often breaking or knocking into things and being verbally rejected by the other children. In this approach, the assessment may be to do with his feelings of lack of self-worth and the diagnosis may well be to work on the rest of the class to include him and congratulate him on anything dexterous he achieves.

When carrying out this type of assessment it is vital to include peer and self-assessment. This will be straightforward if both forms of assessment are used regularly by the class teacher.

What emerges then, as a model of good practice, is a picture of a school where the teachers are able to assess both the child and the environment; their own teaching and the children's learning. If the SENCO can work towards creating a staff group who can say to themselves, 'I wonder if I try . . . if that will make a difference?', they will be close to the model of every teacher a teacher of special needs and they will not, themselves, be seen as the 'testing' or 'phonics' teacher.

Target setting (IEPs)

The statement in the Code of Practice that students should be involved in their own IEPs (Paragraph 2.37, Code of Practice) could lead to some very exciting innovatory practice. Alternatively, it could end up as a sterile exercise, where teacher and child alike simply go through the motions. It depends on what we mean by involvement, and this in turn depends on the school context.

Best practice work, whether the child is withdrawn or supported in the classroom, will combine the systematic approach of task analysis and precision teaching (Ainscow and Tweddle 1988) with the idea of building on children's strengths (Wolfendale 1987), in order to get maximum motivation and involvement (Westwood 1993). Task analysis is about breaking down a global goal, for example 'not knowing letter sounds' into a more realistic achievable goal: to recognise and replicate the sounds of 'ss' and 'mm' by the end of a two-week teaching period. This is helpful for child and teacher alike as they can both see progress towards the bigger goal. Precision teaching monitors the exact progress made by the child over a number of weeks and can produce graphs which help the child and teacher to plot the improvement visually. The obstacle to task analysis is child motivation. Some children see this work as babyish and refuse to participate; others get bored by the repetition which is why peer tutoring as a technique, which allows tutors to achieve *their* targets as well as tutees, is helpful.

Research evidence on motivation shows that there can be a lethal cocktail of 'low self-esteem', 'external locus of control', and 'learned helplessness'. *Low self-esteem* is where children have a negative picture of themselves, such as 'I am a useless reader' which contrasts sharply with a picture of themselves ideally, 'if I were any good I'd be an excellent reader' (Burns 1982, Lawrence 1987, Gurney 1988). *External locus of control* is where children see themselves as having little or no control over life events, especially those associated with academic work, and can result in them being unable to see the connection between effort and outcome (see Maines and Robinson 1988). This may even mean that they attribute success to the support teacher rather than themselves. Such children seem to develop *learned helplessness*. This is a form of dependency which means that children believe they cannot make progress by themselves and that they need the help of others even to try or 'have a go' (McNamara and Moreton 1993).

The result of these motivational factors may mean that children are unable to generalise from specific teaching situations, and appear to make little or no progress, despite a statement and the presence of an extra teacher for the child.

If the support teacher model (see p. 193) is followed, the SENCO may well be doing task analysis or text access on the spot in the classroom whilst working alongside the child. The clear benefits of such an arrangement are that this work, differentiation by task, will be rooted in the curriculum followed by the rest of the class and will take place in context, with the child seated amongst peers.

This approach often results in a whole group of children making better progress, not just the targeted one. However, it soon gives rise to the questions posed by Golby (Golby and Gulliver 1985): Why is it that the materials have to be adapted for the child with a low reading age? Why not present the lesson in another way? Pursuing the answers to such questions may lead to the SENCO supporting the classroom teacher and planning in a collaborative way.

Once two teachers start to plan together they are much more likely to consider all three forms of differentiation – *task, outcome* and *classroom organisation* – the consequence of which may well be experimentation with

- co-operative group work,
- problem-solving group work, and
- group discussion

as alternative ways of delivering the 'body of knowledge curriculum', such as science, history and geography.

It is quite usual for teachers to realise at this point that the majority of the children lack the interpersonal and social skills to do group work. Several writers (e.g. Thacker 1990, Kingsley-Mills *et al.* 1992) have identified the importance of students learning group work skills. Others have seen the development of social skills as being important for children with special educational needs (Tann 1988, Gross 1993). The author has carried out a number of action research pilot studies which clearly show that a carefully structured system of training for the children in primary schools, to learn the skills they need for group work and pair work, leads to real inclusion of children with special educational needs. This system:

- enables all the children to practise these skills whilst gaining access to the whole National Curriculum;
- encourages the more articulate and confident children to review and clarify their conceptual understanding of the whole topic; and
- helps children with learning difficulties to grasp concepts and articulate both current knowledge and new learning (McNamara and Moreton 1993, drawing on the ideas of Vygotsky and the scaffolding of language).

The idea of peer tutoring has been well established in the field of special needs (Goodlad and Hurst 1990, Merrett 1994, Topping 1988, Lewis 1991, Gross 1993), but rarely are the skills for this form of teaching made explicit to all the students including those with special needs. The importance of ensuring that those with special needs are allowed to act as tutors is one observed by Lewis (1991) and identified by Dyson (1995) as good innovator practice.

Record keeping

An isolatory role will see SENCOs going around gathering data and then making decisions on everyone else's behalf because they are the 'experts'. A collaborative approach will see the SENCO co-ordinating information and then sharing it, with parents, pupils as well as colleagues, whilst showing appropriate sensitivity about confidentiality. The information from the records will then be used first to evaluate prior approaches and then to plan another intervention. In such cases the recording may look less elegant than that generated by the 'expert' SENCOs but it may well be more meaningful to all concerned. (Useful ideas for record keeping are offered in Gross (1993), Lewis (1991) and Wolfendale (1987).)

Evaluation

If the SENCO is working on a one-to-one basis with a child then the evaluation will be primarily concerned with the effectiveness of the programme in terms of meeting the targets outlined in the IEP. There is scope for incorporating the child and parent responses in the evaluation and for them to be involved in the next round of target setting.

Another way that evaluation can be approached, however, is by getting all the children to work in pairs to set targets for themselves and for them all to carry out evaluations of their own progress. They can then action-plan according to their own individual progress. The SENCO role becomes one of helping staff to work out teaching methods which teach children to target-set, record and evaluate.

The SENCOs who are consultants in teaching and learning styles will not only be using co-operative group work as part of their daily teaching; they will also be familiar with the ideas of Johnson and Johnson (1987) and will be using assessment techniques, including observations to gather baseline data as a pre-test, before carrying out a piece of intervention work. They will then retest in order to evaluate the effectiveness of the intervention, and to disseminate the results of the research to other staff.

SUMMARY

In this chapter we have identified a 'continuum' of support and provision for the child with special educational needs in the primary school. This continuum will determine the way in which the SENCO role is allowed to develop. The author is quite clear that it is in the interests of the child for all schools to aim to reach the goal of the SENCO as consultant. This chapter has outlined indicators of good practice in order to reach and maintain that model.

Chapter 19

Co-ordinating information technology in the primary school

Jean Underwood

IT IS CLEARLY ESTABLISHED IN OUR SCHOOLS, OR IS IT?

Robins and Webster (1989, p. 35) assert that there is:

> a rapidly growing profile for IT in education . . . . It is doubtful whether any other technological innovation has ever managed to become so popular so quickly and, with a few exceptions, the desirability of learning with and about microcomputers is taken for granted by all concerned.

Information technology (IT) is, therefore, clearly established in our schools, or is it? In reality the picture is less rosy. There are still schools who have yet to take IT on board in any meaningful way and for the majority IT flourishes only in pockets of good practice within the school. There are far fewer schools with clear IT goals which have been put into effective practice. This is the context within which the IT co-ordinator must operate.

THE ROLE OF THE CO-ORDINATOR

It is remarkable how easy it is to draw up a set of guidelines for the support and co-ordination of a curriculum area. There are a number of such documents for IT. Figure 19.1 is a useful working summary based on work by the National Council for Educational Technology (NCET), which emphasises the key roles of school managers and classroom teachers in curriculum change.

Without management backing or classroom support the co-ordinator is at best going to have a frustrating time and at worst will prove ineffectual.

WHY IS THE *IT* CO-ORDINATOR ROLE SO DIFFERENT?

NCET have captured the core roles of all IT co-ordinators but in some schools the IT co-ordinator role has significantly expanded while in others it has become distorted to little more than technician.

The role of senior management

The **head teacher** (*and Governors*) should:

- encourage a sense of shared responsibility for IT within which management and co-ordination roles are clear;
- encourage the development of links with other schools (particularly across phases) and with support agencies;
- exhibit a positive attitude towards IT.

The role of the IT co-ordinator

The **co-ordinator** should:

- promote the integration of IT with all appropriate aspects of teaching and learning;
- act as a link with outside agencies;
- support and encourage colleagues (*staff development officer, curriculum change agent*);
- manage the provision and deployment of IT resources;
- provide the first line of technical support (*resource manager*);
- co-ordinate the evaluation and review of the school's IT policy (*policy implementation and quality control agent*).

The role of individual teachers

Other curriculum co-ordinators should:

- consider the ways that IT can be used in the subject area they are responsible for.

Each **individual teacher** should:

- include planning for IT as an integral part of both long- and short-term planning
- assist the co-ordinator in the monitoring and recording of pupil progress in IT;
- share successes and failures in order to encourage and suport colleagues, helping to develop a shared responsibility for IT.

Figure 19.1 Organising, co-ordination and support

Before examining these core roles further I feel it would be useful to look at the key factors which will effectively define your co-ordinating role in your school. These factors can be summed up in the following questions:

- What style of education are you supporting?
- Are you a teacher or a technician?
- Have you the IT skills for the job?
- Have you the tools for the job?

What style of education are you supporting?

IT is capable of supporting both the most traditionalist and the most avant-garde of educational methods. The style of education you support will significantly affect your role as a co-ordinator. Below is a very brief history of the changing use of IT in primary schools. Although set in this historical perspective, it is still possible to see each of these models of usage within current primary classrooms.

- When computers first came into primary classrooms teachers, lacking IT skills, accepted the software provided with their machine, for example computer generated anagrams (Bleach 1986), and diligently tried to integrate it into the classroom.

Use of such packages makes minimal demands on hardware, teacher or pupil IT capability or indeed your colleagues' skills of curriculum integration.

- There followed a phase in which the message was 'Ask not what you can do with the computer but what can the computer do to support your planned work?' Teachers became more circumspect in their use of IT and often rejected the computer as there was no relevant software for the topic in hand.

A key role here for the co-ordinator is software selection. The use of these content packages will make minimal demands on hardware (unless the software has high-quality graphics), teacher IT capability or indeed your colleagues' skills of curriculum integration.

- Very quickly this was followed by the argument that the computer would provide a new curriculum and its use should not be bound by what had gone before. Seymour Papert (1980) was the leading figure in this movement which, in its less radical form, lead to the exploration of the 'tool' use of the computer (Underwood and Underwood 1990) as opposed to the teacher/tutor role of earlier software. This movement launched a thousand newspapers using NewSpa or Caxton Press.

Tool use of computers places more demands on senior management, the co-ordinator and the classroom teacher. Application packages such as word processors and paint packages require printers to be available and the demand from the pupils is increasingly for colour. Peripheral devices such as printers not only add to costs but also require more technical support and a higher degree of IT capability from both staff and pupils. In addition, if resources are scarce, the teacher is faced with the problem of organising access to the computers.

- At present, we find ourselves returning to the delivery of the core curriculum content but this time through the use of the new multimedia technologies. Currently, NCET is trialling 'GLOBAL LEARNING SYSTEMS', mathematics and English tutoring packages which are designed to support the 'full' mathematics and language curricula from Key Stages 1 to 4, and an integrated learning system through COMPUTER CURRICULUM CORPORATION's mathematics and English SuccessMaker modules.

These large integrated packages place a significant financial strain on school budgets. There is an annual licence fee and the system requires a number of large fast machines (for example a PC 486 with graphics and sound cards) networked together. A network manager is now essential and you, as co-ordinator, will almost certainly need training even if your school provides you with a technician. Your colleagues, on the other hand, may find that they need less training than ever if they can hand their classes over to the IT support unit!

Are you a teacher or a technician?

To be a successful curriculum co-ordinator you need to have a clear understanding of your own role within the school. But it is equally important that your perception of your role matches that of your colleagues including senior management. Although this may appear self-evident, the IT co-ordinator is particularly prone to misinterpretations of role. In no other area of the curriculum do you find the wholesale confusion and merging of the role of teacher into that of technical support staff.

Key questions: How do you prevent yourself from becoming a support technician? How do you stop your colleagues sinking into a state of 'learnt helplessness'?

Have you the IT skills for the job?

IT has a relatively short history in our schools and an even shorter history as a compulsory part of any teacher's education. Many IT co-ordinators are underskilled for the job in hand. Even more disturbing is the level of IT capability among the general staff.

Key questions: What is the current level of your IT skills and that of the staff you are to support? How will you improve your own skills? How will you improve the staff's skills?

Have you the tools for the job?

Level of resource is a vexed question. Few other areas of the curriculum eat at the school's budget in quite the same voracious manner. When budget time comes round the IT co-ordinator is rarely a popular member of staff. Although it may be relatively easy to persuade parents, or even the head, to dip into funds for a new computer, it may prove far harder to obtain funds for peripherals such as colour printers, for new software or for support documentation.

Software frequently breaches schools' equality policies (Agalianos and Cope 1994) and, although such programs as *Granny's Garden* are old in IT terms, they are nevertheless still in active use in the classroom. An important job for the IT co-ordinator is to go through and weed out unacceptable programs. This may be best done with the librarian who will already have faced the problem. Second, choose software which can be tailored to your children. For example, the illustrative child on to which data is mapped in the database *Bodymapper* can be male or female, fair or dark with straight or afro hair. In deference to cultural sensitivity the body can be clothed or not clothed. This allows the teacher to configure the program to his or her own specific needs.

You need to be aware of the hardware demands of any program before you purchase (see Underwood *et al.* (1994) for a fuller discussion of this problem). The Nimbus 186 found in many primary classrooms is unable to run much of the new software. Even if you have a new machine you may find that software runs very slowly or not at all. The new software requires significantly more disk storage space and working memory (RAM) to operate efficiently. For example, *Bodymapper* requires 2 megabytes of working memory while the standard Acorn machine, available at the time the program was launched, was sold with half a megabyte of memory. The software was therefore unusable without an expensive memory upgrade. Although this position has now been rectified it is important to remember that the more your software package can do, especially if sound and graphics are involved, the more memory you will need. Always check the *memory demands* of any program you intend purchasing.

Key questions: Are the resources available to you adequate for the job? Can you tailor your educational goals more effectively to use the resources available to you? Do problems lie with the hardware (computers, printers, etc.), the software or with the skills of you and the staff?

In summary, it is essential that, with the agreement of all your colleagues, you clearly identify what is and is not included in your role of co-ordinator.

A TALE OF THREE PRIMARY SCHOOLS

Ask a number of language or mathematics co-ordinators to outline the key facilities they have to support their subject area and they will start with the reading or mathematics scheme which forms the central pivot point of their resources. The schemes may vary from school to school, there might be heated arguments as to the merit of one scheme over another, the quality and quantity of additional resources might vary, but there will be a common starting point. Ask the same question of IT co-ordinators and they will start by listing the computers in their school yet there might be little comparability between schools. Outlined below are descriptions of three primary schools that I worked with during 1994. They are very similar in that they are all set in the middle of council estates, have a high percentage of parents who are unemployed and a large number of pupils who are on free school meals, but in IT terms they are worlds apart.

School A is a typical 1960s one-tier structure with 400 children aged 5 to 11 years on role and there is a special needs unit. The school owns three BBCs and two new (late 1993) Nimbus 186s. The ratio of children to machines is 80 to 1. The staff are very nervous about computers and the IT co-ordinator is a new graduate two years out of training. No one knows what to do with the 186 machines. Although interested in using information technology (IT) with her own pupils the co-ordinator feels inadequately trained for the role which has been thrust upon her. The IT skills of the staff as a whole are low.

School B is a two-tier structure with again 400 children aged 5 to 11 years on role. This is a 'typical' primary school in that there is a computer for every class, a ratio of 25 children to one machine. The infants have the older BBCs and the juniors work with a range of ACORN Archimedes. The organisation of the computers is interesting in that two or three computers are collected together in an area shared by adjacent classes. The deputy head is also the IT co-ordinator. A keen enthusiast, his Year 6 class have access to three Archimedes and a colour printer. Staff expertise is variable. The co-ordinator is knowledgeable and runs INSET courses for the staff but there are pockets of resistance.

School C is again a typical 1960s one-tier structure with 200 children aged 7 to 11 years on role. This is a technologically rich school with a ratio of pupils to machines of better than 3 to 1. These include BBC Bs and Masters, now largely used for control technology, a PC 286 and a PC 486 network. In addition, there are a substantial number of PC 386 laptop machines available for school and home use. The machines are located in three open access spaces. Staff have a higher than average level of IT literacy and there are key support staff to aid the less advanced teacher. The staff include a full-time and two part-time RSA standard trained computer technicians, in this case 'mums' who have been encouraged to acquire skills and recognised qualifications by the current head of school. The school has a positive policy of integrating the computer fully into the school curriculum.

Each of these schools presents a very different problem to the IT co-ordinator. In School A the development of staff interest, skills and confidence, including that of the co-ordinator, must be paramount. In School B, there are pockets of effective IT use by the children, but those models of good practice need spreading throughout the school. In School C IT is central to the curriculum. The role of the IT co-ordinator here is to maintain the excellent practice through both curriculum development and skills enhancement of colleagues. In addition this co-ordinator supports IT as an administrative and management tool. This is unusual in a primary school, but increasingly common at secondary level.

School A: Jane's role

Jane's colleagues' overt expectations of her as IT co-ordinator are that she knows and understands the school's software and hardware, and that she will be able to sort out their 'technical' problems. Covertly they expect her to 'do' the IT and not make too many demands on them or on the budget.

The peripheral status of IT here is indicated by the decision to nominate a low-status member of staff (a new teacher) as co-ordinator. After two years in post Jane has made little impact on her school. Her own feelings of inadequacy, her inability to obtain resources in competition with more senior colleagues, and the lack of interest and support from 'management' have left her in despair.

Action 1

Jane's first task is to conduct an audit of IT equipment and materials. This sounds so obvious and trivial but it is a task which is often not done! A data base would of course be useful here and a tangible example of the value of IT. Designing a template or form on the word processor (Figures 19.2 and 19.3) might initially prove a less daunting task, however.

The software log should also include the copyright status of the software. Does the school hold one legal copy or more? Is the program freely copyable throughout the school?

Type and model	Extras	Date bought	History	Located
BBC B with single disc drive (dd) using 5.25" discs	LOGO chip	no record	damaged serial port/broken pins/not repaired	Mr. B's room

Figure 19.2 The hardware log

Title and publisher	Curriculum area	Age range	Support	Machine	Other require- ments
STYLUS—word processor with speech—NCET	Cross curricula	All primary and special needs	Easy instruction manual	BBC B or Master	A printer; disks for children's work

Figure 19.3 The software log

Action 2

Next Jane will need to organise her resources. The first thing to do is sort her software into legal and pirated software. The latter should be destroyed. If colleagues object then Jane should ensure that the senior management take responsibility for holding illegal materials. Once the core software is identified, back-up copies should be made and the original software should be stored in a non-magnetic, damp-free environment.

If a program requires a password as in, say, *Wagons West* or *Granny's Garden*, add these passwords to the software log. Documentation does get lost or destroyed and it is very frustrating if a program becomes inaccessible because the key page is missing from the documentation.

Action 3

Jane needs to increase her own confidence and authority by acquiring a greater understanding of IT and its place in the curriculum. She needs help and support to translate her own skills into useful classroom practice.

Action 4

Jane needs to demonstrate to her colleagues the relevance of IT in the classroom by showing good practice in her own classroom and by target-ing and supporting one of her less resistant colleagues. Care should be taken that, in her enthusiasm to gain a convert, Jane does not fall into the role of personal technician to that colleague.

Action 5

Alongside the development of classroom practice Jane must now start to think about how she is to monitor and assess IT in her own classroom.

> Jane's software and hardware audit is the first stage in drawing up an IT policy for her school. This audit should be presented to both senior managers and colleagues for comment.

School B: John's role

In School B the IT co-ordinator is part of the senior management team: IT is seen as relevant, resources are available and progress is being made. John has already met many of the goals that Jane is working towards. His key concerns will be on the need to spread his own good practice throughout the school and to consider the future resourcing within a school which he hopes soon will be actively using computers across the full curriculum and age range. To enable permeation, however, John must first come to terms with the fact that there will be demands on the equipment sitting outside of his classroom. If he encourages teachers to use paint packages they too will want to use the colour printer! John knows he will have to let go of his privileged access to resources.

Action 1

John needs to demonstrate the effective use of the computer through displays of his own and children's work to colleagues.

Action 2

To support his colleagues he needs to provide curriculum relevant ma-terial. John has written some documentation himself as part of the INSET training he is undergoing. He has also swapped material with other 'stu-dents' on his course and reviewed NCET curriculum materials at his local LINK-IT centre.

Action 3

As IT spreads throughout his school, John will be faced with the problem of distributing software. He must identify the level of copyright for each piece of software. Does he have a single copy, multiple copy (i.e. use on a specified number of machines) or site licence?

A key job for John is to identify which programs need to be used throughout the school and which programs can be used in single-licence form. He may only need one copy of an adventure game like *Granny's Garden*, as it will be used in a carousel of activities within the classroom, but a word processing package such as *Caxton* or *Pendown* will be used in all classrooms and funds need to be allocated for this. A typical calculation would be £50 for a single copy and £200 for a multiple copy or site licence. John needs to choose such software with care as it will take a significant part of his budget.

Action 4

John needs to extend the audit Jane has conducted to include staff queries. Are such queries hardware, software or curriculum related? Can John identify key difficulties his colleagues are facing? Are they, in reality, a crisis of confidence, lack of key skills or failures within the hardware and software? By classifying the issues raised by the staff John will be able to design a meaningful training programme for his colleagues.

Action 5

The permeation of IT use through the school means that procedures for monitoring and assessing the use of IT now urgently need to be in place. In the use of tools such as word processors John must ensure that the children's experiences not only lead to more advanced IT skills but also to more effective and demanding use of language.

Action 6

There are significant financial implications of generating increased interest in IT throughout the school in terms of staff training, maintenance and renewal of hardware, insurance and security, and supply of software. John must now begin to develop a financial strategy as part of the IT policy and action plan.

The completion of the audit to include staff attitudes and skills is the next stage of policy planning. This audit will then form the basis for planning and costing the extension and maintenance of IT for the school.

School C: Pam's role

In School C the IT co-ordinator is a valued member of staff. She works in a team with the IT support staff and the head who is very committed to new styles of learning through technology. One key effect of this commitment is that new staff are only appointed if they show an *openness* to IT. They do not need IT *skills*; the school is more than confident in its own training programme, but they must show an enthusiasm and commitment to develop their skills. Staff training is both accepted and appreciated by the staff.

In addition to the goals outlined for Jane and John, Pam is increasingly likely to find herself supporting the day-to-day administration and management of the school. Unless your school has a very strong IT base it is unlikely that you will choose to use a management system other than the one supported by your LEA.

Action 1

The maintenance of the current high standards within the school is Pam's first priority. She needs to ensure staff training is on-going and to complete the development of the monitoring and assessment of children's learning.

Action 2

Pam needs to establish how much it costs to run and maintain her school's computer systems (see, for example, Ding 1994). This will enable her to present a clear development plan to her colleagues and senior managers.

Action 3

Pam must decide how far her role as IT co-ordinator could and should take her away from traditional classroom support and into whole school management.

SUMMARY – THE WHOLE SCHOOL IT POLICY?

Each of our co-ordinators is working towards the development and implementation of an IT policy and action plan. This written document should provide a clear agreed statement on the way in which IT will be used to enhance children's learning, to support staff in their teaching and for administrative and management roles. It should state the resources needed at each stage of development to meet the policy decisions and the financial implications of such resourcing for the school. Finally, the methods of monitoring and evaluating the policies, from children's skills development across the curriculum to the costing of consumables, need to be clearly defined.

Chapter 20

Using help from beyond the school

Margaret Riley

> It is not so much that curriculum is the 'what' of education and the teaching the 'how', as that the teachers' classroom strategies are what transform curriculum from a mere bundle of inert ideas to experiences through which children learn. In this sense, therefore, the 'how' and the 'what' are one.
>
> (Alexander 1992, p. 59)

The relationship between the complex skills and tasks of curriculum co-ordinators and increasing levels of accountability in delivering quality and standards in the curriculum of the primary school make the use of help from beyond the school a crucial component of curriculum change and development, integrating the 'how' and the 'what'. In this chapter we examine how co-ordinators can use external help to aid them in their roles within the school using examples drawn from actual work undertaken in one LEA.

LOOKING BEYOND THE SCHOOL

Curriculum leaders in today's schools have to conduct their business with an eye to the expectations of others who have a legitimate interest in, and indeed responsibility for, the quality of education in primary schools.

The requirements to pay heed to central government initiatives surrounding the implementation of the National Curriculum; the recommendations for action and judgements of Ofsted inspectors; expert professional and academic opinion; the outcomes of recent research studies; curriculum development practice in comparable schools; the views of governors, parents, employers and, wherever possible, the children – all these add to the sheer complexity of the co-ordinator's role.

Strong external pressures for the use of systematic review procedures have developed alongside central government measures for increased accountability at school level. New arrangements for the funding of in-service training, the use of development planning as an instrument for effective management and the introduction of the National Curriculum, together with its later reviews and changes, provide the backcloth to the stage on which the curriculum co-ordinator has to perform.

Co-ordinators have an important part to play in managing the activities of and working with members of staff and external agencies across subjects and key stages within school and outside the school through cross-phase and school cluster collaboration.

It is a salutary thought that for those working in schools to develop the curriculum much of what is written about curriculum leadership arises from sources external to schools themselves. Research studies, educational reports, DfE documents and discussion papers can make a powerful contribution to the work of the school based curriculum leader.

The debate in education during the last five years has also featured a concern for 'quality'. Hargreaves and Hopkins (1991) make suggestions about the characteristics of schools where a quality culture prevails. They cite:

• an ethos which creates both pressure on and support for its members;
• a clear view of the school's main purposes and values;
• a scepticism about its own rhetoric; and finally
• a pre-emptive approach to accountability.

It is these particular aspects of quality which are worthy of consideration by the curriculum co-ordinator in seeking to use external sources of advice, comparison, evaluation and support.

Central to the argument put forward by Hargreaves is the notion that the most effective schools do not wait to be called to account for their internal actions, decisions, strategies and developments.

For many curriculum leaders in schools the challenge lies first in framing the key questions related to curriculum development which will assist them in developing a consistent policy framework. Here, the external consultant can provide assistance which is neutral and objective. Below is an example of a set of key questions developed through collaboration between an external consultant and a curriculum co-ordinator:

DEVELOPING A POLICY FRAMEWORK: Key questions

Aims

• Are there aims which link with other subjects? The SDP?

Resources

• How are these to be organised, deployed, maintained, cared for?
• What schemes are to be used? Published or school made? Will teacher made materials be used to supplement schemes?

> **Equal opportunities**
>
> Are the issues of entitlement and access addressed in terms of curriculum, assessment, gender, race and disability?
>
> **Evaluation and review**
>
> How will the curriculum be monitored? By whom? What are there for feedback?

The external consultant's role is not to provide answers but to enable appropriate questions to be asked so that within the unique context of the school the people most involved can provide their own answers and, indeed, add their own questions. The aim of the process is to generate a specific framework for the curriculum leader then to shape into a working policy.

Alexander *et al.* (1992) in the Discussion Paper *Curriculum Organisation and Classroom Practice in Primary Schools* raised the temperature of the debate which still reverberates around the primary school curriculum in relation to the relative merits of subject expertise, teaching roles and staff deployment. This paper had a significant effect on one very important area of help from beyond the school since it heralded changes to the way in which the national support for curriculum leaders, as manifested through the National Grants for Education Support and Training (GEST), would be delivered.

The authors observed that co-ordinators have 'had a significant impact on whole school planning and resource management, but, because of limited non-contact time and the level of skill and sensitivity which the role demands, have had less influence on actual classroom practice.' (Alexander *et al.* 1992, para. 143, p. 42). This resulted in changes to the GEST priorities for the in-service training of primary co-ordinators. Since 1992, the provision and content of the 20 day programmes for curriculum co-ordination and leadership have reflected the need to:

- strengthen subject expertise;
- train for specialist/semi-specialist roles;
- develop organisational and management strategies;
- train for leadership roles those holding key responsibilities for curriculum quality and standards.

The GEST funded programmes have also illustrated the way in which the institutions of higher education have added value to the necessary understanding of the curriculum. A condition of the grant to support co-ordinator development in primary schools is the involvement of institutes of higher education in the design and delivery of the course programmes. This, together with the recognition given to many participants through a university award, has added to the perceived success of these programmes as vehicles for both training and developmental work in schools.

The GEST programmes represent in many ways a successful partnership between schools, central government, LEAs and institutions of higher education – a 'mixed economy' approach – which has been an effective and efficient method of developing curriculum leadership in primary schools.

EXTERNAL CONSULTANCY

The use of external consultancy can provide a more objective judgement of current practice and quality. Visiting consultants ask questions which those within the school might not ask and they can present a more neutral view of what the school *is* doing and *might* attempt in the future. They can provide, at their best, a detached view of what could otherwise become a very inward-looking, self-contained process. Staff, including curriculum leaders, can fail to see possibilities and weaknesses simply because they are too locked into existing patterns of thought and practice.

The range of consultants available is growing; the services provided are more likely to 'cost'. Indeed cost-effectiveness and value for money may well be crucial considerations for curriculum leaders. LEA inspectors and advisers can and often do act as consultants. They will have expertise and a breadth of experience which assists in the assessment of the effectiveness of school based curriculum initiatives. Other LEA staff who might be approached include staff in curriculum and teachers' centres, advisory teachers, in-service co-ordinators, special needs and second-language teams.

School based curriculum development and review is a theme extensively explored in university education departments and colleges of higher education. Lecturers on education management courses will be able to assist, or identify through their own networks others who can. Schools themselves often contain staff who are well qualified in methods of educational research and development. Alternatively, a well regarded colleague from another school can be an excellent choice as an external consultant.

Working with external consultants does require careful preparation and clear understandings of the consultants' role, what they are expected to comment on and arrangements for reporting to staff (see for example Abbott *et al.* 1988).

The management and practice of development planning have a great deal to offer the curriculum leader. In discussing the use of external perspectives as a strategy in development planning, Hargreaves and Hopkins (1991) cite the way in which different views and external judgements help the school to build up a detailed picture over time and provide benchmarks for gauging school development. They do, however, urge the manager to look carefully at both strengths and limitations of external judgements:

Strengths	*Limitations*
Provides a dispassionate view and a chance for staff to talk through problems with outsiders.	Timing of visits/reviews may be inappropriate for school needs or planning cycle.
Limited time-scales reduce demands on staff.	Might not focus on school's real concerns and may result in breadth not depth.
Tells schools what they are doing well besides highlighting weaknesses.	External perspectives on their own do not necessarily lead to development.
Provides the possibility of bringing new ideas into school and encourages staff to question what they take for granted.	May neglect the existing inner strengths of the school.

In the following example, 'Planning for development', a consultant was used to help a school community come to terms with the process of development planning by designing a whole school audit. The questions in the extract were devised to allow a wide range of people – staff, governors and, in this case, parents – to become involved in the construction of the SDP. Not all the questions relate directly to the work of the subject co-ordinator. Nevertheless they do emphasise that curriculum development takes place within a broader support and accountability framework of school development. The advantage of this holistic approach is that individual co-ordinators can work within a framework which has been agreed by people inside and 'validated' by those with expertise from outside the school.

Planning for Development

Curriculum

Does the school have a clear statement related to the curriculum – philosophy, principles, aims and objectives?

Does the curriculum philosophy encompass National Curriculum programmes of study and locally agreed curriculum principles?

Does the curriculum statement reflect important underlying themes such as special educational needs, assessment strategies, equal opportunities and entitlement?

Does the school have a curriculum 'portfolio' covering all subject areas and including special needs, assessment and recording approaches?

Does the school have a clearly articulated assessment, recording and reporting policy?

Does the curriculum statement reflect an understanding of the time spent on each element of the curriculum which can in turn be reflected in accurate DfE returns?

Does the statement reflect a variety of teaching strategies and learning styles employed throughout the school?

Does the school have clearly identifiable co-ordinators for curriculum areas?

Responsibility, staff development and appraisal structures

Does the school have a system of negotiated, regularly reviewed job descriptions which reflect curriculum and management responsibilities?

Does the school recognise the need to review and evaluate current responsibilities through appropriate consultation with staff at individual and group levels?

Does the school have strategies and approaches which encourage staff participation and ownership of innovation, development and change?

Does the school have a well structured plan for staff development utilising the full range of support available?

Does the school have an identified staff development co-ordinator?

Does the school have a policy and/or strategies for staff development which recognises aspects of induction of new staff, development of subject expertise, team development, teaching techniques, dissemination of new skills and knowledge?

Does the school have a system for teacher appraisal which encourages professional development and meets statutory requirements?

Pupils

Does the school have a carefully considered approach to assessing and recording the achievement and experience of all pupils?

Does the school ensure that each child has a record which reflects the statutory requirements for the National Curriculum?

Does the school ensure through its curriculum planning and delivery that there is continuity of educational experience both within the school and at the point of transfer?

Does the school adhere to planned admission limits?

Does the school have a policy related to individual pupil welfare?

Does the school have a clearly articulated approach to home/school links?

Does the school have a structure of rewards and sanctions – a code of practice which relates to acceptable pupil behaviour and patterns of work?

Does the school have defined procedures for the monitoring of pupil attendance?

Does the school recognise the need to ensure that the whole school community acts to protect and support all pupils both in the context of the whole school philosophy and with due regard to statutory requirements?

Special educational needs

Does the school have a policy for special educational needs (SEN) which ensures appropriate allocation and effective use of resources?

Does the school ensure the delivery of a relevant curriculum for all pupils?

Does the school monitor, evaluate and review the needs of all pupils?

Does the school policy for SEN reflect the needs of able pupils as well as those experiencing difficulties?

Does the school maintain effective mechanisms for liaison with external support agencies?

Does the school involve the parents of children with SEN?

Does the school have an understanding of the requirements and procedures, formal and informal, for assessment, statementing and review of pupils?

Parents, governors and community

Does the school have effective procedures for all aspects of parent/ school relationships?

Does the school have a policy for the involvement of parents in school?

Does the school involve itself in the wider community?

Does the school have a clear policy related to the shared use of premises, resources and facilities?

Does the school have an approach to reporting to parents on pupil progress which reflects the outcomes of key stage assessment?

Does the school offer opportunities for governor involvement in development planning?

Do governor committee/sub-committee/group structures contribute to development planning?

What steps does the school take to ensure that all governors are aware of planning priorities?

The strengths and limitations of this approach have already been referred to above. Evidently, there is a real need for curriculum leaders and school managers to take control of the agenda and to work closely with the external consultant to ensure that the work involved is managed sensibly using methods and time-scales which suit the school.

LOCAL EDUCATION AUTHORITIES

LEAs continue to be involved in the production of good-quality guidance related to curriculum planning and delivery. Whilst it is sometimes difficult to extract specific information from these because they are often couched in terms of subject content, it is increasingly possible to find examples of guidance which consider attitudes, skills, behaviour and methodology. Often these will include advice concerning approaches to assessment and record keeping. LEAs such as Northamptonshire also continue to respond to national initiatives and produce specific and detailed guidance for schools which help them interpret increasingly complex statutory duties as, for example, in 1994 when the consultation process following the publication of the Dearing Report was taking place, and more recently in response to legislation concerning Special Educational Needs provision and the Code of Practice.

LEA ADVISORY AND CONSULTANCY TEAMS

These teams continue to operate in many areas of the country, sometimes as 'arm's-length' trading, business or service agencies. As part of the portfolio of services they offer these teams are often involved in the publication of specialist subject and general curriculum management guidelines as well as the more traditional advice and consultancy roles.

In some areas, curriculum, professional, educational development and teachers' centres have survived cuts to the LEA services. They are often an excellent starting point for the research and development work which curriculum leaders in schools require.

HIGHER EDUCATION

The distinct and significant contribution made by university and college schools of education and departments of continuing education through the provision of and access to their award-bearing course programmes, research initiatives and publications often provides a rich source of advice to curriculum leaders. It is through the HE institutions that subject co-ordinators can seek recognition of school focused curriculum development, both for themselves and for colleagues involved in school. There are good examples of LEA/HE partnership and HE generally has been both persuasive and responsive in its ability to meet the increasingly complex demands which are placed on curriculum managers. Contacts with local providers in the HE field can yield a rich vein of academic, research based subject knowledge which, together with the sharper focus on what happens in schools from the perspective of teachers, can provide a formidable partnership.

INSPECTION REPORTS

Since the inception of the Office for Standards in Education (Ofsted) programme of primary school inspections in September 1994, a steady flow of published and publicly available reports has been produced. These reports comment in some detail on the development and implementation of the curriculum and as such offer insights into the work of curriculum leaders on a national scale. In order to evaluate internal school development, these reports are worth considering as a source of external comparisons.

The reports contain statements and judgements which, while they relate to a specific school context, do nevertheless provide 'markers' or 'indicators' of what is judged to be of good or poor quality in schools. Given the breadth of experience which is represented through the reports they provide a useful set of up-to-date information against which individual schools can judge their own organisation and curriculum provision.

NATIONAL REPORTS AND DOCUMENTATION

For curriculum co-ordinators the publication of yet another report, discussion paper or set of proposals for consultation can be a debilitating rather than an exhilarating experience. The pace of curriculum change, particularly since 1988 and the introduction of the National Curriculum, has accelerated. There is no doubt that the stream of reports from government authorities and agencies has been a prolific one with the consequent dangers of overload and unmanageability for those responsible in schools. These reports are, however, an important area for the curriculum leader to manage and as such should be considered as a help rather than a hindrance.

SUBJECT AND PROFESSIONAL ASSOCIATIONS

The full range of National Curriculum subjects and religious education is represented through specific subject organisations. These groups are influential in the development of the curriculum for they are almost always part of the consultation process when major changes in the National Curriculum are proposed, prepared and drafted. As such, they provide a useful channel of information and communication which can be tapped by the school curriculum co-ordinator.

The *Curriculum Handbook* (NIAS 1993) contains a complete digest of curriculum initiatives from subject groups as well as major national agencies, accreditation agencies, LEAs and HE institutions.

THE VIEWS OF GOVERNORS AND PARENTS

School governors have a direct responsibility for the quality of education provided in the school. It can certainly be argued that the members of the governing body are *not* external to the school and in reality the area where governors often feel least confident in expressing their view is the curriculum. In seeking help from governors, curriculum co-ordinators may have to consider an element of informing as well as obtaining views – a two-way communication. Now that governors have the duty to report to parents and increased powers with regard to the curriculum, often reflected in the sub-committee structures of the governing body, their partnership with curriculum leaders is vital.

Parents too can add a valuable dimension to curriculum development, not least because they are the 'indirect consumers' of what is provided for their children. Some parents working in school on a regular basis as voluntary helpers are in a good position to provide a lay view of curriculum initiatives. Parents and Friends Associations often contribute in very practical ways to developments in school through direct fund raising for vital equipment and resources. Parent governors provide a bridge and a direct line of communication to the wider parent group and as such can add a useful perspective to development in schools.

CLUSTERING, NETWORKING AND PEER SUPPORT GROUPS

With the focus on in-service training and development fixed firmly on the school, one of the most potent vehicles for the provision of external support remains strong in the hands of curriculum co-ordinators – their local, personal, professional and subject networks. Those who forecast less co-operation and collaboration between education professionals as a direct result of local management have largely been proved incorrect. In some areas the almost complete withdrawal of *human* and financial resources in terms of structured LEA support, has in many ways strengthened the resolve of the professionals to fulfil a need to work with colleagues. The way in which a local network, cluster or support group drawn from a discrete geographical area and working in comparably sized schools can draw on the curriculum, professional and interpersonal skills of its members is formidable. Such groups demonstrate their ability to combine individual strengths and abilities, share ideas and expertise and to work in creative and effective ways to develop the curriculum in all the schools involved. The local professional framework available to curriculum co-ordinators should not be underestimated in planning the use of external involvement in internal development.

SUMMARY

Curriculum co-ordinators can manage without reference to external agents or perspectives. However, effective managers utilise a variety of strategies in pursuit of excellence, some of them undoubtedly from outside the school itself. The advantages of such external contacts are considerable and wide ranging. They include the expertise and experience of external consultants, the interpretation and guidance provided by HE institutions and LEAs and, increasingly, the support provided through collaboration with colleagues from other schools.

Chapter 21

Conclusion

Co-ordinating teaching or learning?

John O'Neill

> If learning is about changing one's conceptions, then teaching is about discovering students' conceptions and helping them to change their conceptions.
>
> (Ramsden 1988, p. 21)

In the context of this volume Ramsden's comments are open to a number of interpretations, which suggests that we ought to pause here and focus more closely on what and who we mean when we are referring to the process of teaching and learning with regard to curriculum co-ordination.

The purpose of the authors in many chapters has been to nudge co-ordinators towards a more informed understanding of the nature of their management role, the contexts within which they work, and the anxieties which colleagues are likely to experience when confronting unfamiliar subject and pedagogical challenges in the disparate areas of the formal curriculum. In different ways the various chapters set out to empower co-ordinators so that they can then help classroom colleagues who in turn become, as a result, better able to support the learning of children in the classroom.

Moreover, to return to Ramsden's claim, the learning and the changing of conceptions he refers to may be applied with equal relevance in our present context to subject co-ordinators, classroom teachers and pupils. Teaching in the contexts we have delineated requires co-ordinators to understand and, where necessary, help colleagues to modify their conceptions of the principal concepts underpinning, say, maths or science or history or geography learning. Likewise classroom teachers, as Jarvis suggests in Chapter 9, can themselves be enabled to unpack their pupils' understanding, or misunderstanding, of the core elements of a given subject area and to use this as a starting point for teaching. In the same way that classroom teachers need a detailed understanding of the range of subject content and pedagogical strategies which apply to the particular curriculum area, so too do co-ordinators if they are, in Ramsden's words, to help colleagues change their conceptions. Thus the range of subject knowledge and teaching strategies outlined in Part II of this volume constitute an essential framework within which co-ordinators can assess teachers' understanding and teachers that of pupils.

TOWARDS A SHARED LANGUAGE

Moving towards an informed overview of the curriculum which is rooted in classroom practice is indeed a significant and potentially very threatening undertaking. It is one which rejects the notion of co-ordinators providing necessary but basically anodyne arm's-length support for colleagues by merely digesting documentation on their behalf and organising a suitable repository for shared resources. Just as teachers need to observe pupils working and to talk with them in order to evaluate their understanding of concepts, so do co-ordinators need to engage in observation and focused talk with colleagues in order to make the transition from a dialogue based on written policy and espoused approaches to one grounded firmly in the day-to-day practice of teachers and the received experience of pupils.

Changing their own conceptions requires teachers to open up and confront very personal anxieties about teaching and assessing attainment in areas where they feel less expert, and to acknowledge the misconceptions they may hold about areas of the curriculum as diverse as dance, musical notation, oracy or pulleys and levers. Equally, it requires co-ordinators to develop a sophisticated mix of subject knowledge (the conceptual basis of a given area of the curriculum) and craft knowledge (knowing how best to match specific teaching strategies to that knowledge according to the learning needs of individual children) together with a highly developed range of interpersonal and communication skills. Further, it demands that they adopt a similar perspective with colleagues who themselves are likely to have differing levels of confidence and expertise in each area of the curriculum. In Chapter 10 Dunkley observes that teachers need to ensure that children experience periodic successful outcomes in design technology in order to encourage them to persist with the development of essential problem-solving skills. Perhaps we should require co-ordinators to adopt the same benchmark. Colleagues are more likely to experiment with and adopt novel approaches if they themselves have successful experiences of teaching in new ways and witness at first hand the beneficial effects on children in their classroom.

Of course, one of the most fruitful ways to develop these relationships we have been discussing is through dialogue, the notion of attempting to arrive over time at a shared and articulated understanding of what it is that teachers are trying to do:

Other things being equal, the utility of collegial work and the vigour of the experimentation with teaching is a direct function of the concreteness, precision and coherence of the shared language.

(Little 1982, p. 331)

As you read, then, you may wish to reflect on the degree of precision of the lexicon with which the curriculum is discussed in your subject or the school as a whole. It doesn't seem too outlandish to suggest that the more detailed the level of analysis, the more likely it is that you and your colleagues will be doing two related things.

First you will have spent considerable amounts of time refining and developing the language used in order to question and overcome differences in how you each perceive what is being taught and learnt. Second, you will only have been able to explore different shades of meaning and interpretation by employing the catalyst of observed classroom practice. The likelihood of arriving at a close understanding of the difficulties of teaching or learning essential concepts in, say, music or art or PE is remote if the dialogue is limited simply to a discussion of the content of National Curriculum documentation or the formal language often adopted in school based policy documents. If teachers develop by reflecting on the nature of their practice and their colleagues' and pupils' interpretation of that practice (and I would argue strongly that they do) then the key role of the co ordinator is to facilitate informed reflection.

AN OVERVIEW OF THE WORK OF THE CO-ORDINATOR

Throughout Part I of this book the various contributors have emphasised the ambiguities associated with the role of the subject co-ordinator and the complex nature of the contexts within which they work. The major locus of these early chapters has necessarily been on the relationship between co-ordinator and colleagues and on how to promote a more considered understanding of the needs of fellow teachers.

Galton, for example, highlights the very real difficulties of matching the type of support offered by the co-ordinator to the level of confidence of the individual teacher, an issue made more complex still when the former may be a comparatively junior and inexperienced member of staff whilst the latter a teacher of many years' service or a senior member of staff. Our crude image of 'the classroom teacher' in this support process is given a further subtle shading by Merry who reminds us that the majority of entrants to the profession are now more likely to be returners than they are young graduates with limited experience. The notion of support from co-ordinators may therefore include the management of a potentially threatening reorientation process for mature teachers unfamiliar with the demands of a complex and detailed National Curriculum.

Similarly, the national experiment with school based teacher training schemes serves only to broaden the scope of demands likely to be made on the curriculum co-ordinator 'pit pony'.

Other chapters in Part I have served to sharpen our awareness of the need to understand the nature of school culture, to identify the sources of support which must be gathered within the school, in particular from the headteacher, if the co-ordinator is to have any prospect of success. Headteachers can help by publicly endorsing the work of co-ordinators and, just as importantly, they are the gatekeepers to essential resources such as release time to observe practice. Equally, the co-operation of colleagues is essential if co-ordinators are to be able to work in an effective analytical medium: the rich and vibrant data drawn from observations of actual practice based on the interactions between pupils and teachers within the classroom together with colleagues' perceptions of what they are attempting to achieve. West-Burnham captures this imperative well when he reminds us of the underlying purpose of all this curriculum co-ordinator busyness: to enhance the quality of learning.

In Part II, we presented, in effect, a celebration of the sheer complexity of primary school teaching expertise. The emphasis of each curriculum area in terms of key concepts and preferred teaching approaches is distinctive. Nevertheless each author concisely and coherently unpacks a basic framework of concepts, perspectives and strategies. These serve as a useful starting point from which teachers and co-ordinators can engage with the process of developing their shared language. Equally important is the idea that inexpert or unconfident subject co-ordinators, and according to Whiteside's analysis these may be a significant number of those responsible for developing the curriculum in schools, are able to identify some priorities for their own personal development.

Despite the differences of priority and emphasis and the bewilderingly large subject knowledge base of the primary school curriculum, a persistent theme emerges from these chapters which underlines the basic message conveyed in Ramsden's comments at the beginning of the chapter. Each contribution reinforces the importance of teachers using children's existing knowledge as the basis for teaching and learning. Each suggests that pupils' understanding of essential concepts, their development of necessary skills and their ability to apply these to different situations across the curriculum (the importance of which is alluded to in McNamara's and Underwood's chapters in Part III) are dependent on teachers working from the familiarity of children's own experience and understanding. In some instances this familiarity is a sound basis for the learning of new concepts; in others it is the point at which children need to unlearn misconceptions they have previously developed.

Again, this point mirrors the challenges faced by co-ordinators when working with colleagues. Teachers themselves, as Price and Griffiths point out in relation to maths, may not have been taught the subject well themselves. In these instances co-ordinators need to help colleagues unlearn their own misconceptions; in others their role is to help colleagues acknowledge the strength of their current levels of expertise and the excellence of existing approaches used in the classroom.

Furthermore, as Riley implies in Chapter 20 in Part III, with the gradual diminution, and in some cases wholesale disappearance, of LEA networks of support, co-ordinators may become the major source of expertise and advice for teachers within the school. Co-ordinators, however, especially those who lack confidence themselves, also need support for their personal development. Here, networking with colleagues in other institutions helps to bridge the support gap, for just as co-ordinators can, with the support of staff, challenge misconceptions and disseminate best practice in their own schools, groups of co-ordinators in clusters of schools can develop a shared understanding and pressures for the adoption of good practice across a number of schools. Williams, for example, highlights the benefits of collaboration with regard to the teaching of art across the key stages. Indeed, in the age of autonomous schools it is perhaps this networking aspect of the co-ordinator's work which will emerge as the most significant in the future.

CO-ORDINATING LEARNING

In the introductory chapter we claimed that the book's aim was to improve the management capability of co-ordinators. The final point I wish to emphasise here is that the individual chapters only 'work' when they help readers reconceptualise their role, allow them as co-ordinators to enable teacher colleagues to redefine their personal understanding of the subject area in question and encourage teachers to explore with children their grasp of the key concepts detailed in this volume. If co-ordinators can achieve that then they truly will have captured the essence of excellent primary school teaching and learning.

References

Abbott, R., Steadman, S. and Birchenough, M. (1988) *Guidelines for Review and Internal Developments (GRIDS)*, London: Schools Council Development Committee.

Agalianos, A. and Cope, P. (1994) 'Information technology and knowledge: the non-neutrality of content-specific software', *Journal of Educational Policy* **9**, 1, pp. 35–45.

Ainscow, M. and Tweddle, D. A. (1988) *Preventing Classroom Failure, An Objectives Approach*, London: Fulton Publishers.

Aldrich, R. and Dean, D. (1991) 'The historical dimension in history', in Aldrich, R. (Ed.) *The National Curriculum*, Bedford Way Papers, London: Institute of Education.

Alexander, R. (1991) *Primary Education in Leeds*, Twelfth and Final Report from the Primary Needs Independent Evaluation Project, University of Leeds.

Alexander, R. (1992) *Policy and Practice in Primary Education*, London: Routledge.

Alexander, R., Rose, J. and Woodhead, C. (1992) *Curriculum Organisation and Classroom Practice in Primary Schools: A Discussion Paper*, London: Department of Education and Science.

Allied Dunbar National Fitness Survey (1992) *Main Findings*, report commissioned by the Sports Council and Health Education Authority.

Anderson, C. and Moore, A. (1994) 'Making history happen outside the classroom', in Bourdillon, H. (Ed.) *Teaching History*, London: Routledge.

Anning, A. (1991) *The First Years at School: Education 4–8*, Milton Keynes: Open University Press.

Armstrong, N. and Sparks, A. (1991) *Issues in Physical Education*, London: Cassell.

Barnes, L. R. and Shinn-Taylor, C. (1988) 'Competency and expertise in primary school music and science: a survey of five schools in North East England', *Curriculum* **9**, 1, pp. 28–34.

Barrow, R. (1993) *The Philosophy of Schooling*, Brighton: Harvester Press.

Bastide, D. (Ed.) (1992) *Good Practice in Primary Religious Education, 4–11*, Lewes: The Falmer Press.

Baxter, J. (1989) 'Children's understanding of familiar astronomical events', *International Journal of Science Education* **11**, Special Issue, pp. 502–513.

Bell, B. and Freyberg, P. (1985) 'Language in the science classroom', in Osborne, R. and Freyberg, R. (Eds) *Learning in Science: The Implications of Children's Science*, Auckland: Heinemann.

Benner, P. (1984) *From Novice to Expert: Excellence and Power in Clinical Nursing Practice*, Reading, Massachusetts: Addison-Wesley.

Bentley, D. and Watts, M. (1994) *Primary Science and Technology*, Buckingham: Open University Press.

Berliner, D. (1992) 'Some characteristics in experts in the pedagogical domain', in Oser, F., Dick, A. and Patry, J. (Eds) *Effective and Responsible Teaching: The New Synthesis*, San Francisco: Jossey-Bass Press.

Berrill, M. (1992) 'Structured mentoring and the development of teaching skills', in Wilkin, M. (Ed.) *Mentoring in Schools*, London: Kogan Page.

Bleach, P. (1986) *The Use of Microcomputers in Primary Schools*, Reading: Reading and Language Information Centre, Reading University.

Borko, H. and Livingston, C. (1989) 'Cognition and improvisation: differences in mathematics instruction by expert and novice teachers', *American Educational Research Journal* **26**, 4, pp. 473–498.

British Psychological Society (1992) *Psychological Aspects of Beginning Teacher Competence*, Leicester: BPS.

Brown, A. (1992) *Religious Education*, London: National Society.

Burns, R. B. (1982) *Self Concept and Education*, London: Holt, Rinehart and Winston.

Buzzing, P. (1990) 'Creating returner-positive schools: managing your school to encourage returners to work in it', *Management in Education* **4**, 3, pp. 18–20.

Campbell, R. J. (1985) *Developing the Primary School Curriculum*, London: Holt, Rinehart and Winston.

Cavendish, S., Galton, M., Hargreaves, L. and Harlen, W. (1990) *Assessing Science in the Primary Classroom: Observing Activities*, London: Paul Chapman.

Cheshire County Council (1992) *Mathematics Guidelines*, Cheshire County Council Education Services.

Claxton, G. (1984) 'The psychology of teacher training: inaccuracies and improvements', *Educational Psychology* **4**, 2, pp. 167–174.

Cockcroft Report (1982) *Mathematics Counts*, London: HMSO.

Cole, A. L. (1991) 'Relationships in the workplace: doing what comes naturally?' *Teaching and Teacher Education* **7**, 5/6, pp. 415–426.

Cooper, H. (1992) *The Teaching of History*, London: David Fulton.

Curriculum Council for Wales (1992) *Mathematics in the National Curriculum: Nonstatutory Guidance for Teachers*, Cardiff: CCW.

Day, C., Hall, C., Gammage, P. and Coles, M. (1993) *Leadership and Curriculum in the Primary School. The Roles of Senior and Middle Management*, London: Paul Chapman.

Dearing, R (1993) *The National Curriculum and its Assessment: Final Report*, London: School Curriculum and Assessment Authority.

DES (Department of Education and Science) (1978a) *Primary Education in England*, London: HMSO.

DES (1978b) *Special Educational Needs* (Warnock Report), London: HMSO.

DES (1981) *Education Act 1981*, London: HMSO.

DES (1983) *Cockcroft: An Introduction for Primary Schools*, London: HMSO.

DES (1985) *Mathematics from 5 to 16*, London: HMSO.

DES (1989) *The Teaching and Learning of Mathematics*, London: HMSO.

DES (1989) *The Education Reform Act 1988. Religious Education and Collective Worship*. London: HMSO.

DES (1990) *The Education Reform Act 1988: The Education (National Curriculum) (Assessment Arrangements for English, Mathematics and Science) Order 1990*, Circular 9/90, London: HMSO.

DES (1991) *Art for Ages 5 to 14*, London: HMSO.

DES (1992) *Music in the National Curriculum (England)*, London: HMSO.

DfE (Department for Education) (1992a) *GEST 1993–94 Grant 11: Designated Courses for Primary Teachers*, London: DfE.

DfE (1992b) *Choice and Diversity. A New Framework for Schools*, London: HMSO

DfE (1992c) *Induction of Newly Qualified Teachers* (administrative memorandum 2/92), London: DfE.

DfE (1993) *Education Act 1993*, London: HMSO.

DfE (1994) *Code of Practice on the Identification and Assessment of Special Educational Needs*, London: Central Office of Information.

DfE (1995a) *Design and Technology in the National Curriculum*, London: HMSO.

DfE (1995b) *History in the National Curriculum*, London: DfE.

Dickson, L., Brown, M. and Gibson, A. (1984) *Children Learning Mathematics: A Teacher's Guide to Recent Research*, London: Cassell.

Ding, B. (1994) 'Can your school afford IT?', *Educational Computing and Technology*, October, pp. 40, 47.

Doyle, W. and Ponder, G. (1977) 'The Practicality Ethic and Teacher Decision Making', *Interchange*, **8**, pp. 1–12.

Dyson, A. (1990) 'Effective learning consultancy: a future role for special needs coordinators?', *Support for Learning* **5**, 3, pp. 116–127.

Dyson, A. (1991) 'Re-thinking roles re-thinking concepts: Special Needs Teachers in mainstream schools,' *Support for Learning* **6**, 3.

Dyson, A. and Gains, C. (1993) *Re-thinking Special Needs in mainstream schools: Towards the year 2000*, London: Fulton Publishers.

Dyson, A., and Clarke, C. (1995) *Innovatory Practice in Mainstream Schools*, London: HMSO.

Edwards, A. (1993) 'Curriculum co-ordination: a lost opportunity for primary school development?', *School Organisation* **13**, 1, pp. 51–59.

Eisenhart, L., Behm, L. and Romagnano, L. (1991) 'Learning to teach: developing expertise or rite of passage?', *Journal of Education for Teaching* **17**, 1, pp. 51–71.

Eisner, E. (1972) *Educating Artistic Vision*. London: Macmillan.

Evans, L., Packwood, A. St. J., Neill, S.R. and Campbell, R.J. (1994) *The Meaning of Infant Teachers' Work*, London: Routledge.

Figg, G. (1993) 'Introduction', in Morgan, M. *Art in Practice*, Oxford: Nash Pollock.

Fullan, M. (1991) *The New Meaning of Educational Change*, 2nd edn, London: Cassell.

Galton, M. (1989) *Teaching in the Primary School*, London: David Fulton.

Galton, M. (1994) *Crisis in the Primary Classroom*, London: David Fulton.

Galton, M. and Williamson, J. (1992) *Group Work in the Primary Classroom*, London: Routledge.

Galton, M., Simon, B. and Croll, P. (1980) *Inside the Primary Classroom*, London: Routledge & Kegan Paul.

Galton, M., Fogelman, K., Hargreaves, L. and Cavendish, S. (1991) *The Rural Schools Curriculum Enhancement National Evaluation (SCENE) Project: Final Report*, London: HMSO.

Golby, M. and Gulliver, J. (1985) 'Whose remedies, whose ills? A critical review of remedial education' in C. J. Smith (Ed.) *New Directions in Remedial Education*, Falmer Press.

Goodlad, S. and Hurst, B. (1990) *Explorations in Real Tutoring*, London: Blackwell Education.

Gross, J. (1993) *Special Educational Needs in the Primary School, A Practical Guide*, Buckingham: Open University Press.

Gurney, P. (1988) *Self Esteem in Children with Special Educational Needs*, London: Routledge.

Handy, C. (1994) *The Empty Raincoat: Making Sense of the Future*, London: Hutchinson.

Handy, C. and Aitken, R. (1986) *Understanding Schools as Organisations*, Harmondsworth: Penguin.

Hargreaves, A. (1993) 'Contrived collegiality: the micro politics of teacher collaboration', in Bennett, R., Crawford, M. and Riches, C. (Eds) *Managing Change in Education: Individual and Organizational Perspectives*, London: Paul Chapman.

Hargreaves, A. (1994) *Changing Teachers, Changing Times. Teachers' Work and Culture in the Postmodern Age*, London: Cassell.

Hargreaves, D. (1990) The Management of Development Planning, London: DES.

Hargreaves, D. and Hopkins, D. (1991) *The Empowered School*, London: Cassell.

Hargreaves, D.H., Hopkins, D., Leask, M., Connolly, J. and Robinson, P. (1989) *Planning for School Development: Advice to Governors, Headteachers and Teachers*, London: DES.

Hargeaves, L., Comber, C. and Galton, M. (1996) 'The National Curriculum: can small schools deliver? Confidence and competence levels of teachers in small rural primary schools', *British Educational Research Journal* **22**, 2.

Harland, J. (1990) *The Work and Impact of Advisory Teachers*, Slough: NFER.

Harwood, D. (1992) 'In at the deep end: a case study of the co-ordinator role in a "low-key" innovation', *School Organisation* **12**, 1, pp. 17–28.

HMI (1985) *Mathematics from 5 to 16*, London: HMSO.

HMI (1987) *The New Teacher in School: A Survey by HMI in England and Wales, 1987*, London: DES.

HMI (1992) *The Induction and Probation of New Teachers 1988–1991* (62/92/ns), London: DES.

Hyde, K. (1990) *Religion in Childhood and Adolesence: A Comprehensive Review of the Research*, Birmingham, AL: Religious Education Press.

Inner London Education Authority (1987) 'ILEA Research and Statistics Branch: School Sports Working Party Research Studies 1987', in *My Favourite Subject*, report of the Working Party on Physical Education and School Sports, appointed by ILEA, January 1988.

Inner London Education Authority (1988a) *Children and Mathematics*, ILEA Learning Resources Branch.

Inner London Education Authority (1988b) *Making it Happen*, ILEA Learning Resources Branch.

IPSE (1988) *Implementing Primary Science Education*, Report for the Association of Science Education, Hatfield: ASE.

Jarvis, T. (1993) *Teaching Design and Technology in the Classroom*, London: Routledge.

Jarvis, T. and Cavendish, S. (1994) 'Subject competency of teachers and level of dependency on resource packs to teach levers, gears and pulleys', *Research in Science Education* **24**, pp. 166–172.

Jayne, E. and Stokes, C. (1992) 'Mentoring: an example of a training programme for supporting mentors for teacher returners', *British Journal of In-service Education* **18**, 2, pp. 101–106.

Jenkins, H., Stroud, M., Daniels, W. and Probert, H. (1991) 'Managing maths by mentoring', *Management in Education* **5**, 4, pp. 18–20.

Johnson, D. and Johnson, R. (1987) *Learning Together and Alone: Cooperation, Competition and Individualisation*, 2nd edn, Englewood Cliffs, New Jersey: Prentice Hall.

Kagan, D. (1992) 'Professional growth among preservice and beginning teachers', *Review of Educational Research* **62**, 2, pp. 129–170.

Kingsley-Mills, C., McNamara, S. and Woodward, L. (1992) *Out from Behind the Dash Lens*, LEA.

Kruger, C., Palacio, D. and Summers, M. (1992) 'Surveys of English primary teachers' conceptions of force, energy and materials', *Science Teacher Education* **76**, 4, pp. 339–351.

Lawrence, D. (1987) *Enhancing Self Esteem in the Classroom*, London: Paul Chapman.

Lewis, A. (1991) *Primary Special Needs and the National Curriculum*, London, Routledge.

Lindquist, M. (1994) 'Pre-service and in-service teacher education', in Gaulin, C. et al. (Eds) *Proceedings of the 7th International Congress on Mathematical Education*, Sainte-Foy: University of Laval Press.

Little, J. (1982) 'Norms of collegiality and experimentation: workplace conditions of school success', *American Educational Research Journal* **19**, 3, pp. 325–340.

Little, J. (1990) 'Teachers as colleagues', in Lieberman, A. (Ed.) *Schools as Collaborative Cultures: Creating the Future Now*, Lewes: Falmer Press.

Lofthouse, M. (1994a) 'Religious education in developing economic and industrial understanding in the curriculum', in Kerr, D. (Ed.) *EIU and the Core and Foundation Subjects*, London: David Fulton.

Lofthouse, M. (1994b) 'Religious education in developing environmental education in the curriculum', in Goodall, S. (Ed.) *Environmental Education and Core and Foundation Subjects*, London: David Fulton.

Maines, B. and Robinson, G. (1988) *B/G-STEEM – A Self-esteem Scale*, Bristol: Lame Duck.

Mant, J. and Summers, M. (1993) 'Some primary-school teachers' understanding of the Earth's place in the universe', *Research Papers in Education* **8**, 1, pp. 101–129.

Mathematical Association (1955) *The Teaching of Mathematics in Primary Schools*, London: Bell.

McIntyre, D. (1992) 'Theory, theorising and reflection in initial teacher education', in Calderhead, J. and Gates, P. (Eds) *Conceptualising Reflection in Teacher Education*, London: Falmer Press.

McIntyre, D. and Hagger, H. (1993) 'Teachers' expertise and models of mentoring', in McIntyre, D., Haggar, H. and Wilkin, M. (Eds) *Mentoring: Perspectives on School-based Teacher Education*, London: Kogan Page.

McNamara, S. and Moreton, G. (1993) *Teaching Special Needs*, London: David Fulton.

Merrett, F. (1994) *Improving Reading, A Teacher's Guide to Peer Tutoring*, London: David Fulton.

Moore, J. (1992a) 'Science co-ordination in primary schools: the views of classroom teachers', *Education 3–13* **20**, 2, pp. 33–37.

Moore, J. (1992b) 'The role of the science co-ordinator in primary schools. A survey of headteachers' views', *School Organisation* **12**, 1, pp. 7–17

Mortimore, P., Sammons, P., Stoll, L. D. and Ecob, R. (1988) *School Matters: The Junior Years*, Wells: Open Books.

Nash, W. (1988) *At Ease With Stress: The Approach to Wholeness*, London: Darton, Longman and Todd.

National Council of Teachers of Mathematics (1991) *Professional Standards for Teaching Mathematics*, Reston: NCTM.

NCC (National Curriculum Council) (1993) *Spiritual and Moral Development*, London: NCC.

Newton, D. and Newton, L. (1991) *A Practical Guide to Teaching Technology within the National Curriculum*, Warwick: Scholastic.

Nias, J., Southworth, G. and Yeomans, R. (1989) *Staff Relationships in Primary Schools*, London: Cassell.

Nias J., Southworth, G. and Campbell, P. (1992) *Whole School Curriculum Development in the Primary School*, London: Falmer.

Nussbaum, J. (1985) 'The earth as a cosmic body', in Driver, R., Guesne, E. and Tiberghien, A. (Eds) *Children's Ideas in Science*, Milton Keynes: Open University Press.

Ofsted (Office for Standards in Education) (1993a) *Handbook for the Inspection of Schools*, London: HMSO.

Ofsted (1993b) *The Implementation of the Curricular Requirements of the Education Reform Act*, London: HMSO.

Ofsted (1993c) *Music at Key Stages 1, 2 and 3, First Year, 1992–93*, London: HMSO.

Ofsted (1994a) *Improving Schools*, London: HMSO.

Ofsted (1994b) *Handbook for the Inspection of Schools*, London: HMSO.

Ofsted (1994c) *English Key Stages 1, 2, 3, 4, Fourth Year, 1992–3*, London: HMSO.

Ofsted (1994d) *Religious Education and Collective Worship 1992–1993*, London: HMSO.

O'Mahony, T. and Sollars, R. (1990) 'A personal development programme for advisory teachers', *British Journal of Inservice Education* **16**, 1, pp. 33–38.

Osborn, M. and Black, E. (1994) *Developing the National Curriculum at Key Stage 2; The Changing Nature of Teachers' Work*, Report commissioned by NAS/UWT, Bristol: University of Bristol.

Owen-Cole, W. and Evans-Lowndes, J. (1991) *Religious Education in the Primary Curriculum: Teaching Strategies and Practical Activities*, Norwich: Religious and Moral Education Press.

Papert, S. (1980) *Mindstorms: Children, Computers and Powerful Ideas*, New York: Harvester Press.

Pateman, T. (1994) 'Crisis, what identity crisis?', *Times Educational Supplement, First appiontments*, 14 January, p. 28.

Peel, R. and Bell, M. (1994) *The Primary Language Leaders Book*, London: David Fulton.

Pirsig, R. (1974) *Zen and the Art of Motorcycle Maintenance*, London: The Bodley Head.

Pollard, A. with Osborn, M., Abbott, D., Broadfoot, P. and Croll, P. (1993) 'Balancing priorities: children and the curriculum in the nineties', in Campbell, R. (Ed.) *Breadth and Balance in the Primary Curriculum*, London: Falmer Press.

Pollard, A., Broadfoot, P., Croll, P., Osborn, M. and Abbott, D. (1994) *Changing English Primary Schools? The Impact of the Education Reform Act at Key Stage One*, London: Cassell.

Price, M. (1994) *Survey of Maths Schemes in Leicestershire Primary Schools*, unpublished.

Ramsden, P. (1988) 'Studying learning: improving teaching', in Ramsden, P. (Ed.) *Improving Learning. New Perspectives*, London: Kogan Page.

Robins, K. and Webster, F. (1989) *The Technical Fix: Education, Computers and Industry*, Basingstoke: Macmillan.

Rowntree, D. (1992) *Explaining Open and Distance Learning*, London: Kogan Page.

Russell, T. and Harlen, W. (1990) *Assessing Science in the Primary Classroom: Practical Tasks*, London: Paul Chapman.

SCAA (School Curriculum and Assessment Authority) (1993) *Evaluation of the Implementation of National Curriculum Mathematics at Key Stages 1, 2 and 3: Summary Report*, London: SCAA.

SCAA (1994) *Music in the National Curriculum*, London: HMSO.

Schilling, M., Harlen, W., Hargreaves, L. and Russell, T. (1990) *Assessing Science in the Primary Classroom: Written Tasks*, London: Paul Chapman.

Schon, D. (1983) *The Reflective Practitioner: How Professionals Think in Action*, New York: Basic Books.

Smith, L. N. and Tomlinson, P. (1977) 'The development of children's construction of historical duration', in *Educational Research* **19**, 3.

Smith, R. and Alred, G. (1993) 'The impersonalisation of wisdom', in McIntyre, D., Hagger, H. and Wilkin, M. (Eds) *Mentoring: Perspectives on School-based Teacher Education*, London: Kogan Page.

Stillman, A. and Grant, M. (1989) *The LEA Adviser – A Changing Role*, Windsor: NFER-Nelson.

Stow, M. (1989) *Managing Mathematics in the Primary School – A Practical Resource for the Co-ordinator*, Windsor: NFER-Nelson

Stow, M. and Foxman, D. (1988) *Mathematics Co-ordination. A Study of Practice in Primary and Middle Schools*, Windsor: NFER-Nelson.

Tann, S. (1988) 'Grouping and the integrated classroom', in Thomas, G. and Feiler, A. (Eds), *Planning for Special Needs: A Whole School Approach*, Oxford: Blackwell.

Taylor, R. (1986) *Educating for Art*, Harlow: Longman.

Terrell, C. (1990) 'Practical school experiences: who teaches the student teacher?', in Booth, M. B., Furlong, V. J. and Wilkin, M. (Eds) *Partnership in Initial Teacher Training*, London: Cassell.

Thacker, J. (1990) 'Working through groups in the classroom', in Jones, N. and Frederickson, N. (Eds) *Refocussing Educational Psychology*, Lewes: Falmer Press.

Tizard, B. and Hughes, M. (1984) *Young Children Learning*, London: Fontana.

Tizard, B., Blatchford, D., Burke, J., Farquhar, C. and Plewis, I. (1988) *Young Children at School in the Inner City*, Hove: Lawrence Erlbaum.

Topping, K. (1988) *The Peer Tutoring Handbook*, London: Croom Helm.

Underwood, J. D. M. and Underwood, G. (1990) *Computers and Learning: Helping Children Acquire Thinking Skills*, Oxford: Blackwell.

Underwood, J., Dickinson, D., Lee, K. and Lynch, O. (1994) 'Databases: potential into practice', in Underwood, J. (Ed.) *Computer Based Learning: Principles into Practice*, London: David Fulton.

Wallace, M. (1988) 'Towards a collegiate approach to curriculum management in primary and middle schools,' *School Organisation* **8**, pp. 25–34.

Warnham, S. M. (1993) *Primary Teaching and the Negotiation of Power*, London: Paul Chapman.

Warwickshire County Council (1988) *Primary Schools Art and Design; Questions and Convictions*, Warwick: Warwickshire County Council.

Webb, R. (1994) *After the Deluge: Changing Roles and Responsibilities in the Primary School*, London: Association of Teachers and Lecturers.

Wells, C. G. (1978) 'Talking with young chidren: the complementary roles of parents and teachers', *English in Education* **12**, 15–38.

Wells, G. (1986) *The Hearing Makers*, London: Hodder and Stoughton.

West, J. (1989) 'Thoughts on time charts', in Blyth, J. (Ed.) *History in Primary Schools*, Milton Keynes: Open University Press.

Westwood, P. (1993) *Commonsense Methods for Children with Special Needs*, London: Routledge.

Wheway, D. and Thomson, S. (1993) *Explore Music Through. . .*, Series, Oxford: Oxford University Press.

Wilkin, M. (Ed.) (1992) *Mentoring in Schools*, London: Kogan Page.

Wolfendale, S. (1987) *Primary Schools and Special Needs: Policy, Planning and Provision*, London: Cassell.

Wragg, E. C., Bennett, N. and Carre, C. (1989) 'Primary teachers and the National Curriculum', *Research Papers in Education* **4**, 3, pp. 17–46.

Wray, D. and Medwell, J. (1994) *Teaching Primary English*, London: Routledge.

Index